The Priestly Tribe

The Supreme Court's Image in the American Mind

Barbara A. Perry

Foreword by Abner J. Mikva

PRAEGER

Westport, Connecticut
London

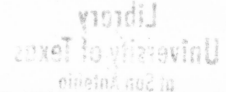

Library of Congress Cataloging-in-Publication Data

Perry, Barbara A. (Barbara Ann), 1956–
    The priestly tribe : the Supreme Court's image in the American
mind / Barbara A. Perry ; foreword by Abner J. Mikva.
        p.   cm.
    Includes bibliographical references and index.
    ISBN 0–275–96598–8 (alk. paper).—ISBN 0–275–96599–6 (pbk. :
alk. paper)
    1. United States.   Supreme Court—Public opinion.   2. Public
opinion—United States.   I. Title.
    KF8742.P3358   1999
    347.73'26—dc21   99–13438

British Library Cataloguing in Publication Data is available.

Library of Congress Catalog Card Number: 99–13438
ISBN: 0–275–96598–8
        0–275–96599–6 (pbk.)

First published in 1999

Praeger Publishers, 88 Post Road West, Westport, CT 06881
An imprint of Greenwood Publishing Group, Inc.
www.praeger.com

Printed in the United States of America

The paper used in this book complies with the
Permanent Paper Standard issued by the National
Information Standards Organization (Z39.48–1984).

10 9 8 7 6 5 4 3 2

FOR HENRY J. ABRAHAM

Inspiring teacher, devoted mentor, loyal colleague, beloved friend

Contents

Foreword

Whether or not it represents the pinnacle of "the least dangerous branch," as its defenders say, or is the den of iniquity that its detractors proclaim it, the Supreme Court of the United States is hardly an institution that generates many neutral feelings. But even more than the passions it brings forth from friends and enemies, it commands awe. From the first moment that I saw the building to all the times that I have been in it as a law clerk, a practitioner, or a spectator, I cannot walk into the Supreme Court building without being overwhelmed by its majesty. This is where nine mere mortals resolve the great disputes of a powerful democracy, where, commanding neither the purse nor the sword, this group of judges commands full faith and credit from all the other players in our government.

Barbara Perry has captured the awesomeness of the institution in *The Priestly Tribe*. From her perch as judicial fellow during the 1994–95 term of Court, Dr. Perry observed everything from the advent of Chief Justice Rehnquist's gold stripes (now nationally famous because of television coverage of the Senate impeachment trial of President Clinton) to the awe of first-time visitors to the Court to the interaction of the nine justices who make up the current complement of the Supreme Court. She writes of her witnessing with enthusiasm and skill. The judicial fellows, a relatively recently instituted group, are insiders to the Court's functions. Professor Perry, as a fellow in the Office of the Administrative Assistant to the Chief Justice, was able to see close-up much that occurred during her term at Court. Of course, no one, save the nine justices, is allowed in the Conference Room, where the real action in the decisional process takes place. But she saw and ably describes the way in which the Court and its personnel perform the other functions of the third branch of government.

Dr. Perry was fascinated (as am I) by the role the architecture of the building has played in its recent history. She researched thoroughly the history of all the places where the Supreme Court was housed, from the New York City location in the Exchange Building to the "potato hole" in the basement of the U.S. Capitol. It even lost the basement home when the British sacked Washington and burned the Capitol building. It was not until 1935 that the Court occupied its very own structure—designed as a court building and fulfilling every expectation of its designers and planners. There aren't many, if any, other buildings in Washington that so ably describe both the function and the aspirations of the agency that occupies it. The Supreme Court building is "as advertised," and a visitor has to be pretty cynical about government as a whole not to be impressed with it.

But even great buildings don't automatically produce great performances. The bulk of Professor Perry's book is about the successes and failures of the cases that were resolved during her term, of the public appearances of the justices, of the press treatment (fair and unfair) of all that occurred. She uses the New Deal period of our country to portray the most recent crisis in the Court's existence—the Court-packing threat advanced by a popular president against "nine old men" who were striking down important legislation passed by the Congress at President Franklin Roosevelt's urging. Since the Court-packing proposal failed, and the Court's personnel changed sufficiently to alter the way New Deal legislation was perceived, the treatment in the book is only an example of the vicissitudes of public perceptions of the Supreme Court.

It is that public perception that is Dr. Perry's focus. How does an institution whose real work is conducted behind closed doors and whose opinions hardly make for interesting reading (I know from having to read them all of my adult life) deal with its image, especially its media relations?

The media have a difficult job in portraying the Court to the American people, despite the fact that there is a press room in the building and a public information officer. The electronic media are limited in their coverage of the Court's most public work: neither radio nor television is permitted to record the Court's oral arguments. Moreover, the justices appear only infrequently on radio or television programs. The print media are allowed to cover the Court; nevertheless, while they can and do report on oral argument, such arguments are seldom newsworthy. The decisions themselves are handed down without any advance notice and the news reporters have to scramble to make their papers' deadlines, and worse yet, try to explain in very little space what the Court said and did in some very important decisions. Frequently, those decisions are set forth with the Court divided into two or more camps, each writing their own opinion as to what the law is or should be. Sometimes the Court is so divided that almost no one, lawyer or newsperson, can figure out what the controlling principles are. There was one important decision, dealing with how juries should be chosen, that had five separate opinions, with no opinion commanding a majority of the Court. While a few journalists who cover the Court are lawyers, it becomes an impossible task to explain in a short space what the Court has said or done.

The justices and their staff are no help at all. While members of Congress and the White House staff are most ready to tell the media at length what they said, what they meant, and what they intend to do, judges cannot and do not explain what they have said and done. I remember hearing the late Justice Hugo Black speak at my alma mater, the University of Chicago, when I was still a student there. Justice Black had just written a most important (and lengthy) opinion in *Adamson v. California*, holding that the Bill of Rights of the federal Constitution was applicable to the states. After the speech, one of the professors asked him a question about a possible interpretation of *Adamson*. Black thought for a moment and responded, "Well, I think I said it as well as I could in the opinion. If I could have been any clearer, I would have." That is pretty much the way most judges respond to questions about their opinions.

That raises the dilemma that becomes one of Dr. Perry's sub-themes: should there be cameras in the Supreme Court? A great controversy exists over whether such showcases as the O.J. Simpson trial shed any light on the judicial process. Some of us believe that the effect on the trials themselves militate against cameras in the courtrooms. Professor Perry believes that similar reasons justify the preclusion of cameras in the Supreme Court (and, presumably, other appellate courts). I would think that the Supreme Court ought to be able to handle the pressure and that such coverage would not influence the outcome of the cases being argued. But Dr. Perry addresses the issue in her usual scholarly fashion, and that has to move the discussion of the issue forward.

This book sheds light on an institution that needs illumination. The Supreme Court may or may not be the least dangerous of the branches, but it is the balance wheel of the whole governmental process. The more people know about how well it works, the better it can perform that role.

Abner J. Mikva, Retired Chief Judge
U.S. Court of Appeals, D.C. Circuit

Preface

This book is dedicated to Professor Henry J. Abraham, whose worldwide reputation in the field of constitutional law was a prime consideration in my decision to choose the University of Virginia over Harvard University as the place to pursue my Ph.D. (The fact that U.Va. offered me a generous fellowship sealed the deal.) Since my choice eighteen years ago, I have experienced nothing but blessings from his bountiful intellect and warm friendship. He has taught me most of what I know about the Supreme Court of the United States, and his support was crucial to the fulfillment of my goal to serve as a judicial fellow at that institution in 1994–95.

The unstinting patronage of Sweet Briar College and its Faculty Grants Committee enabled me to have an entire year's sabbatical in which to write the book. Dean George Lenz willingly granted me permission to disappear from campus for two years to accept the Judicial Fellowship in Washington and then spend a year writing my manuscript. Ken Grimm, Brent Shea, Tom Loftus, and Pat James were especially helpful in working out the administrative details of my leaves.

The perfect setting in which to write this book was provided (along with research funds) by the Virginia Foundation for the Humanities and Public Policy in Charlottesville, Virginia. The VFH assisted the start of my scholarly career over a decade ago and supported my most recent effort on this book. Rob Vaughan, Roberta Culbertson, Susan Coleman, Carol Hendrix, David Bearinger, Andrew Wyndham, the entire staff, and my "fellow fellows" were superb colleagues. They made this work possible and enjoyable.

Virtually anyone who has crossed my path in the past four years has had to endure endless discussions of the Supreme Court's image. Many of them helped me to sort out my thoughts at critical stages of the project. My thanks go to Henry Abraham, Julia McDonough, Paul Weber, A.E. Dick Howard, Bob O'Neil, David Yalof, John Brigham, Gary Jacobsohn, Bob Deyling, Tim Prinz, Janet Adamski, John Blakeman, Steve Bragaw, Pete Knight, and my perceptive senior seminar students at Sweet Briar. Michelle Davis, Jason Robinson, Rick Mayes, and Susannah Silverbrand provided research assistance for material used in the Introduction and Chapter 1. Bob Beck guided the upgrading of my computer, its software, and my skills to use both of them. A host of audiences to whom I have lectured on this topic around the country also contributed to the enterprise.

Unfortunately, one colleague and friend, whose sage counsel on how to approach this subject was particularly decisive, must be thanked posthumously. Air Force Colonel Nelson Drew, a fellow political scientist, and I talked about my project over a long lunch just a few weeks before he lost his life in August 1995 while on the U.S. peace mission in Bosnia. I am grateful to have known such a wise adviser, and I continue to miss his presence in our profession.

Mim Vasan, my editor on two previous books, now retired but still active in publishing, jump-started this project when I became bogged down in revisions. She has been a reliable, encouraging, and sensitive judge of my work on three books, for which I am most grateful. Jim Sabin and John Donohue provided superb editorial guidance on the final iteration of this volume.

Finally, my parents, Louis and Lillian Perry, are the sources of all of my successful endeavors. On this particular project, they maintained a newspaper clipping service for me and participated in countless debates on the image of the Supreme Court. My mother even devoted part of her 1996 summer vacation to proofreading an earlier draft! Their love and encouragement are boundless and always appreciated beyond words. They will claim that the book is error-free, but their "perfect daughter" knows better. The inevitable mistakes that remain are my responsibility alone.

Introduction: "The Brethren" in "Closed Chambers"?

On January 17, 1995, the chief justice of the United States, William H. Rehnquist, emerged from behind the red velvet curtains to ascend the bench of the U.S. Supreme Court and take his seat in its center chair, poised to hear oral argument in the cases before it. He had performed this ritual for almost nine years since his promotion to chief justice in 1986, but that day in January 1995 was different: "the chief" prompted twitters and craned necks from the audience because of a set of four metallic gold stripes affixed to each arm of his black robe. At an institution where tradition, precedent, and the "cult of the robe" reign supreme, the chief's alterations to his judicial garb resulted in a flood of media comment. All of the major newspapers reported the story, which spread throughout the country on the wire services.

Why all this fuss over a few gold appliqués on a judge's otherwise plain black robe? Chief Justice Rehnquist noted bemusedly some months later that the Court is usually a slow news beat for reporters; any variation from routine in the rather staid "marble palace" becomes a hot story. There is more than a kernel of truth in his analysis. Yet the publicity over the stripes, which surfaced again when Rehnquist wore his embellished robe to preside at the 1999 impeachment trial of President Bill Clinton, illustrates a more profound reality about the Court. Almost half a century ago, Judge Jerome Frank wrote about judicial regalia, which he wanted to see abolished: "The robe . . . gives the impression of uniformity in the decisions of the priestly tribe. Says the uniform black garment to the public mind: Judges attain their wisdom from a single superhuman source; their individual attitudes must never have any effect on what they decide."[1] The chief justice's customized robe, which he confirmed was patterned after the lord chancellor's costume in the Gilbert and Sullivan operetta "Iolanthe," challenged the "impression of uniformity." To the extent that it could potentially alter the Court's image, the robe's alteration was indeed newsworthy.

Despite notable controversies in the Court's history (including *Marbury v. Madison, McCulloch v. Maryland, Dred Scott v. Sandford*, conflict over the New Deal, *Brown v. Board of Education*, Abe Fortas's resignation, *Roe v. Wade*, publication of *The Brethren* and *Closed Chambers*, and Clarence Thomas's nomination), the justices have nurtured, and managed to preserve, the image of themselves as a "priestly tribe." In fact, that image of majesty and mystery has allowed the Court to weather occasional storms of protests from the people, the press, the president, and Congress. The Court has cultivated positive symbolic impressions through the language of its opinions, the emblems of its power and physical environment, and the honorable behavior of its justices and support personnel. Although recent academic literature[2] portrays judges as political actors—differentiated from those in the other two branches only by their unique institutional milieu—the "cult of the robe" continues to play a role in the imagery and symbolism of the Court. Scholars will continue, as they should, to explore the "reality" *behind* the Court's famed red curtains; but to the extent that the general public still judges the Court by its *external* imagery, the importance of judicial symbolism must be recognized. Moreover, social scientists have noted that political symbols convey "emotional, moral, or psychological impact" that may not be "independently true" but may "tap ideas people want to believe in as true."[3]

Undoubtedly, the media play a crucial role in the transmission of the Court's image to the American people. Although rampant sensationalism and cynicism characterize the modern media, coverage of the Supreme Court has tended to accentuate the positive without completely eliminating the negative. The justices' decision to remain rather aloof from the media and public at large, however, ensures them some semblance of control over how they are portrayed. Traditional limits on public access to the Court will help to preserve its integrity and legitimacy by preventing the kind of trivialization experienced by the presidency and Congress, which has resulted, at least in part, from overexposure. My conclusion, therefore, counters American popular culture's obsession with microscopic and intrusive examination of all institutions and individuals to the point of obliterating any distinctions between what should be public knowledge and what should remain private or at least off-limits to television. The 1998 revelation of President Bill Clinton's affair with former White House intern Monica Lewinsky generated renewed and heated debates over boundaries between public and private behavior of government officials—with many observers pleading for a return to pre-Watergate norms of investigative reporting.

The Supreme Court—even while deciding some of the legal questions generated by the Clinton scandal—has succeeded in preserving its dignity.

The reviewer of a trio of books on the Court in 1995 concluded, "[A]ll three authors leave this reader wondering why the Court's constitutional and other decisions are such a powerful force in the minds of Americans."[4] *The Priestly Tribe*, which borrows its paraphrased subtitle from Merrill Peterson's classic work *The Jefferson Image in the American Mind*, addresses that question by offering answers to the following queries: What are the primary images and symbols of the Court today? How have they developed and changed over its history? What are the conduits through which the Court transmits its image to the public? What are the respective roles of the Court's administrative offices, the justices, and the media in the transmission process? How does the public's image of the Court manifest itself? Have public perceptions of the Court changed over time? What is the relationship among image, symbolism, and the Court's legitimacy? Can too much public knowledge of the Court, its members, and its processes diminish its legitimacy?

This topic of the Supreme Court's image—how it is generated by the institution, how it is transferred to the public, and how the public receives it—came to the fore several years ago in the aftermath of the controversy over the Library of Congress's release of the late Justice Thurgood Marshall's papers and the subsequent debate over whether audio tapes of the Supreme Court's oral arguments should be commercially disseminated to the public. In both instances, the Court argued against release of materials that would offer the public a rare view of the inner workings of the institution. The irony of the two moments was too delicious to ignore. The Supreme Court usually seeks to work in the quiet isolation of its marble sanctuary, removed from politics and publicity. Yet the Marshall papers and tape incidents prompted the Court—through the chief justice—to challenge publicly the head of the Library of Congress (who had released the Marshall papers upon the justice's death per his request) and Professor Peter Irons (who had commercially distributed the tapes after signing a form at the National Archives barring such release).

Obviously, the Court was concerned about how the incidents might draw attention to it and breach its coveted confidentiality; yet it drew attention to itself by airing its concerns in public. The controversy over the Marshall papers eventually faded, but Chief Justice Rehnquist concluded that the library had displayed "bad judgment" in violating the Court's confidentiality. A few months later, however, the Court surprisingly relented on the tapes and announced that all audio versions of courtroom arguments would be available to the public at the National Archives on a generally unrestricted basis.

A year-long judicial fellowship in 1994–95 allowed me to observe and analyze the Court's image during my tenure in the Office of the Administrative Assistant to the Chief Justice. The 1998 publication of *Closed Chambers*, a scathing indictment of the Court's inner workings by a former law clerk to Justice Harry Blackmun, only reinforced my view that the story of the Supreme Court's public image had to be told in order to understand how it has survived such assaults throughout its history.

Although the Supreme Court is contemporarily associated with the architectural icon that has served as its home since 1935, the tribunal initially had to develop its place in the American governmental system and the public consciousness without a physical presence. As historian Michael Kammen has noted, "Although John Marshall ["the great chief justice" who served from 1801 to 1835] lacked a temple of justice, his greatest legacy may very well have been a template of justice" consisting of "credible and consensual judgments" that could constitute "a gauge and a guide that successors might use in rendering judgments that achieve legitimacy and endure."[5] Despite being overshadowed by the subsequent tenure of Marshall, the Supreme Court in its first decade of existence demonstrably contributed to establishing the high court's place in the constitutional order.[6]

In addition to benefitting from the wisdom and astute strategic reasoning of Marshall and his predecessors, the Supreme Court has always profited from the unique status that the Founders granted to it. As justices constitutionally appointed for "good behavior," they avoid the rigors, pitfalls, and indignities of having to run for elective office (as some state jurists must). They do not have to campaign periodically for reelection or stoop to fundraising or selling themselves to the public. Although the Court's decisions and its members have occasionally become controversial and the subject of adverse public reaction, the justices do not face electoral opponents who regularly take aim at their character. The constitutional requirement that the federal judiciary decide only bona fide cases and controversies means that the Court's role is circumscribed. It may not simply wade into political conflicts prior to the litigation's arrival at its doorstep; even then the Supreme Court now has virtually complete discretion to refuse to hear a case on appeal.

Furthermore, the Court's traditions and mores buttress the advantages of its constitutional structure. Selecting, discussing, and voting on cases within the bounds of strict privacy are a luxury in the modern world. Political scientist John Roche once observed that the secrecy in which the Constitutional Convention itself was conducted in Philadelphia in 1787 allowed the delegates "to retain that freedom of maneuver which is only possible when men are not forced to take public stands in the preliminary stages of negotiation."[7] The same benefit accrues to the justices from the high court's norm of confidentiality. The Supreme Court's policy of opening oral arguments to the public and journalists, but not to cameras, helps to preserve its more stately image. In addition, most of the 108 individuals who have served on the high tribunal have represented the highest standards of professionalism and personal conduct, and they have conducted their public work with civility, rationality, and efficiency.

The substantive and symbolic aspects of the Supreme Court are therefore mutually reinforcing. The Court is a uniquely positioned political institution, whose symbols and images serve to emphasize that it is sui generis. No wonder that the Supreme Court consistently outscores the president and Congress in opinion polls that measure levels of public trust and confidence in the three branches. A 1997 CNN/*USA Today*/Gallup Poll revealed that 71 percent of those polled responded that they had either a great deal or fair amount of trust and confidence in the judicial branch headed by the Supreme Court, compared to 62 percent for the executive branch headed by the president, and 54 percent for the legislative branch headed by the Congress.[8] As political scientists John Hibbing and Elizabeth Theiss-Morse, who have gathered extensive data on public attitudes toward national government institutions, describe this phenomenon, the public views the Court and its members as one entity that is isolated from the president and Congress and the "Washington system." While people envision the legislative and executive branches as mired in the "evil and nasty" system inside the Beltway, they picture the Supreme Court as part of the "constitutional system," a separate and purer element of the political cosmos.[9]

Justice David Souter, in a dramatic voice-over that concludes the Court's film designed for visitors, sums up the reservoir of goodwill that the Supreme Court has managed to maintain during the balance of its history: "Most people are willing to accept the fact that the Court tries to play it straight. That acceptance has been built up by the preceding hundred justices of this Court, going back to the beginning. We are, in fact, trading on the good faith and the conscientiousness of the justices who went before us. The power of the Court is the power of trust earned—the trust of the American people."[10] The justices relied upon this public trust in their first conflict of the modern era—the battle with President Franklin Roosevelt over the New Deal.

NOTES

1. Jerome Frank, *Courts on Trial: Myth and Reality in American Justice* (Princeton, N.J.: Princeton University Press, 1949), 256–57.

2. See the two most influential works, Jeffrey A. Segal and Harold J. Spaeth, *The Supreme Court and the Attitudinal Model* (New York: Cambridge University Press, 1993), and Lee Epstein and Jack Knight, *The Choices Justices Make* (Washington, D.C.: Congressional Quarterly Press, 1998).

3. Barbara Hinckley, *The Symbolic Presidency: How Presidents Portray Themselves* (New York: Routledge, 1990), 4–7.

4. Richard A. Brisbin, Jr., "Toward a Conservative Constitutional Law?" *Judicature* 78 (March–April 1995): 260.

5. Michael Kammen, "Temples of Justice: The Iconography of Judgment and American Culture," in *Origins of the Federal Judiciary: Essays on the Judiciary Act of 1789*, ed. Maeva Marcus (New York: Oxford University Press, 1992), 276.

6. Scott Douglas Gerber, ed., *Seriatim: The Supreme Court before John Marshall* (New York: New York University Press, 1998).

7. John P. Roche, "The Founding Fathers: A Reform Caucus in Action," *American Political Science Review* 55 (1961): 799.

8. "Gallup Puts Judiciary at Top of Poll," *The Third Branch* 29 (November 1997): 7.

9. John R. Hibbing and Elizabeth Theiss-Morse, *Congress as Public Enemy: Public Attitudes Toward American Political Institutions* (New York: Cambridge University Press, 1995), 87–88.

10. York Associates Television, Inc. (producer), *The Supreme Court of the United States* (Washington, D.C.: Supreme Court Historical Society, 1997), video.

Chapter 1

The "Priestly Tribe" or "Nine Old Men"? Images of the Court during the New Deal

March 4, 1933, the last presidential inauguration day to be held in late winter rather than the now constitutionally mandated date of January 20, dawned bright and sunny for Franklin Delano Roosevelt's swearing-in as the thirty-second president of the United States. As FDR faced the crowd to deliver his stirring inaugural message of hope, one governmental symbol was conspicuously absent from the vista across the east lawn of the Capitol grounds. With the trees still devoid of foliage, Roosevelt would have been able to see clearly to the corner of First Street and Maryland Avenue, N.E., directly behind the Capitol. And just what would he have seen looking east from the stage erected on the Capitol steps? A half-completed structure now known as the Supreme Court building. The very institution that Roosevelt would attack after his 1936 reelection did not even have a separate home of its own at the beginning of his first presidential term.

My assessment of the Court's symbolism during this era and throughout this book relies on Barbara Hinckley's 1990 study of "the symbolic presidency," which defined a political symbol as an object that "has a range of meaning beyond itself" and that conveys an "emotional, moral, or psychological impact. This larger meaning need not be independently true, but will tap ideas that people want to believe in as true."[1] The justices' robes, for example, project an "impression of uniformity" in the Court's decisions.[2] In the public mind, the judges' black garments have signified that jurists attain their wisdom from a higher source that trumps their individual attitudes.[3]

Bolstering this "priestly" image (to borrow Judge Jerome Frank's term) was erection of the "marble temple," the Supreme Court's first permanent and separate edifice, which was completed in 1935. The majesty and solidity of the Court's physical structure were emblematic of the tribunal's ultimately successful emergence from the turbulent Roosevelt years. Moreover, the justices of the U.S. Supreme Court (on both sides of the New Deal battle) had clung tightly to their image of impartiality, fairness, and independence throughout the 1930s—even in their most contentious and politically charged decisions. In addition, the media transmitted that image to the public, whose generally favorable opinions toward the Court are evident in polling data from the era.

The Supreme Court had begun its life as the "least dangerous" and most obscure branch of the federal government and only gradually developed into its full partnership with the president and Congress. The Court was the unknown branch for much of the Republic's first century. Yet when Americans did contemplate the Court, they often saw it inextricably bound with the Constitution as one and the same. To the extent that Americans developed reverence for the Constitution, they developed reverence for the Court.[4]

Nevertheless, image and reality of the Court collided during the New Deal crisis. The clash between the justices and FDR embodied two competing strands of the Court's modern history. Inserting itself so boldly and obviously into the governmental process is said to have politicized the Court. In addition, the petty rivalries among justices in the 1940s, which were heavily publicized, humanized the Court, resulting in "justices without halos."[5]

Yet if FDR's Court-packing proposal represented the nadir of the Court's sullied image, its rescue by Congress in defeating the plan helped to restore the tribunal's revered status. Congress's salvaging of the independent judiciary—ensuring that it was beyond the reach of the more political branches—was truly a "defining moment" in the Court's history, to quote Chief Justice William H. Rehnquist.

HOW THE COURT PRESENTED ITSELF: EDIFICE AS IMAGE

In its first 145 years the Supreme Court led a truly nomadic existence. As a permanent exhibit at the Supreme Court notes, "Through the years, the Court was like a poor relation, with meeting space arranged almost as an afterthought."[6] In 1790 the Supreme Court met for the first time under the new Constitution in the then seat of the national government—New York City. The Court convened in the Exchange Building, which was a combination marketplace on the ground floor and meeting space on the upper level. At the end of 1790 the federal government's locale moved to Philadelphia, and the Supreme Court's first half of the 1791 term was spent in the Pennsylvania State House, now known as Independence Hall. The Court convened for the second half of its 1791 term in the newly completed

Philadelphia City Hall. The Court's small wooden chamber—now restored for visitors and modest by today's standards—features simple, early American appointments. Location and decoration were not crucial issues for the Court, however, because during its first several terms, it heard very few cases.

At the turn of the nineteenth century, the peripatetic national government finally settled in Washington, D.C., and a Capitol and executive mansion were the first governmental buildings erected. There were no separate plans for the Supreme Court, however. Architect Benjamin Henry Latrobe's design for the Capitol building included a small room for the Court's use; it would occupy several such niches as it was pushed from one chamber to another in the course of history.

The Court initially occupied a small room in the southwest corner of the Capitol's north wing. Improvements on that wing of the Capitol included a new chamber for the Supreme Court in the building's basement, where it moved for its 1810 term. Just four years later, however, the British stormed Washington during the War of 1812; the Capitol was severely damaged in one of the many fires set by the invaders. In fact, the British ignited a blaze in the Supreme Court chamber itself. The highest court in the land truly followed the old cliché of moving from pillar to post in the years after the War of 1812; it took up residence in a number of sites scattered throughout Washington.

With the restoration of the Capitol, the Supreme Court returned to its basement chamber in early 1819, but by 1859 the "Proceedings of the House of Representatives" declared that "[t]his Congress will not allow the Supreme Court of a Government like ours to sit in the cellar of the Capitol, and have strangers, when they come here and ask to be shown the greatest judicial tribunal of the country, to be taken down [into the] cellar."[7] One observer dubbed the dark, dank chamber a "potato hole"; and visitors joked that the sculpted figure of Lady Justice, usually portrayed with a blindfold to symbolize impartiality, did not need to have her eyes covered because it was so dark she could not see anyway.

In 1860 the Court moved upstairs to a more spacious room just vacated by the Senate for its move to the present Senate chamber. The old Supreme Court chamber in the basement then became a law library for the tribunal. Still, there was no room for the justices to have their own offices, and they therefore worked at home. In 1899 the *Wilmington News* reported to its readers in Delaware that a new building for the Supreme Court had been proposed in Washington. Arguing for the construction of such a structure, the newspaper commented, "There is no sound reason why the court should be cooped up in . . . the Capitol. Let the court have a handsome home of its own."[8]

Nevertheless, the Court remained "cooped up" until 1935 when, as if to assert a physical symbol of its presence, it moved into its current majestic home after almost a century and a half of occupying "borrowed" space in the Capitol building across the street. The very idea that the legislative and judicial branches would share quarters was anathema to a system of separated powers. In ways big and small, sharing space with Congress was a humiliation. For example, when rooms were at a premium, justices initially had to robe in public before oral argument; when they finally did procure their own robing room in the Capitol, it was barely large enough for all nine justices and their assistants. In contrast, the present Court building has a spacious robing room for the justices, where they exchange their symbolic handshake before emerging en masse from behind the burgundy velvet curtains to ascend the bench for their public sessions and sit in order of seniority, the chief justice in the center chair.

As Chief Justice Charles Evans Hughes declared at the 1932 ceremony marking the laying of the Court's cornerstone, "The Republic endures and this is the symbol of its faith."[9] In the depths of the Great Depression, many Americans must have wondered if the country (much less the Court) would indeed endure. At the height of worldwide economic disaster, the architectural undertaking was a sign that the country would survive with its rule of law intact.

On October 7, 1935, the Court opened the first term in its new home— and a fitting home it was. Cass Gilbert, the architect who had taken on the Court's design as his last major project at age 70, planned a stunning visual impact from the Court's front plaza and facade. He chose the classical temple style from the Roman adaptation of the Greek building form. Appropriately for the home of the priestly tribe, Gilbert used Pierre Vignon's "La Madeleine" church in Paris as a modern source of inspiration for the Court. He then surrounded the building's exterior and filled the edifice's interior with a plethora of symbols to augment the Court's majestic image.

The lampposts are adorned with ram heads and lion paws, both of which are meant to represent strength. A peak under the light standards reveals that they rest on bronze tortoises, reportedly signifying the deliberate pace of justice. Eight relief panels in the bronze doors on the Court's front facade depict the growth of the law from ancient Greece and Rome to the early United States. Designed by sculptor John Donnelly, Jr., the doors' style is said to follow that used in the fifteenth century by the Italian artist Lorenzo Ghiberti in his famous "Gates of Paradise" on the Baptistry in Florence. Allegorical figures representing the "Contemplation of Justice" and the "Authority of Law," carved from a 250-ton slab of marble, flank the Court's front entrance. The figure of Justice is blindfolded as a symbol of impartiality and is holding a pair of scales to represent balance and fairness. Flagpoles on the Court's distinctive plaza depict cherubs also displaying scales and swords representing the strength of justice. Other carved angels hold masks and torches to symbolize the ability of enlightenment to uncover the mask of untruth.

The Court's front pediment displays a classical sculptural group of allegorical figures that depict Liberty, Justice, Order, Authority, Council, and

Research Past and Present. Artist Robert Aitken, who sculpted the figures, impishly included the faces of well-known Americans in his depictions. For example, Chief Justice William Howard Taft, whose personal lobbying for the Court's new building was instrumental in its completion, is portrayed as a student at Yale University, his beloved alma mater, in the figure of "Research Present." Taft, the only one of 108 justices in the Court's history also to have served as president of the United States, loved the judiciary and was miserable in the White House. He adored the Court, considered serving on it the attainment of nirvana, and believed passionately that it should have its own home. Taft had remarked to a member of Congress in 1923, "I shall continue to protest against the fact that you do not allow the Supreme Court to have space enough for its records."[10] Fate did not allow him to witness its completion, for he died in 1930, five years before the justices held their first oral argument session in the new building, but it is appropriate that his visage gazes down upon all who enter what can accurately be called "Chief Justice Taft's building." By 1935, Taft's vision of heaven now resided in a neoclassical temple supported by soaring white marble columns. The Court finally had a building that matched its priestly image. As the Supreme Court Historical Society has noted, the "aura of formality is no accident."[11] When Cass Gilbert offered his proposed design for the Court in 1929, he wrote that he planned "a building of dignity and importance . . . suitable for the permanent home of the Supreme Court of the United States."[12]

After climbing up the broad, white steps, stepping under the Corinthian columns, and passing through the foyer, visitors to the Supreme Court enter the impressive "Great Hall." Designed by Gilbert—who also did not live to see his masterpiece—it was meant to dramatize the approach to the courtroom of the highest tribunal in the land. The walls, floor, and modified Doric columns that support the hall were constructed of Alabama marble; 22-foot blocks of stone constitute the monolithic pillars. Massive wooden doors, carved with symbolic figures, grace the entrance to the court chamber at the opposite end of the Great Hall.

In the same year that the Court moved into its new home, it established a Public Information Office (PIO). Thus, the Court institutionalized the presentation of itself to the media and public at large. In 1935, the PIO began giving journalists copies of full opinions as they were announced from the bench. The new procedure made reporting on the Court's decisions easier and presumably more accurate.

HOW THE JUSTICES PRESENTED THEMSELVES: THEIR WORK AS IMAGE

The Court's new structure also gave the justices an enhanced space and opportunity to present themselves through the public component of their work—oral argument. Its sparse quarters in the Capitol building had barely allowed room for spectators. When the Court opened its first term in the new building, however, it looked out on a chamber that could hold some 300 visitors. Chief Justice Taft had also suggested that adequate space be incorporated into the chamber's architectural plans.

The courtroom's design and appointments were as majestic as the entire structure. Gilbert had emphasized that "the location of the chamber itself, in the very heart of the structure, symbolizes the importance of the room in which the Court presides."[13] He imported marble from Spain for the walls and friezes and Italian marble for the Ionic columns that support the room. Gilbert even met with the Italian dictator Benito Mussolini to ensure that only the highest quality Italian marble was exported for the project. The courtroom's elaborate ceiling, designed by mural artist Ezra Winter, displays various styles of plaster rosettes, all highlighted with 23-carat gold leaf. Bronze gates border the room on either side and separate it from two bright colonnades that face exterior courtyards. Each eight-foot gate contains reliefs of lion and eagle heads, torches, and scales of justice. Surrounding the room on all four sides are friezes sculpted by noted artist Adolph Weinman, who depicted a classical procession of "great lawgivers of history," portraying the development of secular law. Hammurabi, Moses, Solomon, Confucius, Mohammed, Charlemagne, Blackstone, John Marshall (the fourth chief justice and only American portrayed in the friezes), and Napoleon are among the historical figures included. The carvings directly above the winged Honduran mahogany bench depict allegorical figures representing Majesty of Law, Power of Government, Wisdom, Justice, and the Defense of Human Rights and Protection of Innocence.

To this day the Court performs at its symbolic best when it convenes for an oral argument session. The courtroom itself, with its marble columns, carved friezes, pews, and velvet curtains, has a church-like quality about it. Spectators speak in hushed tones while they wait for the sessions to begin, and five minutes before the justices enter, the Court's police officers silence the assembly. At exactly the appointed hour, the silence is broken by the crack of the marshal's gavel, and he utters the famous incantation calling the room to order: "The honorable, the chief justice and associate justices, of the Supreme Court of the United States! Oyez, oyez, oyez! All persons having business before the honorable, the Supreme Court of the United States, are admonished to draw near and give their attention for the Court is now sitting. God save the United States and this honorable Court!"

Because only a small number of Americans ever see the Court in session, the tribunal's release of opinions presents one important method of reaching the public. The very concept of "opinions for the Court," which become the law of the land, indicates that decisions are presented on behalf of the institution. Dissents and concurrence, on the other hand, usually reflect the individuality of the author who refers to himself/herself in the first person. In contrast, opinions of the Court are couched in the language of the third person or first person plural, similar to the pope's use of the papal "we." Nonetheless, the propensity of the Court to fracture into closely divided 5–4 and 6–3 rulings on economic regulatory legislation during the 1930s threatened to destroy the Court's ideal of uniformity.

Two cases in 1934 gave New Dealers hope that a narrow majority of the Court would prevail in upholding at least state legislative efforts to ameliorate the effects of the Great Depression. *Home Building & Loan v. Blaisdell* upheld the Minnesota Moratorium Act, giving homeowners and farmers an extension on their mortgage payments during the economic crisis. In concluding his opinion for the five-person majority that the Minnesota statute did not violate the U.S. Constitution's contract clause, Chief Justice Hughes emphasized the Court's neutral image in the realm of public policy. He wrote, "Whether the legislation is wise or unwise as a matter of policy is a question with which we are not concerned."[14] The "Four Horsemen's" dissent, drafted by Justice George Sutherland for Justices Willis Van Devanter, James McReynolds, and Pierce Butler, also invoked the image of the Court as a neutral arbiter of the constitutionality of legislation. Nonetheless, the minority reached the opposite conclusion from the majority and argued in its dissent that the Minnesota statute violated the contract clause.

Following *Blaisdell*, the Court upheld a New York State milk price control law, again with ominous dissents from the "Four Horsemen," in *Nebbia v. New York*.[15] With Justice Owen Roberts writing this time for another close 5–4 majority, the Court reiterated its "function" of applying the pertinent provisions of the Constitution (in this instance the due process clause of the Fourteenth Amendment) to determine the validity of the challenged statute.

The Roosevelt administration's fleeting hopes were dashed, however, at the start of 1935. In early January the Court struck down a portion of FDR's National Industrial Recovery Act (NIRA) on the grounds that Congress had unconstitutionally delegated power to the president to exclude from interstate commerce any oil produced in excess of state regulations. Chief Justice Hughes, who had supported *state* regulatory legislation in the previous year's *Nebbia* case, again made reference to the Court's neutral exercise of judicial review and expanded the image to portray the Court as the guardian of the American constitutional system. As Hughes wrote for a majority that included all but Justice Benjamin Cardozo, "The question is not of the intrinsic importance of the particular statute before us, but of the constitutional processes of legislation which are an essential part of our system of government."[16]

President Roosevelt and his New Deal suffered several more famous blows from the Court before the end of 1935 (most prominently in *Schecter Poultry Corp. v. United States*, which unanimously struck down Section 3 of the NIRA—the very heart of the statute—on the grounds that it unconstitutionally delegated power to the president and ran afoul of the interstate commerce clause),[17] and the new year brought only more judicial defeats for the beleaguered and increasingly frustrated chief executive. During the first week of January 1936, a 6–3 decision by the Court in *United States v. Butler* held unconstitutional the essential provisions of the Agricultural Adjustment Act of 1933, which provided government subsidies to farmers for agreeing to reduce crop production.[18] Money for the subsidy was to come from a tax levied on the processor of the commodity. Justice Roberts's opinion for the Court found Congress's statutory plan to regulate and control production to be beyond the powers delegated to the national government and a clear violation of the Tenth Amendment.

Roberts followed Hughes's lead from the "hot oil" case and argued, "We approach [this case's] decisions with a sense of our grave responsibility to render judgment in accordance with the principles established for the governance of all three branches of the government."[19] Explaining his now-famous explication of a mechanistic and supposedly neutral approach to judicial review, Roberts continued: "When an act of Congress is appropriately challenged in the courts as not conforming to the constitutional mandate, the judicial branch of the government has only one duty; to lay the article of the Constitution which is invoked beside the statute which is challenged and to decide whether the latter squares with the former."[20] Roberts declared, "This court neither approves nor condemns any legislative policy,"[21] thus reiterating the Court's self-described impartiality vis-à-vis public policy.

Justice Harlan Stone's dissent, joined by Justices Brandeis and Cardozo, also noted, as had the majority opinion, "that courts are concerned only with the power to enact statutes, not with their wisdom."[22] Yet Stone called on his brethren to uphold the challenged legislation in an exercise of judicial "self-restraint."[23] In a book published four years later and just before his own appointment to the Supreme Court, Robert Jackson wrote that "[w]hat Mr. Justice Stone was saying, in measured words, was that the decision of the majority was not a legal judgment, but a political and economic judgment, which the Court had no constitutional authority to make."[24] On a collision course then were the image of the Court as an impartial, apolitical arbiter and the perception that a slim majority of the "nine old men" was engaging in unconstitutional public policy-making.

Still to come before the end of the Court's first term in its new building was an invalidation of the Bituminous Coal Act of 1935 (which was Congress's attempt to stabilize the coal industry through regulation of prices, methods of competition, and labor relations) and the negation of a New York State minimum wage law for women. President Roosevelt grew more enraged and frustrated as he saw his initial term of office waning without an opportunity to appoint a new member to the highest court in the land. Nevertheless, he was almost completely silent during the 1936 campaign on what he might do in his second term to eliminate judicial opposition to the realization of the New Deal. Observers speculated, however, that FDR's landslide victory over Republican Alf Landon, and the president's subsequent announcement of his Court-packing plan in February 1937, may well have persuaded two members of the Court, Chief Justice Hughes and Justice Roberts, to change their votes to support economic regulatory legislation. The famous switch in voting line-ups came first in *West Coast Hotel Co. v. Parrish*, which upheld a Washington State minimum wage law for women and minors, and then in *National Labor Relations Board v. Jones & Laughlin Steel Corporation*, which sanctioned the New Deal's National Labor Relations Act.[25]

HOW THE MEDIA PRESENTED THE COURT: JOURNALISTIC IMAGES

Journalistic presentation of the justices during this time generally bolstered the Court's hallowed image from early in the Roosevelt administration and through the judicial negations of New Deal legislation and the subsequent Court-packing debates. An April 7, 1934 article in the popular magazine *Literary Digest* reflects the dignified image of the Court and its members. Despite its headline, "The Supreme Court—Nine Mortal Men," the article's subtitle was more in keeping with the priestly image of the tribunal. The secondary headline read, "Misty, Omniscient, Living in an Intellectual Super-World, the Slow, Awe-Inspiring, Black-Robed Procession Proves to Be Made Up of Warm, Vital Human Beings."[26]

The article described the Supreme Court as "[b]y far the most majestic branch of the Government of the United States," referring to the justices as "half-deified figures" and labeling the sessions of the Court as "awe-inspiring," especially "the slow procession of black-robed, white-haired men to the high-back chairs behind the bench in the small, hushed chamber in the Capitol, and the deliberate unperturbed procedure as they read opinions or listen to arguments."[27] Yet, as if to foreshadow the intense scrutiny to which the institution would soon find itself subjected, the reporter wrote, "[A]s a matter of cold fact, the public should know as much about these nine men as about any others in the Government."[28]

The *Literary Digest* piece, written by Theodore Wallen, also delineated the ideologies and personalities of the Court's nine members. Wallen predicted, with about as much success as his magazine would have in prophesying that Alf Landon would win the 1936 presidential election, that the Court would probably uphold much of the New Deal. The article praised Chief Justice Hughes for his endeavors "to achieve a greater degree of judicial harmony in the apparent hope of reducing the number of 6–3 and 5–4 decisions which impair the weight of the Court's decisions by reminding the public that the interpretation of the Constitution is far from being an exact science."[29] Wallen labeled Hughes and Roberts as "middle-of-the-road justices" and "practical men who apparently feel that in periods of flux the Supreme Court must go part way, at least, with public opinion and Congress and the Executive."[30]

Wallen concluded that "to the politically minded observer the significant fact is that the Supreme Court is moving with the tide."[31] He erred in his prediction by three years, but at least he did relate a more prescient comment about those who argued that if the Court did not follow the public and its representatives, the justices might face "enlargement of the Court" or "some other action which would permanently injure the power of the Court to act as a check on the legislative excesses."[32]

A sample of news articles and editorials from the *Wall Street Journal*, the *Washington Post*, and the *New York Times* on the landmark New Deal cases and FDR's Court-packing plan reveals that these national publications, and the regional newspapers they surveyed, were overwhelmingly deferential to and communicative of the Supreme Court's role as an impartial arbiter of the Constitution. The day after the *Schecter* decision came down, for example, the *Washington Post* hailed its unanimity and stated that the Court had helped "to restore our government procedure to the orderly and constructive lines mapped out by the framers of the Constitution. . . . Thus the traditional balance of power between the legislative, executive, and judicial arms of our Government is restored."[33] Tying the Court's decision so closely to the Constitution demonstrated how the tribunal's image was still inextricably bound with the founding document.

The *Post*'s primary news story on *Schecter* even linked the Court's actions to the physical symbols of its power, history, and prestige. The paper reported that the Court's stunning announcement of its decision in the so-called "sick chicken" case constituted the penultimate time the high tribunal presided in the Capitol building chamber. Gushed the *Post*'s reporter, "Seated where those momentous events, which left their mark on American life, took place and facing the marble busts of all the Chief Justices who ever presided over the court, the nine black-robed jurists with grim faces and without ceremony proceeded to their work. . . . Holding the judicial scales evenly balanced, the Chief Justice recited the nature of the *Schecter* case."[34]

From the *St. Louis Globe-Democrat* came more praise for the Court, which, the paper declared, "exists primarily to guard" the foundations of our political system "that have sustained it [the United States] for a century and a half and that have enabled us to grow and to prosper beyond any other nation under the sun."[35] The *Philadelphia Inquirer* lauded the justices for countering President Roosevelt's "concept of presidential authority," which, so argued the paper, FDR had viewed "as differing widely from those of past executives."[36] Concluded the Philadelphia publication, "[E]mergency or no emergency, Mr. Roosevelt embarked upon a gigantic career of experimentation, at a cost of billions upon billions of dollars, without any misgivings for the legality of his operations."[37] Likewise, the *Kansas City*

Star noted that "[e]ven in the name of emergency it [the Constitution] protects the people and the States as it was designed to do."[38] Moreover, the Kansas City paper hailed the *Schecter* case as proving that "the Constitution is supreme. It cannot be made to mean what it does not say or stretched to cover a broad and virtually unrestricted grant of power."[39] The *New York Times* reported similar "editorial satisfaction" with the *Schecter* decision in newspapers throughout the country.[40]

In addition, Raymond Clapper's syndicated editorial on *Schecter* observed that "[t]alk of blackjacking the Court by enlarging its membership collapsed when all nine justices joined in the decision. That subterfuge of packing the Court, a weak and uncertain one at best, becomes ridiculous to think of now."[41]

The newspapers also reported at length on the press conference convened by President Roosevelt three days after *Schecter* came down. FDR's now famous criticism of the Court as taking the country back to "the horse and buggy stage" of constitutional interpretation appeared prominently in all of the national newspapers. (The widespread quotation of Roosevelt's scathing comment resulted, in part, from the fact that the phrase was the only one the president gave permission to the press to report verbatim. In contrast to the relative openness of today's presidential/press relations, the ground rules of FDR's news conferences maintained the president could "not be directly quoted without his specific permission."[42])

A *New York Times* editorial was typical in its criticism of Roosevelt's demeanor and message at his May 31, 1935 press conference. Dismayed by FDR's uncharacteristic vitriol, the *Times*'s editors responded, "One of the things most admired in Mr. Roosevelt, all through his term, has been his calmness and poise of spirit. Modest in victory, he has been cheerful in defeat. No one could have expected him to betray the pique that appears in his remarks yesterday. It is to be feared that the bitterness of his attitude will frustrate the very purposes he has in mind."[43]

On the other hand, *The New Republic*, with its self-admitted socialist vision of government and public policy, was apoplectic in the days following *Schecter*. It explicitly attacked the Supreme Court and its image, asserting: "The legal fiction is that the Court does not, or should not, concern itself with matters of economic policy. . . . Whatever may be the mental processes of the honorable Justices, however, the practical result of their decisions is often to forbid or reverse important economic policies."[44]

A more famous (or infamous) attack on the Court came from columnists Drew Pearson and Robert Allen's book *The Nine Old Men*. Published in late October 1936, it quickly found its way onto the best-seller lists, was serialized in newspapers throughout the country, and presumably reached a wider audience than the more elitist *New Republic*. The book began with a snide look at the justices' new home, which Pearson and Allen dubbed "The Taj Mahal."[45] The authors offered not a scintilla of documentation for their observations and judgments on the Court as an institution, its members, and its procedures. Historian William Leuchtenburg has commented that "[e]ven critics of the Justices were disturbed by the book's tone and by its inaccuracies."[46]

Thus, when President Roosevelt announced his plans for restructuring the federal judiciary, including his scheme for enlarging the Supreme Court's membership, on February 5, 1937, even *The New Republic* was lukewarm on the proposal. FDR told the American people in one of his famed fireside radio broadcasts, on March 9, 1937, that "[t]he Court has been acting not as a judicial body, but as a policy-making body."[47] *The New Republic* wholeheartedly agreed with the president's assessment, but its editors noted in a column the following week that "neither the president nor anyone else has any marked enthusiasm" for the Court-reform plan.[48]

Indeed, the media had expressed virtually no enthusiasm for the plan from the outset. The *Los Angeles Times* took issue with the president's motives, if not the substance of the reform package, just one day after FDR had sent his plan to Congress. Coming to the aid of the Court, the L.A. paper wrote about the president's blueprint: "These proposals should not pass, even though, in the ordinary course, there is undeniable merit in some of them. It would be better for the United States to suffer stagnation in its judicial system, a breakdown of court processes through congestion and delay, than the independence of the judiciary be destroyed."[49] (Chief Justice Hughes had written to one of the Senate's most influential members, Burton K. Wheeler [D.-Mont.], to oppose FDR's plan and to provide irrefutable evidence that the Supreme Court was completely current in its docket. The case backlog that the president used as one rationale for wanting to enlarge the Court simply did not exist.[50]) Included in the same edition of the Los Angeles paper was an editorial cartoon entitled "The Hands of Dictatorship!" depicting two hands of "the Chief Executive," with one squeezing a man labeled "Legislative Branch of Government," and the other groping hand marked, "Grasping for the Judiciary."[51]

Even the papers normally aligned with the Democratic Party in that era opposed FDR's plan for the judiciary. A 1937 survey by the *Christian Science Monitor* of 76 leading Democratic newspapers revealed that only 20 papers (with a combined circulation of 3,136,198) endorsed the Court bill, whereas 52 papers (with a combined circulation of 13,191,693) opposed the plan. Of the major newspapers that supported President Roosevelt throughout the Court-packing ordeal, the most influential were the *New York Daily News*, the *New York Post*, the *Philadelphia Record*, the *Louisville Courier-Journal*, and the *St. Louis Star-Times*.[52]

Obviously, editorial reactions to the Court-packing plan did not necessarily divide along partisan fault lines. A more likely explanation for journalistic opposition to FDR's scheme—even among normally supportive editors—may well be related to the public image of the Supreme Court in the American democratic system. The *L.A. Times*'s stance is particularly illustrative for its reference to the imperative of preserving judicial independence, and its editorial cartoon reflecting the basic tenets of separation of powers. Indeed, major newspapers throughout the country had lent their stamp of approval to many of the Court's anti–New Deal decisions, which the editors interpreted as a valid judicial exercise of the constitutional construct of checks and balances. In turn, this positive portrayal of the Court only served to reinforce its reservoir of goodwill as the arbiter of America's fundamental governing document.

By the summer of 1937, judicial biographer Merlo Pusey had published a scholarly, yet accessible, rejoinder to Roosevelt's proposal to "reform" the federal judiciary. Addressed to the "average reader," the book's foreword by Senator Edward R. Burke of Nebraska argued "that only a Supreme Court, independent and unawed, stands guard to protect the rights and liberties of the people. If a million American men and women could receive today the message contained within the two covers of this book, the Supreme Court would be saved from pillage."[53]

Of course, the high tribunal was spared from the ill-conceived Roosevelt scheme when the legislation was ultimately removed from consideration by the full Senate on July 22, 1937. Yet, in the meantime, good fortune had finally shone on the New Deal when Chief Justice Hughes and Justice Roberts cast their votes to support state and federal economic regulation and Justice Van Devanter, one of the "Four Horsemen," announced his retirement from the Court in May 1937.

HOW THE PUBLIC PERCEIVED THE COURT: IMAGES IN THE AMERICAN MIND

Throughout the clash between FDR and the Court, the president vowed to take his fight to the people, who he thought would undoubtedly support his position. Public opinion polls of the era, however, reveal less backing for Roosevelt's stance than he assumed. According to William Leuchtenburg, "Most of the nation in 1935 was still either indifferent to the Court question or outrightly opposed to tethering the Court."[54] In fact, the newly established Gallup Poll asked the following question in the fall of 1935: "As a general principle, would you favor limiting the power of the Supreme Court to declare acts of Congress unconstitutional?" The response was: yes, 31 percent; no, 53 percent; and no opinion, 16 percent. The Gallup organization discovered the strongest anti-Court sentiment among those respondents who believed they had been harmed by a particular decision. For example, one man complained bitterly that the Court had "turned" his railroad pension (a reference to the Court's declaring unconstitutional the Railroad Retirement Act of 1934[55]). "But many more thought the justices wise, the system of checks and balances sacred, and Congress mercurial, although their conception of these institutions was sometimes primitive. Asked his view, an Ohio relief recipient said: 'If they didn't know more than the other courts, they wouldn't be called the Supreme Court.' "[56]

Even after Roosevelt's momentous landslide victory in the 1936 presidential election, public opinion showed little variation on its support for the Supreme Court's power. Asked virtually the same question by the Gallup Poll as the organization had posed in 1935, "As a general policy, are you in favor of limiting the power of the Supreme Court to declare acts of Congress unconstitutional?", a third of the respondents answered yes, almost half no, and 17 percent expressed no opinion.[57]

On the issue of FDR's proposal to enlarge the Supreme Court's membership, Gallup Polls indicate that from just after the president announced his plan in February 1937 to the early summer of that year, the highest percentage of respondents favoring the legislation was 45.9 percent.[58] The president's plan reached that public opinion high point (still short of a majority) immediately after Roosevelt's March 9 fireside chat.[59] In that radio address, FDR had compared the Court to the third horse on a team pulling in the wrong direction a plough guided by the American people; the other two horses (representing Congress and the president) were pulling in the direction determined by the popular will.

The low water mark in the Gallup Poll (only 31 percent responding favorably toward Roosevelt's scheme) occurred just after Justice Van Devanter announced his retirement from the bench in May 1937. Although the plan regained some support over the next month, the final Gallup Poll taken on the issue during the second week of June 1937 reflects that less than 38 percent of those polled responded affirmatively to the proposal. Despite his electoral popularity, President Roosevelt never commanded the allegiance of a majority of Americans in the struggle against the Supreme Court.[60]

Miraculously, the priestly tribe had escaped the most direct attack ever on its independence. By 1935 the Court could retreat into the obvious symbol of its bolstered stature—the marble temple at 1 First Street, N.E. in Washington, D.C. Yet even before the justices took possession of their new accommodations, the *New York Times* displayed a photo of the Court building's east pediment just above the Preamble of the U.S. Constitution and placed around the pictures photographs of Chief Justice Hughes and President Roosevelt squared off against each other.[61] Thus, the Court's permanent home and the nation's founding document were linked as a symbol of the Court's role in interpreting and defending the Constitution.

The struggle between FDR and the highest court in the land revealed a tension inherent in the American system, which inevitably observes its hallowed judges descending into the political fray through their exercise of judicial review, but which chooses to perpetuate an image of the Supreme Court above politics. Although the Court was locked in an epic conflict over its status and very composition during the New Deal, the symbols and images of the Court's impartiality, fairness, independence, and dignity survived the battle and allowed it to fight another day.

NOTES

1. Barbara Hinckley, *The Symbolic Presidency: How Presidents Present Themselves* (New York: Routledge, 1990), 4–7.
2. Jerome Frank, *Courts on Trial: Myth and Reality in American Justice* (Princeton, N.J.: Princeton University Press, 1949), 256–57.
3. Ibid.
4. Michael Kammen, *A Machine That Would Go of Itself: The Constitution in American Culture* (New York: St. Martin's Press, 1994). For additional commentaries on the role of the Supreme Court and the Constitution in American political culture, see also Max Lerner, "Constitution and the Court as Symbols," in *Nine Scorpions in a Bottle: Great Judges and Cases of the Supreme Court*, ed. Richard Cummings (New York: Arcade Publishing, 1994), Sanford Levinson, *Constitutional Faith* (Princeton, N.J.: Princeton University Press, 1988), and John E. Semonche, *Keeping the Faith: A Cultural History of the U.S. Supreme Court* (Lanham, Md.: Rowman & Littlefield, 1998).
5. C. Herman Pritchett, *The Roosevelt Court: A Study in Judicial Politics and Values, 1937–1947* (Chicago: Quadrangle Books, 1969), ix.
6. This quotation, as well as the balance of information on the Court's buildings, originates in the script of the Court's exhibit entitled "The Supreme Court of the United States: Its Form and Function." Unveiled in 1994, the display is the first permanent exhibit in the Supreme Court building. I am grateful to the Court's Curator Gail Galloway for generously sharing the script with me.
7. Ibid.
8. Ibid.
9. "The Supreme Court of the United States," prepared by the Supreme Court of the United States, published in cooperation with the Supreme Court Historical Society, 2.
10. "The Supreme Court of the United States: Its Form and Function," script provided by the Supreme Court Curator.
11. Mary Ann Harrell and Burnett Anderson, *Equal Justice Under Law: The Supreme Court in American Life*, 6th ed. (Washington, D.C.: The Supreme Court Historical Society, 1994), 122.
12. Ibid.
13. "The Supreme Court of the United States: Its Form and Function," script provided by the Supreme Court Curator.
14. 290 U.S. 398 (1934).
15. 291 U.S. 502 (1934).
16. *Panama Refining Co. v. Ryan*, 293 U.S. 388 (1935).
17. 295 U.S. 495 (1935).
18. 297 U.S. 1 (1936).
19. Ibid.
20. Ibid.
21. Ibid.

22. Ibid.

23. Ibid.

24. Robert H. Jackson, *The Struggle for Judicial Supremacy: A Study of a Crisis in American Power Politics* (New York: Octagon Books, 1979), 136.

25. 300 U.S. 379 (1937), and 301 U.S. 1 (1937), respectively.

26. Theodore C. Wallen, "The Supreme Court—Nine Mortal Men," *Literary Digest*, 7 April 1934, 9, 45–47.

27. Ibid.

28. Ibid.

29. Ibid.

30. Ibid.

31. Ibid.

32. Ibid.

33. "More Haste, Less Speed," *Washington Post*, 28 May 1935, 8.

34. "All Codes Suspended as Supreme Court Scraps NRA," *Washington Post*, 28 May 1935, 14.

35. "Press of Nation Gives Opinions on NRA Ruling," *Washington Post*, 28 May 1935, 15.

36. Ibid.

37. Ibid.

38. Ibid.

39. Ibid.

40. "Press Generally Sees Ruling as a Victory for Fundamental Law," *New York Times*, 28 May 1935, 12.

41. "Glee Over NRA's End May Be a Bit Premature," *Washington Post*, 29 May 1935, 2.

42. "Roosevelt Sees Social Setback of 50 Years in Court Decision; Calls on People to Face Crisis," *Washington Post*, 1 June 1935, 4.

43. "An Imprudent Speech," *New York Times*, 1 June 1935, 14.

44. "Social Control vs. the Constitution," *The New Republic*, 12 June 1935, 117.

45. Drew Pearson and Robert Allen, *The Nine Old Men* (New York: Doubleday, 1936).

46. William E. Leuchtenburg, *The Supreme Court Reborn: The Constitutional Revolution in the Age of Roosevelt* (New York: Oxford University Press, 1995), 119.

47. Franklin D. Roosevelt, "Reorganizing the Federal Judiciary," 9 March 1937, in *Free Government in the Making: Readings in American Political Thought*, 3d ed., ed. Alpheus Thomas Mason (New York: Oxford University Press, 1965), 800.

48. "The President Faces the Court," *The New Republic*, 17 March 1937, 154.

49. "Packing the Supreme Court," *Los Angeles Times*, 6 February 1937, 4.

50. See text of the Hughes letter in Elder Witt, *Guide to the Supreme Court*, 2d ed. (Washington, D.C.: Congressional Quarterly Press, 1990), 963.

51. "Packing the Supreme Court."

52. E. Kimbark MacColl, "The Supreme Court and Public Opinion: A Study of the Court Fight of 1937" (Ph.D. diss., UCLA, 1953), 224–25.

53. Merlo Pusey, *The Supreme Court in Crisis* (New York: Macmillan, 1937), vi.

54. Leuchtenburg, *The Supreme Court Reborn*, 94.

55. *Railroad Board v. Alton R. Co.*, 295 U.S. 330 (1935).

56. Leuchtenburg, *The Supreme Court Reborn*, 94.

57. Kammen, *A Machine That Would Go of Itself*, 325.

58. Lee Epstein et al., *The Supreme Court Compendium: Data, Decisions, and Developments* (Washington, D.C.: Congressional Quarterly Press, 1994), 605.

59. Gregory A. Caldeira, "Public Opinion and the U.S. Supreme Court: FDR's Court-Packing Plan," *American Political Science Review* 81 (December 1987): 1146.

60. Epstein, *The Supreme Court Compendium*, 605.

61. "End of NRA," *New York Times*, 2 June 1935, Sec. 4, 1.

Chapter 2

From "Potato Hole" to "Marble Palace": How the Court Presents Itself

A third of a century would pass before another chief justice in the William Howard Taft mold would focus so determinedly on the Court's physical presence and image in the American mind. Warren Earl Burger, who served in the Court's center chair from 1969 until his retirement in 1986, "was a passionate proponent of any and all efforts to increase public awareness of the role of the Judiciary, and particularly of the Supreme Court in our system of government."[1] Upon Burger's death in 1995, his colleagues eulogized him as a chief justice who emphasized judicial administration during his seventeen-year tenure as "the chief," Burger's favorite appellation. At his funeral, Justice Sandra Day O'Connor, after reminiscing warmly about Burger's kindness and consideration to her at her 1981 investiture "when he [Burger] took my arm and led me down the steps at the front of the Court to confront the battery of press," noted how beautiful the interior appointments of the Court building are thanks to Burger's attention to historical and decorative detail.[2] He supervised the restoration of several rooms on the Court's second floor that are now used as a formal dining room for guests and a smaller, yet equally elegant, dining area for the justices. The rooms are filled with period antiques and paintings. In addition, Burger suggested that the official portraits of previous justices be displayed in the corridors of the publicly accessible ground floor. Visitors and staff alike may feel surrounded by judicial specters when walking beneath the gazes of such Supreme Court notables as Oliver Wendell Holmes, Louis Brandeis, Hugo Black, Thurgood Marshall, and William Brennan.

Chief Justice Burger was also responsible for helping to found several entities that contribute to the maintenance of the Court's physical structure and the presentation of the highest court in the land to the public. The

Supreme Court Historical Society (SCHS) operates closely with the Court but is a separate, private, non-profit organization headquartered on Capitol Hill. Two of Burger's other legacies—the Curator's Office and the Office of the Administrative Assistant to the Chief Justice—are part of the Court's official structure and are located in the building at 1 First Street, N.E.

THE SUPREME COURT HISTORICAL SOCIETY

Incorporated in 1974 at the recommendation of an ad hoc committee of lawyers, legal scholars, and other concerned citizens appointed to advise Chief Justice Burger, the SCHS is funded through membership contributions, gifts, grants, and an endowment. As of 1997, approximately 5,200 members belonged to the SCHS. The Society's stated purpose is to expand public awareness of the history and heritage of the Supreme Court of the United States. Toward that end the SCHS collects and preserves the history of the Court, supports historical research, collects antiques and artifacts relating to the Court's history, and publishes books and materials to increase public knowledge of the nation's constitutional heritage.

Among the Society's historical research projects is the ongoing preparation of the multi-volume *Documentary History of the Supreme Court of the United States*, which reconstructs the historical records of the Court's initial decade. The project has accumulated over 20,000 documents, including private letters, newspaper reports of judicial proceedings, and other records that cover many gaps in the story of the Court's earliest years. Five of the proposed eight volumes had been published by 1997.

The first volumes in the series provided interesting insights into early Supreme Court cases and the additional duties of the justices, which initially included arduous, and sometimes dangerous, circuit riding. Although Congress had established circuit courts (the intermediate level of courts in the federal system located on the judicial hierarchy between the U.S. district courts and the U.S. Supreme Court) through the Judiciary Act of 1789, it did not create circuit *judgeships* until 1891, when it formed the modern circuit courts of appeals. Until then Supreme Court justices had to preside twice yearly over the circuit courts located throughout the country. In the earliest days of the Union, this duty meant traveling by such primitive means as stagecoaches over rutted roads, which could turn into quagmires of mud when it rained. (In fact, a stagecoach crash suffered by the eminent Chief Justice John Marshall while riding the circuit hastened his death in 1836.) Room and board were often taken at crowded inns that held many travelers but little charm. One benefit of the circuit court scheme was its introduction of the federal judicial system to the American people at the grassroots level.[3] Yet many years would pass before the Supreme Court and its members would penetrate the American consciousness on a regular basis.

Since 1975, the SCHS has produced and distributed to its membership a quarterly newsletter containing short historical articles on the Court and photographs and narratives of Society events. The newsletter's history lessons used to take the form of short trivia quizzes compiled by the late law professor Bernard Schwartz. The questions read like a prep session for the game show *Jeopardy!*: Who was the first justice to wear trousers beneath his Supreme Court robe? (Chief Justice Roger Taney, who served from 1836 to 1864. Lest the reader assume that previous members of the Court conducted their judicial duties *sans* pants, earlier justices actually wore knee breeches.) Which justice appointed the first female law clerk? (Associate Justice William O. Douglas, who would also hold the record for most marriages—four—the last three to women considerably younger than he.) Who was the biggest member of the Court? (Chief Justice William Howard Taft—who was the only member of the Court ever to serve as chief executive as well—also maintains the dubious distinction of being the most rotund president of the United States.) Who was the smallest member of the Court? (Justice Alfred Moore, who served in the early 1800s, was a mere four-and-a-half-feet tall and weighed less than 90 pounds.)

Yet the balance of the Society's work and contribution to maintaining a worthy public image of the Court is anything but trivial. A committee of the SCHS works to identify and acquire antiques and artifacts relating to the Court's history and places them on permanent loan to the Court, where the curator incorporates some of these items into historical displays for the benefit of visitors. Two of the most attractive rooms in the Court—the East and West Conference Rooms—display paintings of each of the fifteen former chief justices. Another artifact recovered by the Society is the original printing of the majority opinion in the landmark *Dred Scott* case.

The Supreme Court Historical Society also sponsors special educational events or participates in ongoing programs to reach the public and provide it with information on the Court and its history. The Society has organized public lecture series covering the Supreme Court during the Civil War, the careers of the Jewish justices who have served the Court, the New Deal era, the impact of World War II on the tribunal, and the history of civil rights. Well attended by Society members and the interested public, many of the lectures were also broadcast on C-SPAN.

A program initiated in 1995, sponsored by the Society and conducted by the Washington-based Street Law, Inc., may have an even broader impact on the public's understanding of the Supreme Court. The Supreme Court Summer Institute for Teachers offers a five-day intensive course on the history and development of the Court, the appointment process for justices, the role of the Court in American life, and selected cases from the current term. The seminar encourages the participants to develop curricular units on the Court for use in their own classrooms and for sharing with their colleagues who teach similar courses in their communities.

One California teacher, from an innovative law and government "magnet" school, has developed a lesson for simulating the "cert. pool," which is the process by which law clerks at the Supreme Court apportion, analyze, and write summary memos to the justices on the over 7,000 petitions for *certiorari* now received by the Court each year. In the 1997–98 term, the Court decided with full opinions fewer than 100 of those cases appealed to it through the *certiorari* process; so, as the teacher from California wrote, "I hope the simulation gives students some sense of the difficult decisions made by both clerks and justices."[4]

Many of the teachers reported that the highlight of the 1995 summer institute was a reception held in one of the Court's impressive conference rooms and hosted by Justice O'Connor. The educators had attended a session of the Court that morning, where the justices handed down their decision in the case of *Vernonia School District v. Acton*, appropriately for the teachers, a case involving the constitutionality of random drug testing of student athletes in an Oregon public school district. That evening, surrounded by portraits of former chief justices and the ornate decor of the conference room, which includes exquisitely carved paneling, a crystal chandelier, and a gilded ceiling, the teachers were inspired by Justice O'Connor's account of how one of her teachers in Arizona motivated her decision to pursue a career in law. No wonder that after such a day one of the participating teachers was moved to write to the Supreme Court Historical Society, "I know that the effects of my participation will last beyond a single academic year."[5] In fact, he estimated that by conducting his annual seminars and symposia throughout his state, he would reach 175 teachers, who would then implement his suggested lesson plans on the Court for more than 5,000 students. The Supreme Court institute for teachers has become so successful that it has doubled in size, accepting 60 participants each summer.

Another of the Society's projects that reaches a large audience is *The Supreme Court Justices: Illustrated Biographies, 1789–1993*, which includes biographical portraits of all the justices who have served on the Court, along with rare photographs and other illustrations. The only one-volume treatment of the lives of the justices, this book sells well through its publisher Congressional Quarterly and through the Society-sponsored Gift Shop at the Court, which attempts to provide high-quality merchandise at a reasonable cost.

The shop is undoubtedly one of the most tasteful among Washington's tourist attractions. Every year it expands its educational materials available for sale, especially its growing list of book titles, including judicial biographies, histories of the Supreme Court, and books on the Constitution and civil rights and liberties. The shop also carries an expanding collection of children's books about the Supreme Court, among them a workbook in the "Travels With Max" series. Previous volumes in the series, intended for readers six to twelve years of age, have taken children on imaginary tours of the White House and the Capitol. The "Max" book on the Supreme Court was commissioned by the SCHS. In it the title character Max, who looks like a koala bear, introduces children to the basic historical facts about the founding of the United States and the creation of the Supreme Court. It paints a picture of the Court as a special, dignified place, where visitors are told not to bring food or drinks and not to run or yell in the building; to be polite and say "please" and "thank you" when asking a question and to remain patient in line; and to have an "awesome time" because "it is an honor and privilege to visit the Supreme Court."[6] The book reinforces standard lessons about etiquette for children while emphasizing that they should be on their best behavior in such an "awesome" edifice.

A 1998 addition to the Gift Shop's collection for children is a storybook entitled *Marshall, the Courthouse Mouse,* which explains to youngsters the judicial process through the "tail" of Marshall J. Mouse, "the chief justice of the Supreme Court of the United Mice of America." Cleverly illustrated with black-robed mice playing the nine justices, the book describes how the mouse Court strikes down a law ("unani-mouse-ly") that mandates which cheese mice can eat.[7]

For adults, the Gift Shop sells a popular 165–page illustrated history of the Court entitled *Equal Justice Under Law* (the words carved on the Court's front pediment) and subtitled *The Supreme Court in American Life.* The SCHS calculates that the book annually introduces tens of thousands of readers to the history and operation of the Supreme Court and that the publication is the most widely distributed history of the Supreme Court now in use. Illustrated with glossy color photographs of the modern Court as well as historical illustrations, the book is produced in cooperation with the National Geographic Society. Indeed, the work brilliantly encapsulates the iconography of the Court. The opening chapter, "A Heritage of Law," begins with one of the most stunning vistas of the Court—a photograph taken on a summer evening when the building is typically bathed in a warm, golden glow from the setting sun's reflection off the facade's marble. The next photograph offers an all-American family portrait of a young couple with their two small children gazing upward in awe at the giant marble columns supporting the Court's front pediment. The caption reads, "Visitors stand at the threshold of the Nation's citadel of law, the Supreme Court."[8]

The second chapter in *Equal Justice Under Law* is entitled "Decisions for Liberty," and narrates the story of the Court's early years—a story that the book's foreword promises is "replete with controversy and courage."[9] A description of John Jay, one of the Founding Fathers and the Court's first chief justice, relies on the following encomium from one of Jay's contemporaries: "He [Jay] was remarkable for strong reasoning powers, comprehensive views, indefatigable application, and uncommon firmness of mind." The book adds about Jay that "[t]he Federalist statesman set lasting standards of judicial excellence during five years of service as Chief Justice," and

that "his tenure on the bench launched a tradition of high-minded dignity
that continues to distinguish the Supreme Court."[10]

Chapter 2 also describes the 34-year tenure of the Court's fourth head,
"the great chief justice," John Marshall, during which "the Court assumed
its role as a coequal and independent branch of the federal government."[11]
As the book notes, "When Marshall gave the Presidential oath to his cousin
Thomas Jefferson in 1801, the Supreme Court was a fortress under attack.
It had become *a shrine* when he gave the oath to Andrew Jackson in
1829."[12] Depicted in his trademark tattered knee breeches on one of his
circuit court visits, Marshall is described as persuasive, genial, charming, and
capable of holding a room full of lawyers spellbound. An admirer once noted
that to try to describe Marshall's eloquence "would be an attempt to paint
the sunbeams."[13] In addition, the book quotes from a newspaper that reported upon Marshall's death, "Next to [George] Washington, only, did he
possess the reverence and homage of the heart of the American people."[14]
This tribute came from a publication that typically opposed Marshall's rulings.

The Supreme Court Historical Society's hottest selling history of the
Court portrays the tribunal in heroic terms and places its members in a
judicial pantheon. Yet it also recounts the disastrous consequences of the
decision by Marshall's successor, Chief Justice Roger Taney, in the *Dred
Scott* case, which prompted vitriolic outbursts against the Court among ab-
olitionist journalists and leaders of the antislavery movement. As the book
remarks, such "attacks . . . have never been surpassed in bitterness."[15] President Lincoln, whom Taney swore into office in 1861, distanced himself
from the most unreasoned broadsides against the Court, but he added ominously: "If the policy of the Government, upon vital questions affecting
the whole people, is to be irrevocably fixed by decisions of the Supreme
Court, the instant they are made, in ordinary litigation . . . the people will
have ceased to be their own rulers."[16] Of course, it took a civil war to solve
the "vital question" of slavery, and the Court suffered more humiliations
in its aftermath at the hands of a Congress controlled by Radical Republicans.

The SCHS's account of the Court's modern history attests to the tribu-
nal's recovery of its preeminent place at the head of the "third branch."
The book points out that during the Court's battle with FDR over his New
Deal and Court-packing plan in 1937, "the people chose to sustain its
power and dignity . . . in one of the Supreme Court's greatest crises."[17]
Equal Justice Under Law lives up to its title by then briefly chronicling the
Court's landmark decisions in the realms of civil and criminal rights, free
speech, and separation of church and state. Filled with poignant black-and-
white photographs of plaintiffs in a host of cases where they were denied
basic human rights, the book cites numerous instances where, as the text
explains, "the judges were the best guardians of liberty. Chosen for learning,

ability, and impartiality, judges were safer guides than any other men. Courts were wiser than crowds."[18] Although the book concedes that the apogee of the civil rights cases during the 1950s and 1960s prompted the display of billboards and bumper stickers calling for the impeachment of Chief Justice Earl Warren, the conclusion of the history section proclaims that "through all its history, the Supreme Court has been the ultimate guardian of the rights we enjoy and the obligations we accept as free people."[19]

The book draws to a close with a chapter on "the Court today." It focuses on many of the aspects of the Court's physical structure and professional norms described in my chapter on the Court during the New Deal. With references to the tribunal's "majestic setting and moments of sheer ritual," it emphasizes that the pomp and circumstance are a crucial part of the Court's patina. On the subject of judicial attire, the book states that "when he or she takes the oath to uphold the Constitution and dons a robe, a Justice can enjoy an almost Olympian detachment." Moreover, "the pressure makes for an air of aloofness, but that is part discipline, part *illusion*."[20] The chapter continues, "Formality, courtesy, and dignity are not empty custom; they are vital to colleagues who are compelled to disagree publicly in print, expressing their deepest convictions, but always respecting the equally deep convictions of their fellow Justices."[21] Thus, the Court's mores facilitate relatively smooth relations among the justices, but also provide an image of dignified jurists handing down wise judgments from the heights of "Olympus."

THE OFFICE OF THE CURATOR

Fostering that impression on a daily basis is the Curator's Office, added to the Court's administrative structure during Chief Justice Burger's tenure. In addition to overseeing the day-to-day preservation of the Court's history, the Curator's Office schedules tours and briefings for visitors, keeps a meticulous collection of Court memorabilia (including photographic chronicles of most Court events), and organizes exhibits. Although the Supreme Court lags far behind Washington, D.C.'s most visited attraction (the National Air and Space Museum, with over eight million tourists each year), the Court now attracts 800,000 visitors annually. By comparison, the White House welcomes just over one million guests.[22] In addition to accommodating the casual tourist who walks in off the street, the Curator's Office at the Court receives thousands of requests for special tours. Such requests are filled for guests of the justices, Court employees, federal agencies, and Congress, as well as academic/tour groups. The Curator's Office also provides lectures for visitors to the Court and staffs information desks for providing answers to tourists' questions. The curator's staff arranges special briefings, usually delivered by the judicial fellow. In 1994–95, I briefed over 3,000 visitors, including foreign guests from at least 70 different countries. The Court goes out of its way to make guests, however ordinary or exalted, feel equally welcome and to provide for them high-quality tours, lectures, and briefings led by superb student interns, permanent Court staff, or the judicial fellow.

Interns in the Curator's Office are chosen through a competitive selection process and receive rigorous training for guiding visitors through the Court. Neat and professional, they present a basic history of the Court and provide the public with an overview of how the institution functions. Their presentation, which is prepared by the Curator's Office, is noticeably devoid of laudatory language regarding the Court. Nevertheless, the interns point out the magnificent appointments of the courtroom, where most public lectures are delivered, and then let the atmosphere speak for itself. The presentations also emphasize that the justices do their own work—albeit with the help of capable clerks. Visitors are also told candidly about the Court's tradition of barring cameras and recording equipment from the courtroom when the Court is in session. In this era of budget debates over bloated federal government expenditures, most groups express surprise and admiration that the Court returned $94,000 of the original $9.7 million appropriated for construction of the building. A deflationary economy during the 1930s allowed the Court to complete the project under budget. The Court also managed to furnish and decorate the new edifice and still return a substantial portion of the original allocation to the federal treasury.

In 1994 the curator mounted an exhibition of the Court and its justices during World War II to commemorate in 1995 the fiftieth anniversary of the conflict's end. The display highlighted the roles played by the justices of the World War II era, some of the cases they decided related to the war, and the experiences of future justices at war and on the home front. Tourists seemed especially drawn to this exhibit, with its portrayal through photos, artifacts, personal memorabilia, and lively narratives of the Court's activities between 1941 and 1945. The donations of retired Justice Lewis F. Powell, Jr., were particularly detailed. He preserved most of the components of his uniform, as well as items of olive drab clothing knitted by his wife for him and a pair of socks on which his mother had sewed his name, as if she were sending him off to summer camp. He also offered for display the spoils of war, such as a Nazi flag that he acquired as the Allies swept across Germany at the war's end. Assigned as an ULTRA intelligence officer, the future justice participated in successful efforts to break the German code, and for his exceptional service he received the Legion of Merit, the Bronze Star, and the Croix de Guerre with Palm.

The wartime stories of Byron White, nominated to the Court in 1962 by his prewar and wartime friend John F. Kennedy, were also engaging and heroic. In the display of White's memorabilia was a famous photograph of a handsome JFK, as a young navy lieutenant (j.g.), posing shirtless with his crew of the ill-fated PT-109. It was his friend Lt. (j.g.) Byron White who, as a naval intelligence officer, wrote the official report on the sinking of the

109 when it was rammed by a Japanese destroyer off the Solomon Islands, and the subsequent rescue of the surviving crew members. White himself barely escaped death during the Okinawa campaign when he was on two ships that on separate occasions were struck by kamikaze attacks. Another future justice, John Paul Stevens, served with equal distinction in the U.S. Navy where, after Pearl Harbor, he was a watch officer analyzing intercepted Japanese communications at the site of one of America's most infamous defeats. "For services in the Communications Intelligence Organization, the nature of which cannot be divulged," Stevens was awarded the Bronze Star.

The display did not sidestep one of the most ignominious stories of the period and the Court's history—the majority's sanction of the internment of Japanese-Americans from the West Coast in *Korematsu v. U.S.* Ironically, it was future chief justice and civil libertarian Earl Warren who, as attorney general of California, urged that Japanese-Americans be relocated to internment camps because he believed (as did many Americans) that they posed a threat to national security after Pearl Harbor. Many years after the war, Warren regretted his part in the relocation of Japanese-Americans and termed it "one of the worst things I ever did." Although this part of the exhibit could have brought opprobrium upon the Court, it served as an example of the tribunal's willingness to highlight even an ill-conceived decision and its unwillingness to hide from its own history, however occasionally shameful.

The World War II exhibit's denouement, which covered American participation in the Nuremberg Trials, reinforced the United States' devotion to the rule of law. Quoting from Justice Robert H. Jackson's opening statement at the trials, where he was on a leave of absence from the Court to serve as American chief counsel, the display's concluding panels declared, "That four great nations, flushed with victory and stung by injury stay the hand of vengeance and voluntarily submit their captive enemies to the judgment of the law is one of the most significant tributes that Power has ever paid to Reason." In addition, Jackson admonished observers of the "judgments at Nuremberg" that "the world yields no respect to courts that are organized merely to convict." Of the twenty-two defendants—representing the highest levels of the German war machine that had wreaked death and destruction on Europe—twelve received the death penalty, seven were imprisoned, and three were acquitted.

No doubt because of its popularity among visitors to the Court, the World War II exhibit was chosen by the Curator's Office to be featured on a special two-and-a-half-hour segment of C-SPAN's *Washington Journal* one morning in late July 1995. Curator Gail Galloway offered the tour of the exhibit for the C-SPAN reporter and his cameras.

On the same program, Jane Yarborough, the visitor program coordinator in the Curator's Office, gave a tour of the East Conference Room and its portraits of the first eight chief justices. The interviewer initially drew her attention to the imposing painting of John Marshall at one end of the grand room. Yarborough commented that he is known as the "great chief justice," in part, for his opinion in *Marbury v. Madison*, which established the Court as a coequal branch with the president and Congress. Chief Justice Roger Taney received short shrift as the author of the disastrous *Dred Scott* opinion. More positively portrayed was Chief Justice Fuller who established the tradition of the collegial handshake, which, Yarborough explained, signifies that even though the justices may disagree, "they are here to uphold the Constitution."[23] (Even those symbols of the Court that remain hidden from the public are celebrated for their contribution to the stature of the institution.)

The C-SPAN correspondent returned the camera's attention to the John Marshall portrait, and Yarborough explained that it was painted by the renowned American artist Rembrandt Peale in his "porthole" style, in which the subjects are framed by a painted representation of a round stone window and which Peale reserved for his paintings of the most illustrious Americans. Written as if carved into the stone porthole is a Latin inscription, which translates to "Let justice be done." On the mantle, just below the Marshall portrait, is also a bust of the fourth chief justice; Yarborough added that the object d'art is removed when the fireplace, directly beneath it, is in use. It would not do to scorch the "great chief justice."

A few months later, the C-SPAN cameras were back at the Court, where the visitor program coordinator offered a more extensive tour of the building. The feature ran one hour and allowed Yarborough to instruct the viewer on the history, architecture, and processes of the Court through her own narrative and her responses to an off-camera correspondent. They began on the front steps of the Court, where Yarborough noted that the plaza constitutes the "grandest entrance to the building"—one befitting the "dignity and importance of the Court."[24] She also recalled the nomadic existence of the justices prior to the 1935 completion of the Court's first permanent home. Cameras then focused on the imposing bronze doors at the Court's entrance, and Yarborough made reference to two of the scenes depicted in its panels: the signing of the Magna Carta (the "Great Charter" of English rights) and another portrayal of John Marshall.

Once inside the Court, the cameras panned the expansive Great Hall as the visitor program coordinator explained the "politics" of the building project which Chief Justice (and former president) Taft so expertly engineered. Yarborough observed that the money budgeted for the edifice alone was also used to furnish the Court, with $94,000 returned to the federal treasury. Illustrating the collective spirit of the place, she declared, "We're rather proud of that point."[25]

Inside the Court chamber itself, Yarborough detailed the proceedings in oral argument, noting that the process is a "grueling" one for lawyers arguing before the bench, but that occasionally a witty remark from a counsel or, more likely, a justice will prompt laughter and break the tension momentarily. As the cameras captured the atmosphere of the high court, Yarborough explained that the justices sit on the bench in order of seniority in chairs that are custom made for them in the Court's own carpentry shop. Before Chief Justice Burger came on the bench, justices could choose any style of black leather office chair they wished; but, ever with an eye toward aesthetic detail, Burger required all of the chairs to be the same size and height so that they would offer an image of uniformity. Even after hours, the chairs are always perfectly aligned, never the least askew. Justices sometimes leave the bench briefly during oral argument, as Rehnquist does frequently to relieve his chronic back pain. Lest a chair appear out of line, one of the Court messengers, who sit behind the bench during arguments, immediately realigns the chair.

The private corridor, which runs behind the bench and the velvet curtains that block the public's views, contains a fireplace, a complete set of the *U.S. Reports* (the official version of Supreme Court cases), and the justices' pewter water glasses arranged by their names—in order of seniority, of course.

Responding to the correspondent's questions regarding cameras in the courtroom during arguments, Yarborough confirmed that they are not allowed, that the justices have discussed the matter and decided to maintain the status quo, and that the policy would not change "anytime soon." The cameras then zoomed in on the carved friezes, described as both allegorical and historical, with John Marshall again given top billing. Before leaving the chamber, the reporter queried Yarborough about her personal impressions of the room, and she replied that its "magnificence," "dignity," and the importance of the work undertaken there had the most impact on her.[26]

The tour made a brief stop at the Court's library, which is normally off-limits to the general public. Intricately carved wood forms the walls and bookcases, all highlighted by another gilded ceiling. The next segment took the viewer through the permanent exhibit on the Court's architectural history, which depicts the building throughout its various stages of construction. Yarborough noted the photographs of, and the memorabilia from, the cornerstone ceremony and invoked Chief Justice Hughes's stirring utterance regarding the Court as a symbol of the Republic's faith. The exhibit's photos reveal that upon completion, the Court's size and beauty may have been even more striking than today because the site was not yet landscaped with the towering trees that surround it presently.

Yarborough pointed out the scale models of several rooms of the Court that appear in the exhibit because they are off-limits to the public. A replica of a justice's chambers, the robing room, and the conference room give viewers a sense of how these rooms appear. On the subject of the robing room, the visitor program coordinator reported on Chief Justice Rehnquist's procurement of the four gold stripes, which "added interest" to his black robe. Yarborough also remarked on the model of the Court's famous spiral staircases, which are rare architectural and engineering masterpieces found in only a few other grand buildings around the world, including the Vatican and the Paris Opera. Another part of the exhibit displays representations of the animals used throughout the building; Yarborough noted that the owl signifies wisdom and that the lion symbolizes majesty, strength, courage, justice, and law. This one broadcast encapsulated all of the important symbolic and substantive features of the Supreme Court, as presented by an articulate and knowledgeable member of the Court's staff.

OFFICE OF THE ADMINISTRATIVE ASSISTANT TO THE CHIEF JUSTICE

Created in 1972 by congressional statute, the administrative assistant to the chief justice supports the planning and leadership responsibilities of the chief, whose non-adjudicative duties include chairing the Judicial Conference, which has been described as a "board of directors" for the federal judiciary. The Conference, consisting of representative circuit and district court judges, meets twice yearly at the Court and decides policy for the federal courts. The chief justice also oversees two other judicial agencies— the Federal Judicial Center (responsible for research, development, and training for the judiciary) and the Administrative Office of the United States Courts (which administers the federal judiciary). In a more honorific vein, the chief justice of the United States also serves as the chancellor of the Board of Regents of the Smithsonian Institution, and trustee of the National Gallery of Art and the Joseph H. Hirshhorn Museum and Sculpture Garden. Although these positions would seem primarily ceremonial, they can take on a substantive component. For example, the chancellorship of the Smithsonian drew the chief justice into the 1994–95 controversy surrounding a proposed Air and Space Museum exhibition of the "Enola Gay," the airplane that dropped the atomic bomb on Japan at the end of World War II. As constitutionally required, Chief Justice Rehnquist presided over the Senate's 1999 impeachment trial of President Bill Clinton. Rehnquist's administrative assistant helped him prepare for this historic duty and sat just to the chief's left throughout the trial.

The Office of the Administrative Assistant to the Chief Justice (called the "A.A.'s Office" for short) does not exist primarily to present the Court to the public. Nevertheless, it often must consider public ramifications for duties it performs. In my entire year as the judicial fellow based in the A.A.'s Office, however, no member of the office ever talked to me about how I presented the Court in my public briefings nor did any supervisors ever attend my presentations. As a college professor, I felt at home with the equivalent of academic freedom that was afforded my oral presentations. The presumption, quite rightly, seems to be that professionals accepted into the Fellows Program, after careful screening by the A.A.'s Office staff and the Judicial Fellows Commission (which consists of distinguished judges, attorneys, business leaders, and academics appointed by the chief justice) will present the Court in an equally professional manner.

Perhaps the care with which the Court screens applicants helps to explain why virtually the entire Court staff, numbering a little over 300, from police force members to cafeteria staff to personnel employees to clerical workers, is especially industrious, efficient, and pleasant. Because the Court is a relatively small governmental entity, housed under one roof, there is a familial air about the work force. By and large, the Court's reflection through its employees is one of professionalism and pride in work. Most who labor at the Court comprehend that it is truly a special institution; they are genuinely proud to be a part of it. Moreover, the Court fosters this unity of purpose with an annual Employee Recognition Day, where longevity and special diligence are honored at a ceremony in one of the ornate conference rooms.

When the A.A.'s Office is called upon to participate in planning public occasions, it meticulously schedules and prepares such events. In October 1994, Justice Stephen Breyer was invested as the 108th justice of the Supreme Court of the United States. In addition to a brief ceremony held in the courtroom and attended by his guests, as well as President Clinton who had nominated him, the event included Breyer's presentation to the media on the front steps of the Court building and a reception held in both conference rooms. The A.A.'s Office spent days attending to every detail of scheduling, security, press relations, and menus. Consequently, the investiture proceeded without a hitch and displayed the Court at its very finest.

On a sadder occasion, the A.A.'s Office assisted in the preparation for ceremonies commemorating Chief Justice Warren Burger after his death in June 1995. The Curator's Office maintains files of previous funerals for members of the Court—both retired and active—along with binders of photographs from Court, church, and graveside ceremonies. An institution that is wedded to precedent in its adjudicative duties also follows tradition in its ceremonial life. A protocol has developed for deceased members of the Court to lie in repose (only government officials receiving a state funeral technically "lie in state") in the Court's Great Hall. Chief Justice Warren Burger and Justices Brennan, Marshall, Powell, and Blackmun have been so honored.

Chief Justice Burger's ceremony at the Court was simple, yet elegant. On the somber, grey, drizzly morning of June 28, 1995, a hearse pulled up to the front plaza of the Court at exactly the appointed hour—9:30 A.M.—and pallbearers, who were former clerks to "the chief," carried the flag-draped coffin up the steps. They passed the members of the current Court, as well as retired justices well enough to attend, who were carefully lined up on alternating steps leading up to the Court's front entrance. After a brief invocation by a Protestant cleric, Court employees filed past the coffin that rested on the historic Lincoln catafalque, which had been brought from storage in the Capitol. Ex-Burger clerks stood guard at the coffin, along with members of the Supreme Court police force. The scene contained flower arrangements and the official portrait of Chief Justice Burger. Over the entrance to the courtroom, at the opposite end of the Great Hall, hung a swag of black crepe. Members of the general public, along with Burger friends and colleagues, paid their respects throughout the day. For 30 days after the ex-chief's death, the flags on the Court's front plaza flew at half-staff in tribute to the deceased chief justice.

The funeral service was an equally dignified ceremony held at the National Presbyterian Church in northwest Washington. Heartfelt eulogies by ex-Burger clerk (now federal judge) A. Michael Luttig, Justice Sandra Day O'Connor, and Chief Justice William Rehnquist were accompanied by brief prayers and stirring patriotic music, such as "The Battle Hymn of the Republic." Attended by President Clinton and other high-ranking officials from all three branches of the government, the service was covered by C-SPAN, as had been the lying-in-repose ceremony the previous day. Indeed, the meticulously planned events that presented the Court in such a stately light were a tribute to the chief justice who, first as head of the highest court in the land and then as chairman of the Bicentennial Commission, contributed his best years to the honorable exhibition of the Supreme Court of the United States and the Constitution that established it.

It was a particularly fitting farewell for Burger, who epitomized the very essence of the public's image of a chief justice. As journalist James J. Kilpatrick remembered "the chief," in an editorial after his death, "Burger could have been sent from Central Casting to play the role. He had a Rushmore forehead and a mane of white hair, and especially in his last years his every movement conveyed a deep sense of *gravitas*."[27] Kilpatrick failed to mention Burger's rich, deep baritone voice that turned his utterances from the bench into authoritative-sounding pronouncements.

PUBLIC INFORMATION OFFICE

In 1982, Burger had hired as head of the Public Information Office (PIO) Toni House, a former reporter for the now defunct *Washington Star* newspaper, because, as she later stated, Burger "was looking to change his image." House, who died in 1998, believed that Burger had started off "on the wrong foot with the press because he was not Earl Warren." She reported that Burger had been a stringer for his hometown newspaper, the *St. Paul Pioneer*, in his younger days, which, she claimed, helped him foster favorable relations with members of the press who knew him.[28] Nevertheless, he remained suspicious of journalists and even once commented that if he wrote his memoirs it would be to correct all the mistakes that the media had disseminated about him.[29] In his last formal interview in the summer of 1994, Burger compared the public attacks made on Thomas Jefferson during his political career with the current political atmosphere: "You had congenital liars [then] who would put in writing something that just never happened because it made a good story. But it's worse today. You've got more media and more reporters and more people who want to write a book. . . . We've got too many damn lawyers in this country, too many law schools and too many reporters."[30] Toni House always avoided responding to questions about whether Burger actually had offered her advice regarding how to portray his image. She used to note that by the time he served as chairman of the Bicentennial Commission, after retiring from the chief justiceship in 1986, he had "learned how to use the press" for sending a message to the public.

Burger also effected a number of changes in how the Court as an institution presents itself to the public. The Public Information Office had been in existence since its creation as the Press Information Office in 1935—just as the Court moved into its new building and just prior to the battle royal with FDR over the New Deal. Reportedly, journalists had asked the Court to appoint a "press contact man" to facilitate the gathering of news on the tribunal and its decisions. Burger took the concept several steps further. He provided more physical space for credentialed journalists in the courtroom by moving the press section from in front of the bench (where only six reporters could be accommodated) to a set of benches to the left of the bench, which can seat close to 30. On overflow days when a popular case is heard, the press is also offered space in the corridor running on the left side of the Court chamber.[31] Although filming of oral arguments is forbidden, reporters may take notes (unlike members of the general public), and artists with press credentials may sketch the proceedings.

In addition, Burger established the practice of having the reporter of decisions, who supervises the official publication of the Court's record, add summaries, including the voting line-up, to the initial printing of decisions for release to the press and public. Journalists working against tight deadlines find the summaries useful, especially at the end of the Court's term when several important cases can come down in one session. Yet reporters still complain, with justification, that they are swamped as the term nears its end.

Reporters and scholars have offered their assessments of the PIO's relationship with the press,[32] but how does the Public Information Office view its own representation of the Court to the press and public, which it must undertake on a daily basis? Toni House firmly believed that "the Court speaks for itself" through its opinions. The PIO makes these opinions available to the press and public immediately upon their release by the Court, but the office does not interpret the decisions for the press. In fact, a packet of information distributed by the PIO to members of the press states explicitly, "We think you will understand why we will not interpret the Court's orders and opinions." The Public Information Office acts as a conduit for channeling documentary records of the Court to the press in the form of opinions, orders, briefs, petitions, and oral argument transcripts. It also maintains a file of justices' speeches, although each member of the Court determines which texts, if any, to deposit in the PIO.

In addition, the Court furnishes a pressroom for resident and visiting journalists. Reporters with permanent Court press passes make themselves at home; they have access to the pressroom after the normal working hours of the Court, they often lunch with the public information officer or the clerk of the Court in the building's cafeteria, and even use the employees' restrooms. And like employees of the Court, journalists relish their assignment at the nation's highest tribunal. The pressroom, while not luxuriously appointed, does contain cubicles, tables, phones, and a copier for press use. The Court also maintains six broadcast booths for assigned reporters to file taped reports. So-called television "stand-ups" and interviews on Court-related subjects are allowed in front of the Supreme Court building with prior permission from the PIO. (The image-making power of television was always evident to me as I walked past journalists preparing for or filming their "stand-ups." On the TV screen, the reporter would appear perfectly coifed [undoubtedly as the result of copious amounts of styling spray I saw one reporter applying to his hair] and larger than life [resulting from reporters perching on small boxes just beneath them and out of camera range].)

Although Toni House liked to claim that her office did not engage in "spin doctoring," she acknowledged that the Court exudes an "aura": "People are respectful [toward the Court] and we encourage that." On occasion, for example, rowdy school children have been asked to leave because of their disruptive behavior.[33] (Apparently, the students had not read Max the koala bear's admonitions regarding proper etiquette while visiting the Court.) House also saw the role of the PIO as one of helping the public to understand the Court. She believed that the biggest public misconception about the institution is that justices can simply reach out and select a case. House used to appear periodically on C-SPAN to explain the procedural aspects of the Court's work.[34]

The public affairs network often featured House just before the start of a new term. She appeared the week before the opening of the 1994–95 term, on film taped in the Court's library, to describe the sense of "anticipation" everyone at the institution experiences prior to the commencement of oral arguments on the first Monday each October. She also emphasized that the Court works year-round in accepting petitions for *certiorari* and emergency requests to justices, each of whom is assigned at least one circuit of the federal judiciary from which such pleas are generated. In addition, House reported that during the summer the justices lecture, teach, travel, and take vacations. Nevertheless, as long as they can be reached by phone, they can expedite the response to an emergency petition. If a justice is unavailable, the next most junior justice handles the matter.

After delineating the Court's procedures for processing over 7,000 petitions for *certiorari* ("cert. petitions") that the justices receive annually, House was asked in 1994 about the upcoming investiture of Stephen Breyer as the 108th justice of the Supreme Court. She described plans for 300 guests to be present in the courtroom for a swearing-in ceremony, where, she said, Breyer would enter the chamber and sit before the other eight justices in a chair that had once been used by John Marshall (clearly the patron saint of the Court). Chief Justice Rehnquist would then swear the newest justice into office using a Bible that had belonged to Justice John Marshall Harlan, who served on the bench in the late nineteenth and early twentieth centuries. House effectively conveyed the importance of history, ritual, and tradition in the Court's ceremonial life.

When asked what the PIO does to prepare for the new cases each term, the public information officer commented that her office tries to keep abreast of topics of interest to the press and public and enables the former to cover the Court competently by providing them with all relevant documentary material. She reiterated her much-stated belief that "we [the PIO] don't tell the press what's important. We don't tell them what the case is about when it comes out. (We're a very weird office!) We do provide the opinions immediately after they're released from the bench, and, in that case, we don't issue a press release. We say, 'Here's the opinion, read it and decide for yourself what the Court has done.' And sometimes that's not easy!" Quizzed about her own job at the Court, House enthused that it is a "fascinating institution" and a "terrifically enthralling place to work!"[35] When House died of lung cancer at age 55 in September 1998, members of the Supreme Court press corps remembered her as a convivial and ebullient spokesperson for the Court, but one who was adamant that the institution spoke for itself through its opinions.

The Public Information Office offers a number of printed explanations of the Court, its operation, and its members. Those who pay a visit to the Court will find stacks of brochures entitled "Visitor's Guide to the Supreme Court" greeting them at the entrance to the Great Hall. After welcoming guests to the Court, the brochure describes the institution as the "final arbiter of the law," which is "charged with ensuring the American people the promise of equal justice under law, and thereby, also functions as guardian and interpreter of the Constitution." With an eye toward the many foreign visitors to the Court, the pamphlet declares that "few other courts in the world have the same authority of constitutional interpretation and none have exercised it for as long or with as much influence."

The brochure then explicitly remarks on the importance of the physical atmosphere of the building, which it describes as "majestic in size and rich in ornamentation," serving "as both home to the Court and the manifest

symbol of its importance as a coequal, independent branch of government."
The text also highlights several of the Court's "design details symbolizing
both American and legal themes."

For guests who attend oral argument at the Supreme Court of the United
States, the PIO publishes a second pamphlet that dispenses slightly more
detailed material on the procedural aspects of such sessions. In addition to
explaining briefly how cases come to the Court and how they are decided,
the brochure includes description of all the participants in the courtroom.
It also provides the adult version of Max's rules for children who visit the
Court. Under the heading "Court Etiquette," the PIO begins, "This is your
Supreme Court and we hope you enjoy your visit. . . . In order to maintain
the atmosphere one might expect in the nation's highest court, we would
appreciate your cooperation." Visitors are asked to refrain from smoking
and taking food or beverages beyond the cafeteria. They also are asked to
maintain a quiet decorum and not to wear sunglasses, identification tags,
display buttons, or inappropriate clothing.

The Public Information Office, in conjunction with the Supreme Court
Historical Society, publishes a lengthier introduction to the institution entitled, straightforwardly, "The Supreme Court of the United States." I often
gave these small booklets to foreign visitors. They served as both informational literature as well as a souvenir of their visit to the Court. Another
photograph of the Court bathed in warm twilight graces the cover of the
booklet. It is followed by the ubiquitous Hughes quote, "The Republic
endures and this is the symbol of its faith."

A short introductory section on the Court and constitutional interpretation cites the French sociologist Alexis de Tocqueville, who wrote in the
1830s that a "more imposing judicial power was never constituted by any
people." The booklet then observes that the "unique position of the Supreme Court stems, in large part, from the deep commitment of the American people to the Rule of Law and to constitutional government." In a
section on the Court as an institution, the booklet displays several of the
symbols found around the building, including the striking bronze tortoises
supporting the courtyard and exterior lampposts.

The booklet also describes briefly the traditions of the Court, such as the
wearing of judicial robes, and its procedures. After displaying portraits and
short biographical sketches of the current justices, the publication concludes
with information about the building, and like the PIO's brochure, it describes the primary symbolic and architectural features of the Court. Many
of the visitors I briefed were pleased to have a short explanation of the Court
and were particularly impressed with the relative diversity and outstanding
credentials of the current members of the Court.

Visitors who do not have special tours or briefings arranged for them can
still learn about the Court through an informational film shown continuously throughout the day in a small theater located on the ground floor.

The current version, released in 1997, is a 24-minute explanation of how the Court operates, told primarily from the point of view of the nine current justices. C-SPAN aired the film on its network in 1998 and then took viewer calls for Professor A.E. Dick Howard of the University of Virginia Law School. Howard, who was a law clerk to Justice Hugo Black in the early 1960s and who interviewed the current justices on camera for the film, gave informative answers to the queries. Several guests remarked on how much they had learned about the Court from the segment.

CLERK OF THE COURT

Although this office would seem to have little to do with "public relations" per se, it does deal with the public, both the legal community and the wider populace, who flood the Court with thousands of petitions each year. In addition, the current clerk (not to be confused with the "law clerks" who serve individual justices), William K. Suter, meets with many groups of visitors to the institution and travels around the country and abroad to give presentations on the Court and how it operates. Some of these discussions are more technical in nature, as when the clerk attends state bar association meetings and outlines for attorneys the procedures for appealing a case to the Supreme Court. At the Court, Suter, a retired career army officer from the Judge Advocate General Corps, who rose to the rank of major general and served as acting judge advocate general, often speaks to groups of visiting foreign dignitaries. Well over six feet tall, and still maintaining his military bearing, he cuts an imposing figure before audiences. His presentation is packed with statistics and illustrative stories of how the Court operates and its history, and he relates all of this material with razor-sharp precision and good humor. The latter might be particularly welcomed by attorneys preparing to argue before the Court. Suter provides a brief orientation for them, one hour before argument begins, on what to expect and how to conduct themselves before the justices. No detail is too small for his office to handle, and he announces to the nervous advocates the availability of aspirin, throat lozenges, and sewing kits if they need them.

Suter's public speaking skills were in evidence on the same *Washington Journal* program of July 1995 that included appearances by other officers of the Court. He explained how his office staff of "highly qualified and outstanding employees" manages the constant inundation from the thousands of petitions that arrive each year. Suter proudly described the new automated system that allows for more efficient case management. Lest the system appear too mechanical, he emphasized that all petitions "are treated with the same degree of dignity."[36] Such respect would be afforded petitions on the paid docket, which requires a $300 filing fee, as well as those on the unpaid docket, which arise from petitioners who have demonstrated pauper status and have the filing fee waived. In addition, the Clerk's Office treats equally petitions filed by lawyers on behalf of their clients and those filed *pro se*, that is, by individuals without attorneys.

After elaborating on how the Court decides to accept cases, Suter sifted through a stack of the briefs that had been submitted for a case placed on the Court's oral argument docket. The institution is so thoroughly organized that each type of document (briefs on the merits of the case, briefs in opposition, reply briefs, *amicus curiae* briefs, joint appendices) must be submitted according to the Court's mandated color code. Each brief can then be identified immediately as to its type simply by looking at the color of its cover page. The Clerk's Office can easily assemble the color-coded documents into stacks to be routed to each justice.

The Clerk's Office must also sort and organize the 5,000 applications for entrance to the Supreme Court bar received each year. The clerk, who sits in a specially designated box just to the left of the bench in the courtroom, announces the appearance of attorneys present for induction into the bar and then swears them in as a group after each is introduced to the justices by a sponsor.

Although the Clerk's Office must stand or fall on its ability to process paperwork, William Suter describes his job in more inspirational terms. When asked by a C-SPAN correspondent about the most edifying part of his job, he responded, "Seeing the Court every morning when I drive to work, what it stands for, the respect that it has—not just the legal community—I think the entire country respects the Court as an institution. It's not political." He then referred to the inscription above the front doors— "Equal Justice Under Law"—and concluded, "I'm inspired to have the opportunity to work here and know the Court deals with dispensing justice."[37]

The Supreme Court presents itself to the public through a number of offices, foundations, and multi-media outlets. Although these various channels are not necessarily coordinated in the message they deliver, the image of the Court portrayed through them is strikingly similar: a picture of the institution emerges as a physically beautiful structure, guided by highly qualified justices and staff, who, while not infallible, have succeeded in steering the Court through the rough waters of American history and occasional storms of public protest. As told by the Court and its related organizations, the tribunal's history is inextricably bound with the political controversies that have shaped the nation; yet, the Court as an institution is portrayed above quotidian politics. As Justice Ruth Bader Ginsburg has related, quoting the late constitutional law scholar Paul Freund, "[T]he Court must be aware of the climate of the era, not the weather of the day."[38]

NOTES

1. Leon Silverman, "A Letter from the President," *The Supreme Court Historical Society Quarterly* XVI, No. 2 (1995): 2.

2. Sandra Day O'Connor, *America and the Courts*, C-SPAN, 2 July 1995.

3. Mary Ann Harrell and Burnett Anderson, *Equal Justice Under Law: The Supreme Court in American Life*, 6th ed. (Washington, D.C.: Supreme Court Historical Society, 1994), 18.

4. Mark Elinson, letter to author, 9 August 1995.

5. As quoted in Lee Arbetman, "Teachers Unanimous in Praise for Summer Institute," *The Supreme Court Historical Society Quarterly* XVI, No. 3 (1995): 6.

6. Nancy Ann Van Wie, *Travels with Max! The Supreme Court* (n.p.: Max's Publications, 1994), 5.

7. Peter W. Barnes and Cheryl Shaw Barnes, *Marshall, the Courthouse Mouse: A Tail of the U.S. Supreme Court* (Alexandria, Va.: VSP Books, 1998).

8. Harrell and Anderson, *Equal Justice Under Law*, 8–9.

9. Ibid., 5.

10. Ibid., 16.

11. Ibid., 5.

12. Ibid. (emphasis added).

13. Ibid., 40.

14. Ibid.

15. Ibid., 47.

16. Ibid., 48.

17. Ibid., 83.

18. Ibid., 79.

19. Ibid., 104.

20. Ibid., 128 (emphasis added).

21. Ibid.

22. "Attracting Tourists," *Washington Post*, 10 March 1995, A7.

23. *Washington Journal*, C-SPAN, 28 July 1995.

24. C-SPAN, 7 October 1995.

25. Ibid.

26. Ibid.

27. James J. Kilpatrick, "A Last Talk with Burger," Universal Press Syndicate, June 1995.

28. Toni House, talk to Public Leadership Education Network, U.S. Supreme Court, January 1994.

29. Warren E. Burger, talk to University of Virginia class, U.S. Supreme Court, October 1982.

30. James S. Rosen, *Washington Post*, 10 December 1995, p. C5.

31. See Richard Davis, *Decisions and Images: The Supreme Court and the Press* (Englewood Cliffs, N.J.: Prentice-Hall, 1994), 35–37.

32. See, for example, ibid.

33. Toni House, PLEN talk.

34. See "The U.S. Supreme Court: Transition and the New Justice," C-SPAN 2, 24 August 1993; *America and the Courts*, C-SPAN, 24 September 1994; and *Washington Journal*, C-SPAN, 28 July 1995.

35. House, C-SPAN, 24 September 1994.

36. *Washington Journal*.

37. Ibid.

38. Ruth Bader Ginsburg, "Informing the Public about the U.S. Supreme Court's Work," *Loyola University Chicago Law Journal* 29 (Winter 1998): 228.

Chapter 3

High Priests or "Nine Scorpions"? How the Justices Present Themselves

In June 1995, just eight months after he was sworn in as the 108th justice of the Supreme Court, Stephen Breyer presided over the swearing-in ceremony of the new directors of the Holocaust Museum in Washington, D.C. The seventh Jewish member to serve on the high court in its history, Breyer was an obvious choice to read the oath of office for each new director.

Breyer spoke briefly, movingly, and extemporaneously after the ceremony, which C-SPAN broadcast on its *America and the Courts* series some days later. His juxtaposition of the powerful symbolism of the Holocaust Museum with the awe-inspiring nature of his new job at the Court is revealing. Standing in the museum's Hall of Remembrance, with its eternal flame flickering in the background, Breyer began with a remembrance of his first tour through the museum. Like many others who have taken the several-hour journey, he was overcome with emotion and rendered speechless. In addition to an emotional reaction based on his own Jewish background, he was also preoccupied by thoughts related to his status as a lawyer and a judge. He recalled that there were laws, lawyers, and judges in Nazi Germany, but that they had not prevented—indeed they had sometimes facilitated—the terror and annihilation that marked the horrific reign of Hitler's Third Reich. He noted that Americans often express frustration over the inefficiency of the U.S. government, but Breyer reminded his audience that our frustration results from the separation of powers, which the Founders designed to curb the kind of unrestrained power that was exercised by Nazi Germany in the twentieth century.

Finally, Justice Breyer spoke of his new job at the Supreme Court in a voice filled with passion and awe:

I go into this courtroom—this amazing room—and I'm . . . looking out across this courtroom and there I feel this history. This is the room in which *Brown v. Board of Education* was decided. This is the room in which so many things of historic importance have transpired. And I look across this room and the feeling that you get—that you get, that I get—is a feeling of responsibility. I must take part in an institution that has to transmit from the past these traditions and values to the next generation. That is the responsibility of a trustee.

Breyer then analogized his position as a justice to the role of the new trustees for the Holocaust Museum.[1]

Justices often have such opportunities to relay messages regarding the Court's role to the public. Justice Anthony Kennedy, in a November 1994 talk to a group of graduate students from the University of Virginia, spoke no longer than ten minutes because he was due on the bench for oral argument that morning, but he managed to summarize succinctly the source of the Court's power and prestige. He noted that the Court is set apart from the other branches of government because it speaks a different language from the political institutions. Next he commented that there is "tremendous support in society for our role." He believes that the American public recognizes the importance of the Court's function because over its history it has decided cases important to the political and economic development of the United States. Kennedy cited the 1824 case of *Gibbons v. Ogden*, in which Chief Justice John Marshall protected free competition through a broad definition of commerce. More recently, First Amendment and civil rights decisions have had similar impacts on the public consciousness. The justice observed that the Court has accumulated political capital and goodwill that it must not squander.

Justice Kennedy also pointed to the high quality of U.S. judges drawn from the best ranks of the American bar, and he recognized the role of law schools in the United States, which have helped to create a unified law profession. U.S. law schools provide a stable curriculum and national common language for legal practitioners that is the envy of many other countries. Having spent some time in Argentina just prior to the talk, Kennedy recalled that the South American country has no bar association and that most attorneys there have only undergraduate degrees in law. He concluded that the American tradition of courts adhering to judicial precedent was crucial to maintaining the strength of the Supreme Court. Precedent imposes both retrospective and prospective restraint on courts. Justices must look to the past in deciding new cases and must realize that they will have to live with their own precedents in the future.

Justice Kennedy taught for many years at the McGeorge School of Law at the University of the Redlands in California. His presentation to the Virginia students was polished yet warm. He is a charming man who represents the finest qualities of the Court while putting visitors to the imposing building at ease. When members of the Supreme Court enter a room, police officers who accompany them always ask the audience to rise out of respect. Kennedy and Justice David Souter appear slightly embarrassed at this tradition, and they sheepishly ask visitors to be seated. Visitors often seem beguiled by the compelling combination of a justice's prestige and humility.

Justices possess numerous and varied opportunities to convey to the public impressions about themselves and the institution they serve. The most obvious and voluminous outlets for justices' presentations are the opinions they pen while on the Court. As Justice Ginsburg has stated, "The Court speaks principally through its opinions, which today are instantly available by electronic transmission." Yet Ginsburg acknowledged another fact of life—that Court opinions "have a limited audience: the legal profession and the press."[2] (Undergraduates in constitutional law classes should be added to the list.) Another transmission point for the Court to reach the public is its oral argument sessions. Through the several hundred people who witness each argument, and the thousands more who have experienced the historic moments of past arguments through the Peter Irons tapes, the Court reaches additional members of the public. No doubt the Court's largest audiences are assembled for speeches, lectures, and presentations delivered by the justices at the Court and throughout the country, which are transmitted to interested observers via television, newspapers, and legal periodicals. Justices have also written articles and books about their personal perceptions of the Supreme Court's history and procedures.

JUDICIAL OPINIONS

Opinions released by the Court since its establishment over two centuries ago now fill more than 500 volumes, printed and disseminated as the official record of the Court's work by the U.S. Government Printing Office. These volumes, known as the *U.S. Reports,* are available in most public and academic libraries of any size. Commercial publishers also make the opinions available to their subscribers in printed form or on-line. In addition, Supreme Court opinions are now retrievable from various sites on the Internet. This study concentrates on nearly 100 commonly accepted "landmark" cases and/or highly publicized decisions released by the Court in the modern era (since the mid-1930s).

Occasionally in these cases, a justice commented on the very symbols being conveyed by the Court itself. In the famous symbolic speech case involving compulsory flag salutes by public school students in West Virginia, Justice Robert Jackson wrote in the majority opinion:

Symbolism is a primitive but effective way of communicating ideas. The use of an emblem or flag to symbolize some system, idea, institution, or personality, is a shortcut from mind to mind. Causes and nations, political parties, lodges and ecclesiastical groups seek to knit the loyalty of their followings to a flag or banner, a color or design. The State announces rank, function, and authority through crowns and maces, uniforms and *black robes*, the Crucifix, the altar and shrine, and clerical raiment.[3]

In a 1980 dissenting opinion, then Associate Justice Rehnquist foreshadowed future changes that he would make in his own black robe with a reference to the Gilbert and Sullivan operetta "Iolanthe." Rehnquist criticized the multiple opinions supporting the judgment of the Court in the *Richmond Newspapers* case, involving the closing of a Virginia murder trial to the public, as reflecting "more than a little of [the] flavor" of the play's lord chancellor who lyrically proclaimed: "The Law is the true embodiment of everything that is excellent, It has no kind of fault or flaw, And I, my lords, embody the law."[4]

Much less explicitly, but much more frequently, however, the Court reveals a sense of itself through the tone of its opinions. In a 1936 case addressing whether Congress could delegate embargo power to the president (in this instance, Franklin Roosevelt, who subsequently used the power to issue a ban on the sale of arms to two warring Latin American countries), the Supreme Court's 8–1 decision in favor of the president exhibited a tone that can only be labeled magisterial in the majority opinion written by Justice George Sutherland. The opinion takes for granted the Court's long-recognized prerogative to delineate the powers of the other two branches of government and, then, discourses authoritatively on the origins of congressional and presidential powers in the U.S. Constitution.[5]

When the Court operates in controversial and emotional territory, as it often must in civil rights and liberties cases, it is especially prone to employ its omniscient tone, particularly to convince a skeptical audience of a dubious point. In the highly charged Japanese internment case, handed down in the midst of World War II, Justice Hugo Black, writing for a six-person majority, dismissed the criticism that the U.S. government had forcibly resettled Japanese-Americans in "concentration camps." He euphemistically labeled the internment camps "relocation centers" and wrote indignantly that "we deem it unjustifiable to call them concentration camps with all the ugly connotations that term implies."[6] Justice Black also relied on both a substantive and symbolic tactic that the Court, by its very nature, enlists in opinions. As a symbol of its continuity, consistency, cumulative wisdom, and self-restraint, the Court usually tries to base its decisions on precedent. Indeed, it views itself as bound—barring some unusual and collective change of mind—by the substance of its previous decisions. Thus, Justice Black bolstered the Court's decision in *Korematsu* by reference to the precedential *Hirabayashi* case in which "we gave [the pertinent issues] the serious consideration which their importance justified."[7] Black continued: "In light of the principles we announced in the *Hirabayashi* case, we are unable to conclude that is was beyond the war power of Congress and the Executive to exclude those of Japanese ancestry from the West Coast war area at the time they did."[8] Note the reference to "principles" rather than a more neutral term, such as "conclusions."

Combining the issue of civil rights with another basic aspect of the American governmental framework, namely, federalism, the Court pulled out all the symbolic and substantive stops in its 1958 opinion upholding the *Brown* desegregation order against the state of Arkansas' attempts to circumvent it. First, the opinion in *Cooper v. Aaron* was unanimous (like *Brown*), and each justice signed the judgment in an unprecedented effort to signify the Court's solidity behind the ruling. In fact, the opinion reminded readers that *Brown* was a unanimous decision garnered "only after the case had been briefed and twice argued and the issues had been given the most serious consideration."[9] In addition, the Court remarked, three new justices had joined the bench, and they were "at one with the justices still on the Court."[10]

Second, the Court quoted several times from Chief Justice Marshall's opinions, including his landmark declaration in *Marbury v. Madison* that "it is the duty of the judicial department to say what the law is."[11] The Court combined Marshall's reasoning with the principle that Article VI of the Constitution makes the document the "supreme Law of the Land" to argue that "the federal judiciary is supreme in the exposition of the law and the Constitution."[12] Thus, it followed that the Court's precedent in *Brown*, which applied the Fourteenth Amendment's equal protection clause to strike down state segregation in public schools, "is the supreme law of the land."[13] The Court concluded eloquently, "Our constitutional ideal of equal justice under law is thus made a living truth."[14]

A host of additional cases on separation of powers, civil rights and liberties, and federalism reveals numerous other examples of the Court's use of history, precedent, tone, and jurisprudential debates on judicial power to express a vision of itself to the public. An important separation-of-powers case from the early 1950s, for example, served as a vehicle for discussing the nature and extent of the Court's power. Although Justice Felix Frankfurter agreed with the majority's ruling against President Harry Truman's seizure of the country's steel mills when they were struck during the Korean War, he took the opportunity to write in a concurring opinion that the "Framers . . . did not make the judiciary the overseer of our government," and he called for "rigorous adherence to the narrow scope of the judicial function."[15]

Justice Robert Jackson also concurred with the decision in the steel seizure case, but wrote a separate opinion to urge that the Court not "lose sight of enduring consequences upon the balanced power structure of our Republic."[16] In addition, he included a footnote that countered positions he had taken as FDR's attorney general in favor of presidential seizure of industries during World War II. Touching on the ubiquitous theme of judicial impartiality, Jackson wrote in the 1952 case, "I shall not bind present judicial judgment by earlier partisan advocacy."[17]

Justice Frankfurter had also expressed these themes of judicial self-restraint and impartiality in another 1952 case, *Rochin v. California.* His majority opinion overturning the conviction of a drug dealer, whose stomach had been pumped to retrieve morphine capsules police had seen him swallow upon entering his bedroom, warned that

we [the Court] may not draw on our merely personal and private notions and disregard the limits that bind judges in their judicial function. . . . To practice the requisite detachment and to achieve sufficient objectivity no doubt demands of judges the habit of self-discipline and self-criticism, incertitude that one's own views are incontestible and alert tolerance toward views not shared. . . . They are precisely the qualities society had a right to expect from those entrusted with ultimate judicial power.[18]

When the Court continued the Warren era pattern of activism into the 1960s, the justices carried on a debate among themselves in their opinions over the proper function and power to be exercised by the institution. In *Baker v. Carr,* the Court, via Justice William Brennan's majority opinion, held for the first time that claims regarding unequal apportionment of state legislative districts could be adjudicated. Preferring to see such "political questions" answered by the legislative branch of government, Justices Frankfurter and John Marshall Harlan II dissented in two separate opinions. Harlan concluded by asserting that observers who believe that the Supreme Court should act as the mediator of all possible injustices would applaud the opinion of the Court. He added in closing, however, that "those who consider that continuing national respect for the Court's authority depends in large measure upon its wise exercise of self-restraint and discipline in constitutional adjudication, will view the decision with deep concern."[19] In the succeeding apportionment case of *Reynolds v. Sims* in 1964, Harlan again dissented, proclaiming that "this Court, limited in function . . . , does not serve its high purpose when it exceeds its authority, even to satisfy justified impatience with the slow workings of the political process."[20]

Even as it continued to break new ground in the 1960s in the realm of criminal rights, the Court tried to base its precedent-setting decisions on previous precedents. Thus, in *Mapp v. Ohio,* where the Court applied the exclusionary rule (barring unconstitutionally seized evidence from trial) to state court proceedings, Justice Tom Clark's majority opinion argued that the Court's decision was the "logical dictate of prior cases" and was founded on "reason and truth."[21]

When the Court overturned precedent in the 1963 case of *Gideon v. Wainwright,* it attempted to justify its departure from the 1942 *Betts* decision by asserting in Justice Hugo Black's majority opinion that "the Court in *Betts v. Brady* made an abrupt break with its own well-considered precedents."[22] Black achieved a double victory of sorts by championing the Sixth Amendment right to counsel in non-capital cases, for he had dissented from the Court's opposite ruling 21 years earlier in *Betts*.

In another criminal justice precedent from the 1960s, Chief Justice Warren tried to head off criticism (unsuccessfully, as it turned out) of the Court's pathbreaking ruling in *Miranda v. Arizona*, which established the now-famous list of procedural rights about which suspects must be informed prior to any police questioning, by appealing once again to precedent. Warren commenced the opinion for the Court "with the premise that our holding is not an innovation in our jurisprudence, but is an application of principles long recognized and applied in other settings."[23] Once more, Justice Harlan disagreed and offered yet another ode to self-restraint in his dissent from the *Miranda* decision.

Also in the 1960s, the Court took perhaps its most innovative step in maintaining that the right of privacy, which it discovered as an implicit guarantee in various parts of the Bill of Rights, invalidated a Connecticut law barring the use of birth control devices and dissemination of information about them. Justice Douglas's opinion for the 7–2 Court in *Griswold v. Connecticut* insisted that the justices were not sitting as a "superlegislature."[24] In a concurring opinion, Justice Arthur Goldberg also tried to blunt criticism that the justices had departed from the principles of judicial self-restraint and objectivity. He agreed that "in determining which rights are fundamental, judges are not left at large to decide cases in light of their personal and private notions."[25]

As the Court forged ahead in the 1970s under a new chief justice, Warren Burger, and with increasingly complex issues before it, the justices continued to rely on precedents in majority opinions while their brothers in dissent maintained a running commentary on the virtues of self-restraint. In the 1971 church–state ruling, which established the now much-maligned but still extant (if diluted) *Lemon* test, Chief Justice Burger gleaned the three-pronged standard for determining a violation of the First Amendment's establishment clause from the "cumulative criteria developed by the Court over many years."[26] The *Lemon* criteria determine that a state action does not violate the First Amendment's Establishment Clause if the action (1) has a secular purpose, (2) neither advances nor inhibits religion, and (3) does not promote excessive entanglement between government and religion.

One year later, in the famed death penalty case *Furman v. Georgia*, the Court was so splintered that it could not forge a majority opinion, nor even a plurality position. Instead, the justices struck down capital punishment, as then applied in Georgia, by a 5–4 vote with each of the nine members of the Court filing a separate opinion. All of the dissenters from the Court's judgment, including Chief Justice Burger and Justices Rehnquist, Powell, and Blackmun, focused on their conception of the proper role of the judiciary in a democratic system, the need for judicial self-restraint, the distinction between the role of the Court and that of a legislature, and the need to eschew resorting to personal views as a basis for judicial decision-making. Burger and Blackmun, still known at that time as the "Minnesota Twins," for their common state of origin and their propensity to vote together, both commented that if they had been legislators, they would have voted against the death penalty statute.

Justice Blackmun tried to rely on precedent in bolstering the seven-person majority opinion in the 1973 abortion decision of *Roe v. Wade*, which a quarter century later still sparks controversy. Although conceding that "the Constitution does not explicitly mention any right of privacy," Blackmun cited case after case establishing that guarantee upon which the Court based a woman's fundamental right to an abortion, at least during the first trimester of pregnancy.[27] Justice Rehnquist's dissent, however, characterized the majority's trimester test as "far more appropriate to a legislative judgment than to a judicial one."[28]

On occasion in the early 1970s, more conservative justices appointed by Richard Nixon held firmly to the principle of self-restraint and refused to use the Court's power to remedy a perceived wrong appealed all the way to the high bench. In a 1972 commerce case, *Flood v. Kuhn*, challenging baseball's reserve clause (which allows professional baseball teams to confine a player by contract to his club or assign his contract to another club) as a monopolistic practice in violation of a federal antitrust act, Justice Blackmun's opinion for the Court rejected the challenge and upheld pro baseball's right to practice such a policy in light of precedent and Congress's failure to overturn baseball's exemption from antitrust legislation.

One year later, in a 1973 case from San Antonio, Texas, that claimed that the state's method of financing public schools violated the equal protection rights of children living in poorer school districts, Justice Powell's opinion for a five-person majority refused to increase the level of judicial scrutiny for such decisions made by the state of Texas. Powell argued that the Court "would, indeed, then be assuming a legislative role and one for which the Court lacks both authority and competence."[29]

Justice Thurgood Marshall, champion of the downtrodden, first as an NAACP attorney and then as a member of the Court, wrote a vigorous dissent from the San Antonio decision, in which he was joined by Justice William Douglas. Marshall argued that the right of every American to an equal education was so vital as to make it completely insufficient to subject the indigent children, on whose behalf the case was appealed to the Court, "to the vagaries of the political process."[30] Therefore, Marshall would have utilized the power of the Court to scrutinize strictly the funding methodology then used by the state of Texas to fund public schools.

One year later the country and the Court experienced the most serious constitutional crisis since the Civil War. In the midst of the Watergate scandal, and with President Richard Nixon facing impeachment proceedings in the Congress, the Supreme Court agreed to decide whether Nixon must release his secretly taped conversations for use in the criminal trials of several members of his administration. Nixon, who had been named an unindicted coconspirator by a federal grand jury, argued that the right of executive privilege protected his confidential papers and records from subpoena. In such a highly publicized and politicized case, the Court was under intense pressure to live up to its image as an impartial arbiter of presidential power.

Justice Rehnquist recused himself from the case because of his association with the indicted Nixon subordinates when he worked at the Justice Department prior to his appointment to the Supreme Court. Although three of the remaining eight justices who heard the case were Nixon appointees, including the chief justice, the Court decided unanimously against Nixon, ruling that his qualified executive privilege to protect diplomatic and military secrets did not apply to the taped conversations at issue. It was especially significant that the Court was unified against Nixon's contention because he had argued that the separation of powers doctrine precluded judicial review of his executive privilege claim. The Court's opinion, delivered by Chief Justice Burger, was particularly careful to assert in the strongest language—quoting from the revered John Marshall—that "it is emphatically the province and duty of the judicial department to say what the law is."[31] With the whole nation—indeed the entire world—watching, the Supreme Court and Congress stood firm against the president, who resigned shortly after the decision in *U.S. v. Nixon* was announced.

Throughout the remainder of the 1970s, in a variety of cases, Justices Brennan and Rehnquist went toe to toe, or pen to pen, over their respective perceptions of the role and power of the Court. Each called upon precedent, and interpretation of history and founding documents, to bolster his position. In a rather technical case, *National League of Cities v. Usery*, that caused little stir among the general public, Justice Rehnquist led a narrow, five-person majority in striking down Congress's attempt to extend provisions of the Fair Labor Standards Act to employees of states and their political subdivisions. He cited numerous precedents, including John Marshall's seminal decision in favor of federal regulation of interstate commerce, but ultimately ruled for the states, relying on the Tenth Amendment's reservation of power to them. In dissent, Justice Brennan pointedly argued that Rehnquist's decision for the Court repudiated settled principles of constitutional interpretation, which had been in place since Chief Justice Marshall, and that his colleague had taken such insupportable action in the very bicentennial year of the nation's independence. Brennan asserted that Rehnquist's opinion restrained Congress's commerce power, which could only be limited through the "political process not . . . the judicial process."[32] Without basis in precedent or the Constitution, the Rehnquist-led majority, according to Brennan, had impermissibly allowed the Court "to erect a mirror of its own conception of a desirable governmental structure."[33]

Also in 1976, Brennan and Rehnquist clashed over the Court's ruling in *Craig v. Boren*, which created a "heightened" judicial scrutiny standard for sex-based classifications. This time Rehnquist was in dissent in the 8–1 case, and it was he who took the Court to task for creating "out of thin air" an equal protection standard that would "invite [the use of] subjective judicial preferences or prejudices."[34]

Rehnquist, again in dissent, angrily refuted Brennan's majority opinion in an early affirmative action case from 1979 in which the Court upheld a private hiring plan favoring black steelworkers despite the 1964 Civil Rights Act's prohibition of racially determined hiring practices. The Court's interpretation of the statute included references to the "spirit of the law" (and its intention to help blacks) rather than its explicit wording, which prompted Rehnquist to accuse the Court of engaging in judicial legislation.[35]

Such refutations might seem to undercut the majority's logic, and opponents of the Court's decisions can always look to dissenting opinions for ammunition to attack the case's outcome. Nevertheless, the justices generally follow a linguistic protocol in their opinions. Majority opinions carry the added weight of being written in the institutional third person ("this Court") or the first person plural ("we") so that in the contretemps between Justices Brennan and Rehnquist, whichever one was in the majority could express his position as that of "the Court." In addition, dissenting opinions almost always refer, not by name to the justice who authored the majority opinion, but to the arguments of "the Court." Moreover, the dissenting justice is left to label an opposing view as his or her own by the conventional use of the first person singular "I" in the minority opinion. Whether or not readers of the Court's opinions are swayed by such dueling pronouns, on the level of symbolic messages, the majority opinion has the benefit of presenting the position of the highest court in the land.

It is often the case that the broader the sweep of the Court's decision, the more the author of the majority opinion attempts to ground it in precedent and couch it in terms of judicial restraint. Such was the case in *I.N.S. v. Chadha*, after which headlines in national newspapers trumpeted that the Court had struck down over 200 pieces of legislation in one fell swoop. The reported number of laws invalidated as a result of the 1993 *Chadha* case was all the more amazing in light of the fact that the Court had voided fewer laws of Congress in the whole of its history of exercising judicial review.

Chadha, which questioned Congress's inclusion of one-house vetoes in its laws, produced a majority opinion authored by Chief Justice Burger, who noted that his predecessor, Chief Justice Marshall, had once written in a case that the Court may wish to avoid difficult questions, but it cannot do so. Instead, it must "conscientiously" perform its duty.[36] Moreover, Burger's opinion called for restraint on the part of the judiciary in performing such duties as reviewing federal statutes. Finally, invoking the Founding Fathers by individual names and cumulatively, Burger relied on their wisdom to support the Court's claim that one-house veto provisions, liberally sprinkled throughout numerous federal laws since the New Deal, violated the Constitution.

When the Court limits the reach of previous precedents, as it tended to do in the 1980s in the realm of criminal rights, it goes out of its way to claim that it is not overturning past decisions. In the controversial area of the exclusionary rule, which opponents argued was a judge-made technicality that often allowed criminals to go free, the Court welcomed an opportunity to limit the rule's use through a 1984 case, *U.S. v. Leon.* Justice White's opinion in the 6–3 ruling seemed particularly concentrated on tight reasoning to fashion a "good faith exception" to the exclusionary rule. Thus, if law enforcement officers act in "good faith," evidence that they collect should not be barred from trial because of a technicality. Asserting that the new exception turned on "objective reasonableness," the Court assured skeptics that the decision was "not intended to signal our unwillingness strictly to enforce the requirements of the Fourth Amendment."[37]

Nevertheless, the Court has a more difficult time maintaining an image of consistency if it overturns a recent precedent, particularly if dissenters on the Court point out its erratic behavior. The 1985 *Garcia v. San Antonio Metro. Transit Authority* case, which explicitly overruled the *Usery* decision, carried the added burden of having a justice write the opinion for the Court using logic he had voted against in the previous case.

The mercurial nature of Justice Blackmun's change of heart in the intervening nine years between *Usery* and *Garcia* provided an obvious target for dissenters, who attacked his majority opinion in the latter case. Blackmun's opinion for the Court in *Garcia* acknowledged that "we do not lightly overrule recent precedent," but it nevertheless did so.[38] The Blackmun flip-flop prompted the lead dissenting opinion, written by Justice Powell, to lift a direct quote from Blackmun's concurrence in *Usery*, which directly contradicted the posture Blackmun now assumed for the majority in *Garcia!* Explicitly citing the dangers for the Court's public image inherent in Blackmun's behavior, Powell declared, "The stability of judicial decision, and with it respect for the authority of this Court, are not served by the precipitous overruling of multiple precedents that we witness in this case."[39]

The Court also explicitly fretted about public perceptions one year later in a highly controversial decision in the Georgia sodomy case. In *Bowers v. Hardwick* a narrow 5–4 majority refused to extend the Court's previous precedents on privacy rights to create a fundamental right to engage in private, consensual, homosexual sodomy. The Court, via Justice White's

majority opinion, revealed that over the years, as it had recognized rights
qualifying for heightened judicial protection, it had strived "to assure itself
and the public that announcing rights not readily identifiable in the Constitution's text involves much more than the imposition of the Justices' own
choice of values."[40]

Unfortunately, the Court's proclamations eschewing personal predilections in this case were eventually overshadowed by the much-publicized
story that Justice Powell had switched his initial vote in the case to the side
upholding the Georgia statute forbidding adult consensual sodomy between
heterosexuals or homosexuals. Powell even acknowledged his vote switch
some years later and admitted that it had probably been a mistake.[41] His
initial vote would have invalidated the Georgia sodomy statute by forming
a different five-person majority on the Court to extend the right of privacy
to cover sodomy.

Powell, the very embodiment of a swing-voter on the Court, voted on a
case-by-case basis in each decision. In his last opinion for the Court in
McCleskey v. Kemp, authored just before his 1987 retirement, he wrote his
approach to judicial decision-making into a ruling rejecting the use of statistics by the judiciary to make determinations of alleged racial bias in the
imposition of the death penalty. Statistics, by their very nature, provide an
aggregate picture of an issue; therefore, Powell argued for the Court that
statistics were suited to the legislative branch's policy-making role rather
than the judiciary's case-by-case determinations for individuals. In other
words, the Court refused to accept aggregate statistics as proof of bias in a
particular imposition of capital punishment.

The Court also deferred to legislative power at the state level in another
fractious abortion decision in 1989, *Webster v. Reproductive Health Services*.
Writing for a plurality of justices, now Chief Justice Rehnquist refused to
judge the preamble of a Missouri law, which included pro-life findings as a
prelude to a statute placing limitations on access to abortion in the state.
Citing a 1990 precedent, Rehnquist's opinion declared that the Court "is
not empowered to decide . . . abstract propositions."[42] In upholding several
components of the Missouri statute, Rehnquist, for the plurality, labelled
the trimester system from *Roe* "unsound" and "unworkable."[43] Although
the plurality did not directly overrule *Roe* in its entirety, it noted that adherence to precedent (while a cornerstone of the American legal system)
"has less power in constitutional cases, where, save for constitutional amendments, this Court is the only body able to make needed changes."[44] That
argument, borrowed from the Blackmun-authored majority opinion in *Garcia*, was a dig at *Roe*'s author; Rehnquist had dissented in *Garcia*, which
had overturned his reasoning in *Usery*.

Justice Scalia's concurrence in *Webster*, which advocated overturning *Roe*
outright, was an explicit discourse on the Court's role vis-à-vis the public
and the democratic process:

Alone sufficient to justify a broad holding [against *Roe*] is the fact that our retaining control, through *Roe*, of what I believe to be, and many of our citizens recognize to be, a political issue, continuously distorts the public perception of the role of this Court. We can now look forward to at least another Term with carts full of mail from the public, and streets full of demonstrators, urging us—their unelected and life-tenured judges who have been awarded those extraordinary, undemocratic characteristics precisely in order that we might follow the law despite the popular will—to follow the popular will.[45]

On the opposite side of the issue, Justice Blackmun dissented from those parts of the judgment that limited *Roe* in any way, and he expressed his fear that the plurality's seeming insensitivity to the impact of their decision on women would prove to be "profoundly destructive of this Court as an institution."[46] Ironically, Scalia's belief that the Court should overturn *Roe* but did not, and Blackmun's belief that the Court in effect had overturned *Roe* but should not, resulted in their feelings of trepidation regarding the public image of the Court.

A case that came to the Court that same year of 1989—and over a symbol, no less—produced similar debates among the justices on the role of the Court. In *Texas v. Johnson*, Justice Brennan led another narrow 5–4 majority in striking down a Texas flag desecration statute that had been violated by a political protester who had burned an American flag in a public demonstration. Brennan's opinion for the Court upheld Johnson's right to engage in symbolic speech—even to the point of destroying a revered political, cultural, and patriotic symbol.

Reluctantly joining in the majority vote, but spurred to write a separate concurrence, Justice Kennedy revealed the personal pain he had experienced in voting to uphold the right of flag burners. With another reference to how a justice must put aside his personal predilections, he admitted

that sometimes we must make decisions we do not like. We make them because they are right, right in the sense that the law and the Constitution, as we see them, compel the result. And so great is our commitment to the process that, except in the rare case, we do not pause to express distaste for the result, perhaps for fear of undermining a valued principle that dictates the decision.[47]

Chief Justice Rehnquist, writing a bitter dissenting opinion, joined by Justices White and O'Connor, emphasized the over 200-year history of the flag's "unique position as the symbol of our Nation" and the fact that "millions and millions of Americans regard it with an almost mystical reverence."[48] Attacking the majority's vision of the place of the Court in the American democratic system, the chief justice granted that "the Court's role as the final expositor of the Constitution is well established, but [Rehnquist argued] its role as a platonic guardian . . . has no place in our system of government."[49] He would have deferred to the Texas legislature's right to follow public opinion and protect the flag from desecration.

Moving from the 1980s into the last decade of the century, the Court experienced the most rapid turnover of its membership since the 1940s. Between 1990 and 1994, four justices (Brennan, Marshall, White, and Blackmun) retired. The White House also changed hands and political parties with the election of Democrat Bill Clinton over Republican George Bush in 1992; each had an opportunity to nominate two justices prior to 1995. George Bush named David Souter to replace William Brennan in 1990, and despite the former's assumed conservative credentials, he has become a reliable vote for liberal causes. In contrast, the Thurgood Marshall seat that passed to conservative Clarence Thomas obviously changed ideological hands. President Clinton's nomination of moderate liberal Ruth Ginsburg has produced a slight liberal gain over the ideologically mixed votes of Justice White. Stephen Breyer, another moderate liberal named by Clinton to the high bench, usually replaced Blackmun's liberal vote. Therefore, despite the rapid turnover in the Court's membership, it remained closely divided on controversial issues, with the justices continuing to debate in their opinions the role of the Supreme Court in American democracy.

In 1992, a 5–4 Court, led by the unpredictable Justice Kennedy, ruled against officially sanctioned, clergy-led prayers at public high school graduation ceremonies because they violated "a cornerstone principle of our [the Court's] Establishment Clause jurisprudence."[50] Returning to the 1962 precedent that had struck down state-sanctioned and state-drafted prayers for public school students, the Court's majority opinion 30 years later reiterated that the government may not sponsor prayers for the American people to recite without violating the First Amendment's Establishment Clause. The Kennedy-led majority found that the officially sanctioned graduation prayers applied unacceptable psychological coercion to high school students attending their graduation ceremonies.

Justice Scalia's pointed dissent labelled the Court's creation of a psychological coercion test an "instrument of destruction" and a "bulldozer" of "social engineering," which illustrated why "our Constitution cannot possibly rest upon the changeable philosophical predilections of the Justices of this Court, but must have deep foundations in the historic practices of the people."[51]

Not surprisingly the Court was at its most agitated on these questions of the nature of its power in yet another abortion decision, this one from Pennsylvania. The badly splintered *Casey* ruling also provoked the justices to write into their opinions their perceptions of the Court's image and legitimacy in the eyes of the public. The controlling opinion, which reflected the unusual practice of being penned by three different justices (O'Connor, Kennedy, and Souter), upheld four of five limitations on access to abortion in the Pennsylvania statute. As historian David Garrow has written, "symbolically invoking the powerful precedent of *Cooper* [*v. Aaron*], Justices O'Connor, Kennedy, and Souter issued their plurality decision in *Casey* as an explicit trio opinion."[52] Nevertheless, with two additional justices (Blackmun and Stevens) joining them, a majority bowed to precedent and reaffirmed the "central holding" of *Roe*, that a woman's choice to end her pregnancy is based upon her constitutionally protected guarantee of personal liberty. The plurality opinion, however, rejected the trimester framework of *Roe* and substituted the so-called "undue burden" test, which was defined as one that "has the purpose and effect of placing a substantial obstacle in the path of a woman seeking an abortion of a nonviable fetus."[53]

The trio of justices, who found themselves wedged between the more liberal Justices Blackmun and Stevens and the more conservative Chief Justice Rehnquist and Justices Scalia, Thomas, and White, acknowledged the controversy surrounding the abortion debate and hinted at their own opposition to the procedure but emphasized their "obligation . . . to define the liberty of all, not to mandate our own moral code."[54]

They then presented a highly unusual exegesis of the Court's history of deciding controversial issues and overturning precedent. O'Connor, Kennedy, and Souter recalled that the Court "lost something" by its stubborn adherence to anti–New Deal jurisprudence and admitted that "the Court-packing crisis only magnified the loss."[55] They agreed that a new understanding of facts had finally prompted the Court to reverse its economic regulation precedents in 1937 and its civil rights precedents in 1954. But they quoted Justice Potter Stewart, who once had written on the question of precedent that "a basic change in the law upon a ground no firmer than a change in our membership invites the popular misconception that this institution is little different from the two political branches of the Government. No misconception could do more lasting injury to this Court and to the system of law which it is our abiding mission to serve."[56] The threesome continued:

The Court's power lies . . . in its legitimacy, a product of substance and perception that shows itself in the people's acceptance of the Judiciary as fit to determine what the Nation's law means and to declare what it demands. . . . The Court's legitimacy depends on making legally principled decisions under circumstances in which their principled character is sufficiently plausible to be accepted by the Nation. . . . The country can accept some correction of error without necessarily questioning the legitimacy of the Court. . . . The legitimacy of the Court would fade [, however,] with the frequency of its vacillation. . . . It is true that diminished legitimacy may be restored, but only slowly. Unlike the political branches, a Court thus weakened could not seek to regain its position with a new mandate from the voters. . . . Like the character of an individual, the legitimacy of the Court must be earned over time. . . . The Court's concern with legitimacy is not for the sake of the Court but for the sake of the Nation to which it is responsible. . . . A decision to overrule *Roe*'s essential holding . . . [would come] at the cost of both profound and unnecessary damage to the Court's legitimacy, and to the Nation's commitment to the rule of law.[57]

Justice Scalia, not surprisingly, returned to his theme from *Webster*, this time in dissent, and confronted the plurality with his own view of how the *Casey* decision would influence public perceptions of the Court. He wrote that on the abortion issue

so many of our citizens . . . think that we Justices should properly take into account their views, as though we were engaged not in ascertaining an objective law but in determining some kind of social consensus. . . . As long as this Court thought (and the people thought) that we Justices were doing essentially lawyers' work up here—reading text and discerning our society's traditional understanding of that text—the public pretty much left us alone. . . . But if in reality our process of constitutional adjudication consists primarily of making *value judgments* . . . then a free and intelligent people's attitude towards us can be expected to be (*ought* to be) quite different.[58]

Scalia concluded, sarcasm dripping from every word, that the people ought to demonstrate to reveal their own values to the justices and that senators ought to convey to Court nominees their constituents' most favored and least favored constitutional rights.

With abortion missing from the Court's more recent dockets, the justices have avoided a repeat of a *Casey*-style debate over its role and image. Nevertheless, important cases have continued to produce 5–4 splits and passionate opinions from the justices. Chief Justice Rehnquist's highly technical majority opinion in the 1995 *Missouri v. Jenkins* case narrowed the role of district court judges in school desegregation plans and prompted Justice Souter to write in dissent that "the Court's process of orderly adjudication has broken down in this case."[59] Justice O'Connor's equally technical plurality opinion in the minority business preference case (*Adarand v. Peña*) from the 1994–95 term overturned two precedents, and she was forced to distinguish her perceptions of *stare decisis* in this case from her discourse on the doctrine in *Casey*. She also took the highly unusual step of addressing her colleague Justice Stevens by name in countering his criticism of her opinion in his dissent.

Although two more landmark cases from the 1994–95 term were also closely divided, the Court held to its more traditional tone of authoritatively citing precedent, history, constitutional language, and intentions of the Founding Fathers in striking down state imposition of term limits on members of Congress (*U.S. Term Limits v. Thornton*) and in invalidating the Gun-Free School Zones Act of 1990 (*U.S. v. Lopez*). Of course, dissenting opinions in each of these 5–4 decisions read the precedential, historical, and constitutional records differently, but the justices avoided the kind of public soul-searching so evident in *Casey*.

That 1992 public display of disaffection prompted journalists and scholars alike to speculate about whether the traditionally collegial Court was coming apart at the seams. In fact, internal conflicts among the justices are not new to the highest court in the land.[60] Even so, the increased willingness to display personal and ideological differences before the public in published opinions and speeches is a worrisome phenomenon for the image of the institution. Moreover, Justice Scalia returned to his strident ways in two highly publicized dissents from the 1995–96 term in the Colorado gay rights case (voiding a state constitutional amendment that barred local ordinances banning discrimination on the basis of gender orientation) and the Virginia Military Institute decision (declaring unconstitutional VMI's male-only admissions policy).[61] In both dissents, Scalia accused the majority, among other things, of advocating politically correct causes of the legal elite. Still, compared to the other two branches of government, the Supreme Court has managed to maintain a public persona of collegiality.[62]

As Justice Lewis Powell argued in a 1976 article, "differences of opinion" on the Court "are inevitable, and in my view reflect a strength—not a weakness—of the Court. The very process of dissent tends to minimize arbitrary decision making, assures a rigorous internal testing of the majority view, and bespeaks the vitality of the Court as an institution."[63]

In 1980, then Justice Rehnquist wrote on this same issue of perceived lack of unity and disharmony on the Court, much reported in the press at the time. He compared the Burger Court to the Vinson Court of the 1940s and 1950s, and he noted that President Truman had nominated his charming friend, Fred Vinson, to serve as chief justice in the hope that he would unify the conflicted Court and therefore improve its public image. Vinson failed to do so, but this was not surprising considering that lack of unanimity on the Court had been one of its defining features since the early nineteenth century. While noting that the percentage of unanimous opinions had declined markedly after 1935, Rehnquist's primary point was that, in light of the varied and controversial cases brought to the Court, unanimity is neither feasible nor desirable.[64]

In fact, Rehnquist maintained that the harmony of pursuing a common aim—"to uphold the Constitution and laws of the United States"—actually "underlies the discord reflected in our opinions."[65] He concluded that "while we may overdo dissents and separate concurrences, those who would insist on an artificial unanimity may mistake the rancorous exchanges in a particular case for a malfunction of the system. . . . Dissenting and concurring opinions, when not overdone, are comparable to the spirit of checks and balances which permeates the Constitution."[66]

Admittedly, Rehnquist's position on dissents may have been self-serving given that he had earned the nickname "Lone Ranger" (along with a doll from his clerks depicting the erstwhile cowboy hero) for his numerous solo dissents from majority opinions. Nonetheless, Rehnquist's position that the justices do have unity of purpose, if not always result, in upholding the Constitution is telling. For, although more skeptical observers point to passionate debates on the Court as evidence that the institution is all too human, one would be hard pressed to find congressional or presidential debates undertaken at such a high level of sophistication.

ORAL ARGUMENTS

Likewise, attending an oral argument session at the Court and a typical floor debate in either house of the U.S. Congress provides a stark contrast. First-time visitors to the House or Senate are shocked to find only a handful of senators or representatives in attendance, often giving half-hearted attention to their colleagues debating at the podium. Even if a congressional debate is well attended or the members pay closer attention to their colleagues, they and the public audience in the chamber or through television may be treated to a bombastic harangue or, in 1994, to Senator Alphonse D'Amato (R.-N.Y.) singing his rendition of "Old MacDonald Had a Farm" with words that parodied the Clinton administration. The public might even see members of Congress criticizing the very institution in which they serve.

Attorneys who have appeared before the Court make the case that oral argument is a thrilling experience for them and spectators in the courtroom. Sarah Weddington, who argued *Roe v. Wade* on behalf of Jane Roe, has commented about her trip to the Court, "When you approach the Supreme Court, of course, you see those levels of marble steps, reaching up to the entrance. And when you go up them and stand at the entrance to the Supreme Court building, there are a number of columns that seem to just reach into the sky."[67] Weddington, the daughter of a minister, continued, "The chamber holds about 350 people, so it is not a really large room, and in fact the way it's done, it has a very intimate feeling. When you come in at the back, there are very heavy red velvet curtains. And just as you go through those curtains, there are three sections of what look like church pews."[68]

As in the Court's opinions, much of the discussion in oral arguments, from both the attorneys and the justices, centers around the institution's position at the apex of the federal judiciary and its role as the arbiter of the Constitution and the laws of the land.[69] For instance, the oral argument in *Cooper v. Aaron* reflected the position of the Court that it ultimately took in its unanimous opinion regarding the supremacy of the Constitution and the Court's interpretation of it.

The advocate for the state of Arkansas argued that the governor could borrow time before carrying out the mandate of *Brown* if he was uncertain about how to apply the landmark decision. An audibly annoyed Justice

Frankfurter responded, "The governor's calling out of troops [to stop desegregation] isn't the same thing as the uncertainty of what the law is. That has nothing to do with the uncertainty of the law. That's the action of the governor under what he thought was his refusal to abide by the law."[70]

The Arkansas attorney then tried a different tack, positing that if the governor of a state declared that a U.S. Supreme Court decision (in this instance, *Brown*) was not the law of the land, then the people of the state had a right to doubt just what the law of the land was until it was resolved. An equally annoyed Chief Justice Warren exploded from the bench, "I have never heard such an argument made in a court of justice before, and I've tried many a case, over many a year. I never heard a lawyer say that the statement of a governor, as to what was legal or illegal, should control the action of any court."[71]

Following attorney Thurgood Marshall's argument for the students in the case, Solicitor General J. Lee Rankin spoke as a "friend of the court" in defending the United States' position in the lawsuit. He urged the members of the Arkansas school board "to carry out the obligations of the Constitution of the United States as interpreted by this Court." Rankin then concluded eloquently with a reference to the symbol on the front pediment of the Court. "[O]n this Supreme Court building is the carved inscription, 'Equal Justice Under Law.' All Americans take pride in this controlling principle of our government. It is there as a reminder of the great objective of this Court in all of its decisions."[72]

In *Baker v. Carr*, the 1962 reapportionment case, the Court again faced the issue of its position in the trinity of the branches of government and the federal system. Archibald Cox, famed lawyer and solicitor general of the United States at the time *Baker* was argued, emphasized to the Court the lasting importance of the dispute over redrawing state legislative districts. Because the main question at issue in *Baker* involved whether the judiciary should even take and decide such previously declared "political questions," Cox stressed to the Court the need for it to intervene in order to protect its own power, as well as the legitimacy of the constitutional system itself.

The Court heard a similar position expressed in *U.S. v. Nixon* by Leon Jaworski, the Watergate special prosecutor. He began his oral argument before the justices with the following query: "When boiled down, this case really presents one fundamental issue: Who is to be the arbiter of what the Constitution says? . . . [T]his nation's constitutional form of government is in serious jeopardy if the president, any president, is to say that the Constitution means what *he* says it does, and that there is no one, not even the Supreme Court, to tell him otherwise."[73] In summing up, Jaworski returned to his contention that "if the courts are the ultimate interpreters of the Constitution and can restrain Congress to operate within constitutional bounds, they certainly shouldn't be empowered any less to measure presidential claims of constitutional powers."[74] The Court agreed with Jaworski's reasoning in ruling against President Nixon.

Throughout the 1960s and 1970s, in cases involving individual rights, the arguments before the Court turned repeatedly to the theme of the Court's unsurpassed power in interpreting Bill of Rights guarantees and congressional statutes. By 1963, five years after the Court reasserted its supremacy over state actions in *Cooper v. Aaron*, and just one year after it declared state-sponsored prayer in public schools to be unconstitutional, a much more deferential attorney pleaded his case before the nine justices on behalf of the Abington School District in Pennsylvania. The state legislature in Pennsylvania had mandated in 1959 that "ten verses from the Holy Bible shall be read" every day in public schools throughout the state. At oral argument, the Abington attorney argued that the reading of Bible verses constituted a few moments of moral instructions, not a religious ceremony. That line of reasoning prompted Chief Justice Warren to inquire whether a full hour of mandated reading of biblical verses could also be labeled instruction in morality. Learning the lesson of the Court's role in determining the constitutionality of such state activities, the Abington attorney replied that such a "problem would be for the Court to determine."[75] The Court determined in the Abington case that even a few moments of organized, state-sponsored Bible reading in public schools constituted a devotional exercise in violation of the First Amendment's Establishment Clause.

That same year of 1963 found the Court facing another state policy, this time in the criminal realm, where Florida provided counsel to indigent defendants only in capital cases. From the bench in oral argument, Justice Hugo Black explicitly stated his desire to overturn *Betts v. Brady*, which had upheld such state policies, and he asserted the Court's power to tell states "what they can do to comply with what this Court says the Constitution requires."[76] Abe Fortas, who would be nominated to the Supreme Court two years after arguing the case as a Court-appointed attorney for his indigent client Clarence Earl Gideon, concluded with eloquent oral advocacy for Justice Black's position, which the Court subsequently adopted unanimously. Fortas summarized: "I think *Betts against Brady* was wrong when decided; . . . time has prepared the way so that the rule, the correct rule, the civilized rule, the rule of American constitutionalism, the rule of due process, may now be stated by this Court."[77]

In 1964 the counsel for the Heart of Atlanta Motel tried to utilize the accepted role of the Court, as the final arbiter of state/federal relations and the constitutionality of congressional acts, to the advantage of his client, who had challenged the 1964 Civil Rights Act's ban on racial segregation in public accommodations. Focusing on the Tenth Amendment's reservation of powers to the states, the attorney argued that the Court's role was "to maintain the balance of powers" between the state and federal governments.[78] Moreover, he argued, the Court must declare which acts of states and which acts of Congress are constitutional. Despite the attorney's explicit acceptance of the Court's historical role as the final arbiter of constitutional disputes (an acceptance that just six years previously the attorney for Arkansas had so boldly and unsuccessfully dismissed in *Cooper v. Aaron*), the Court used its power to rule against his client, the Heart of Atlanta Motel, in declaring that Congress did indeed have the power to regulate racial policies in public accommodations through its interstate commerce prerogative.

In another of the many cases on racial discrimination that the Court heard in the aftermath of *Brown*, the tribunal used its power to reach a different result in 1971. The case of *Palmer v. Thompson* challenged Jackson, Mississippi's closing of public pools on the grounds that it did so with discriminatory intent and in violation of the Fourteenth Amendment's Equal Protection Clause. Attorneys for the black citizens of Jackson called upon the Court to view the city's closing of public pools as the same kind of activity outlawed by the Court's precedent in *Brown*. Famed advocate William Kunstler pleaded with the Court to view Jackson's actions also as a violation of the Thirteenth Amendment, outlawing slavery. Putting himself in the Court's place, Kunstler concluded "that we as a Court have just as much responsibility as Congress, just as much responsibility as the executive, in wiping out these badges [of inferiority], because unless they are wiped out, no black person can feel secure in the United States." In addition, Kunstler described a perception of the Court "in the public's mind" that is close to the truth. He declared, "I submit that . . . this Court is really nothing more than an extension of the American personality, an extension of the American sociology."[79] Although Jackson, Mississippi's lawyer was not in the same league as Kunstler, admitting before the high court that he was "a little nervous—in fact . . . scared," he persuaded a narrow majority of justices that his city's closing of its public pools to all residents was *not* a violation of the "equal protection of the laws."[80]

In 1972 another interesting religion case came before the high court, offering more insights regarding the tribunal's image contained in the oral argument session. *Wisconsin v. Yoder* raised the question of whether the state could force Amish children to attend school until age sixteen despite their sect's beliefs that they should leave formal schooling after the eighth grade to participate in and learn more about family farming and domestic chores. Wisconsin's advocate placed the question squarely before the Court to determine the rights and obligations of Amish parents. In summing up his position on behalf of those parents, the Amish respondents' lawyer was equally confident in the role that the Court would play to delimit the power of the state in matters related to the free exercise of religion and education. He concluded, "The Amish do not come here as fearful supplicants to this Court. They come here with confidence, believing in this Court as their brothers in justice, in love, in goodness, in belief in constitutional liberty."[81]

The Amish's confidence in the Court was well placed, for, with only one justice dissenting, Chief Justice Burger wrote in the majority opinion that to apply Wisconsin's education policy to the Amish would violate their freedom to exercise their religion as guaranteed under the First Amendment.

Not surprisingly, one of the most revealing oral arguments occurred in *Roe v. Wade.* So intriguing is the oral session that C-SPAN has presented it in its entirety, with identifying portraits of justices and counsel who can be heard on the audio tape. Occasionally, the Court orders further argument after the initial session. *Roe* was one such case. It was actually argued twice before the high bench. The first time *Roe* was argued, two seats had been empty, owing to the deaths of Justices Hugo Black and John Marshall Harlan II in the fall of 1971. Early in the first argument, Justice Potter Stewart stressed the commonly stated role of the Court to the counsel for Ms. Roe. He urged her to move beyond the policy implications of Texas's antiabortion law to tell the Court "what provisions of the Constitution you rely on [to counter the law]. Because, of course, we'd like to sometimes, but we cannot here be involved simply with matters of policy, as you know."[82] Responding to a Texas assistant attorney general, who argued before the Court for his state, another justice (whose voice cannot be identified) reemphasized Stewart's point, "Policy questions are for legislative and executive bodies, both the state and federal governments. But we have here a constitutional question," which must be decided.[83]

In the first *Roe* argument the Texas assistant attorney general began on the wrong foot with a weak and sexist attempt at humor. Approaching the podium, the advocate began with the traditional greeting to the Court, "Mr. Chief Justice, may it please the Court." He then unadvisedly continued with a reference to the two female attorneys arguing for Roe: "It's an old joke, but when a man argues against two beautiful ladies like this, they're going to have the last word."[84] On the tape of the argument there is dead silence following the remark. Another Texas assistant attorney general replaced his colleague for the second argument.

During the subsequent hearing, the Court again returned to the issue of the proper forum for the abortion issue. Justice Blackmun, who ultimately would write the Court's majority opinion in *Roe*, queried the Texas assistant attorney general about how the question of personhood of the unborn should be decided: "Is it a legal question, a constitutional question, a medical question, a philosophical question, a religious question, or what is it?" The Texas advocate initially answered that the issue of when a fetus becomes a human being should be left to a legislature, which could sift through medical evidence presented to it. Yet on the constitutional issue, the advocate for Texas argued that the question was "fairly and squarely before this Court, adding rather gratuitously, "we don't envy the Court for having to make this decision."[85] Another unidentified member of the Court reemphasized: "If you're right that an unborn fetus is a person, then you can't leave it to the legislature to play fast and loose in dealing with that person."[86] In other words, the Court would have to decide the constitutional issues related to state abortion statutes. Decide it did in 1973 with mighty repercussions for the Court, which it spelled out so dramatically almost twenty years later in *Casey.*

On another matter of life and death, namely, capital punishment, the Court again grappled with its role, and that of public opinion, in the oral argument of *Gregg v. Georgia* in 1976, which challenged new death penalty statutes passed by the state legislature after the U.S. Supreme Court had invalidated Georgia's capital punishment laws four years earlier. Robert Bork, who would be an unsuccessful nominee for the high court in 1987, argued as the U.S. solicitor general and a friend of the Court in *Gregg.* He asserted that the case was "merely the latest in a continuing series seeking to obtain from this Court a political judgment that the opponents of capital punishment have been unable to obtain from the political branches of government."[87] But Chief Justice Burger had an exchange with Bork's counterpart on the influence that political considerations and public opinion should have in the Court's judgment of whether capital punishment violated the "cruel and unusual" component of the Eighth Amendment. The lawyer arguing against the death penalty maintained that "plebecites" on capital punishment should have no bearing on the case. He also argued that it was not his side in the case that was asking the Court to "use subjective gut feelings, to be a superlegislature" and that "the only coherent analytic position" was that "the death penalty is a violation of the Eighth Amendment."[88] Ultimately, the Court disagreed, upholding capital punishment statutes that guarantee due process.

The merging of symbol and substance in this most public work of the Court is unmistakable. As Chapter 1 indicates, the setting for Supreme Court oral arguments simply cannot be surpassed in its ceremony, iconography, ritual, and symbolism. From the decor of the chamber itself, to the reverential tone of the audience and the attorneys, to the explicit acceptance of the Court's role as the final arbiter, to the image of the black-gowned justices, to their efforts to portray the Court as a non-political branch of government, oral arguments project the institution in its finest light. Even the occasional sniping that may occur among the justices on the bench or the more recent efforts at humor, which lighten the somber atmosphere, cannot diminish the "priestly" image of the place and its people.

JUSTICES' SPEECHES, ARTICLES, AND BOOKS ON THE COURT

Justice Felix Frankfurter once complained in an after-dinner speech delivered during his tenure on the Court that he was suffering from "judicial lockjaw."[89] To anyone who knew the verbose Frankfurter, always the professor ready to launch into a lecture from the bench and in conferences, the very idea that he could suffer from lockjaw—of the judicial variety or otherwise—was an absolute impossibility. Frankfurter explained that he felt restrained as a justice in the topics that he could publicly discuss. A few years later, Justice William Brennan quoted a chief justice from his home state of New Jersey who had been asked by a reporter to explain a portion of his court's opinion that had been widely discussed in the press. The chief justice replied: "Sir, we write opinions, we don't explain them."[90] Justice Stephen Breyer has reiterated a similar position: "The judicial opinion explains itself; that's its whole point."[91]

Nevertheless, throughout its history, the Court's members have written and spoken in extra-judicial commentaries about the Court. Especially in the modern era, justices have taken numerous opportunities to speak, lecture, and write about the Court's procedures, organization, and history; about criticism of its decisions; and about proposed reforms to change its operation or jurisdiction. In doing so, the justices have not only revealed interesting facts about the Court as an institution, but they have also provided insights into their own personalities and their feelings about their service on the highest court in the land. In the process, they have almost universally contributed to the positive image of the Supreme Court. Justice Breyer's moving tribute to the Court and its traditions delivered in the Holocaust Museum, or Justice Blackmun's reference to the Court as his "institutional hero," or Justice Kennedy's stirring challenge to the forces of terror and incivility in the wake of the 1995 Oklahoma City bombing are illustrative.

Long before justices began to have their public speaking engagements televised, they accepted invitations to lecture to bar associations and specialized professional organizations, and at commencement exercises, dedications, judicial conferences, and assorted other professional and social gatherings. Often these speeches were published in legal periodicals or more generally circulated journals. One of the earliest speeches by a justice in the Court's modern era, on the topic of the Court as an institution, is a set of extemporaneous remarks by Justice Harold H. Burton delivered to the 1947 Annual Meeting of the National Association of Women Lawyers. Blandly entitled "The United States Supreme Court," it might have been called "The Court Is Special!"[92]

Justice Burton stressed to the women lawyers that part of the Court's unique nature derives from its continuity—the historical fact that the Court has had a "continuous existence from its inception to the present day." Congress changes its membership and numbered sessions every two years; presidential administrations transform every time a new occupant of the White House is elected; but as Burton noted, "we still have with us the original Supreme Court of the United States."[93] He argued that "out of this continuous service has come an independence and a stability of thought that has done much to preserve this nation for 158 years."[94]

Burton linked the nation's founding documents to the Court in observing that "our Constitution, with its Bill of Rights, is . . . only as strong as it is interpreted to be by the Supreme Court of the United States." Foreshadowing Justice Breyer's trusteeship theme in his 1995 Holocaust Museum speech, Burton elaborated, "this in turn places upon our Court a high obligation of trusteeship for the benefit of all the people, all the time."[95] Just a decade after the Court had emerged triumphant from the battle with FDR and during a period of intra-Court fighting that had broken into the press, Burton's more illustrious image of the high tribunal was all the more important to convey in a public setting.

Just one year later, a retired justice who had been a key figure in the battle with FDR over the New Deal delivered an advocacy piece regarding the Court to the New York City Bar Association. Owen Roberts, who by 1948 was serving as the dean of the University of Pennsylvania Law School, admitted that he felt entirely free as a private citizen to speak in public about the Court, which he had served for fifteen years from 1930 to 1945. He spoke openly in support of several constitutional amendments, which he thought would protect the place of the Court in our "triune form of government."[96] Two proposals touted by Roberts that day were intended to guard the non-partisan, non-political image of the Court. One amendment would have banned any member of the Court from future service as president or vice president of the United States. To hold intra-Court jockeying to a minimum, Roberts added that he would like to see a ban on any associate justice's promotion to chief justice. In addition, Roberts wanted to see a prohibition on any justice serving in any other governmental or public office or position. Like many of his predecessors, Roberts had served at the behest of two different presidents on two commissions whose work was not of a judicial nature. He believed in retrospect that such service had not been good for his work as a justice or for the Court as whole.

In a tribute to Roberts when he died in 1955, Justice Frankfurter, attempting to spare his former colleague's reputation regarding the Court's famous switch to a pro–New Deal posture in 1937, argued that Roberts had not changed his position out of deference to the prevailing political mood of the country as reflected in FDR's landslide victory in 1936. The tribute, which originally appeared in the *University of Pennsylvania Law Review*, also gave Frankfurter the opportunity to defend the Court's adherence to confidentiality. He realized that attempting to dispel the story about Roberts's actions in 1937 was a delicate operation. As Frankfurter put it:

Disclosure of Court happenings not made public by the Court itself, in its opinions and orders, presents a ticklish problem. The secrecy that envelopes the Court's work is not due to love of secrecy or want of responsible regard for the claims of a democratic society to know how it is governed. That the Supreme Court should not be amenable to the forces of publicity to which the Executive and the Congress are subjected is essential to the effective functioning of the Court.[97]

Frankfurter's justification for the institution's aloofness was especially important at a time when the Court was under attack for its 1954 school desegregation decision in *Brown*.

Less salutary for the Court's public perception during the 1950s was a brief, but fascinating, article by a future member of the Court in the widely circulated *U.S. News and World Report*. Entitled "Who Writes Decisions of the Supreme Court?" the short piece by young William H. Rehnquist appeared in the magazine at the end of 1957, several years after he had completed his clerkship at the Court with Justice Robert Jackson. Acknowledging that some of the "mystery and rumor" surrounding the Court's work must remain intact in order to protect the confidentiality of the tribunal, Rehnquist proceeded to describe the role of Supreme Court clerks in sorting through *certiorari* petitions and researching and drafting opinions. While downplaying the role of clerks in the final decisions of the Court, he reported that they were much more likely to influence the justices' positions on whether to accept a case on appeal.

The most damning part of the article was the conclusion in which the future associate justice and chief justice vented his political spleen by accusing the majority of his fellow clerks of occupying a position on the ideological spectrum that "was to the 'left' of either the nation or the Court."[98] To the extent that the clerks' biases crept into the Court's work, via their role in the *certiorari* process, Rehnquist argued that "some of the tenets of the 'liberal' point of view which commanded the sympathy of a majority of the clerks I knew were: extreme solicitude for the claims of Communists and other criminal defendants, expansion of federal power at the expense of State power, great sympathy toward any government regulation of business—in short, the political philosophy now espoused by the Court under Chief Justice Earl Warren."[99] In the midst of the Red Scare of the 1950s, some of Rehnquist's remarks could have been labeled "fighting words."

Justice Tom Clark's published comments to a conference on judicial administration sponsored by the American Judicature Society in 1959 returned to the more typical version of judicial and judicious comments about the Court. Clark delineated the external and internal limitations on the Court and discussed the behind-the-scenes procedures of conferences. He described the contrast between the austere majesty of the courtroom and the warm intimacy of the oak-paneled conference room. He also mentioned the prominent display of Chief Justice Marshall's portrait in the latter chamber, describing him as the "fourth Chief Justice by number but the first in stature."[100]

As have virtually all justices who have described the conference procedure,

Clark informed his audience that *only* the nine justices are present at the meetings to discuss *certiorari* petitions and cases heard in oral argument; he stressed the absolute need for conferences to operate in secrecy. In addition, Clark reminded his audience of the traditional handshake among all of the justices that symbolizes their collegiality and dates back several generations.

In 1963, Justice Charles E. Whittaker, who had retired from the Court with nervous exhaustion after serving only five years on the high bench, wrote even more glowingly than Clark of the institution that had taken such a toll on his physical and mental health. He noted that justices not only shook hands before conferences but anytime they encountered each other in the building. Whittaker observed that he thought the custom was a good one; "it is conducive to good will, for one is not likely to have or retain ill-will toward another who extends a warm handshake every time they meet."[101] Even when justices differed on cases and did so in strong language in their opinions, "mutual respect is such that this is always done without personal rancor or ill-will."[102]

Whittaker then addressed criticism of the Court, which had grown so heavy in the Warren era, quoting President Calvin Coolidge, who said: "It is not necessary to prove that the Supreme Court never made a mistake; but, if the power is to be taken from them, it is necessary to prove that those who are to exercise it would be likely to make fewer mistakes." The retired justice added, "It is of the essence of orderly government that the Court's decisions, so long as it is charged with the responsibility of decision, be accepted and obeyed. It is too obvious for serious discussion that any other course can only result in chaos and calamity." He ended rather poignantly (especially in light of the anguish that serving on the Court had brought to him) with reference to one "Professor Sutherland of Harvard," who had explained that the Court was bound to attract abuse, "and if the abusive custom seems a little hard on nine devoted . . . men . . . holding, as they perform their essential public duties, a middle course through the cross-currents of public opinion, we . . . can perhaps, now and then, pause to say that we understand and value their work and respect their endurance." Despite the fact that Justice Whittaker apparently had no endurance for the criticism and unrelenting pressure that serving on the Court entailed, he begged his audience to "at least respect . . . the good faith of their [the justices'] efforts."[103]

Yet in the tumultuous decade of the 1960s, when all institutions of government and society in general were exposed to the most public and microscopic inspection, criticism of the Court expanded. In the aftermath of the 1968 presidential campaign, during which Richard Nixon made the tribunal a key campaign issue, Justice Tom Clark, who retired from the bench in 1967 when his son Ramsay became attorney general, noted that there had always been "open season" on the Court, but by 1970 there were "more hunters and more game with fewer applicable game laws." Although he viewed the U.S. Supreme Court as the "world exemplar" of "law, the only dependable force for man's freedom," he acknowledged that the tribunal was "suffering its darkest hour at a time when it deserves admiration for its most glorious day."[104]

Citing the power of judicial review and interpretations under the Fourteenth Amendment as two fundamental reasons for public furor over the Court, Clark zeroed in on the cases involving segregation, criminal law, legislative apportionment, and school prayer as specific issues that had ignited political criticism of the Court's work. In the final category of school prayer, he complained that the press had so distorted the Court's 1962 ruling striking down state-sponsored and -drafted prayer in public schools that he had felt compelled to abandon his policy of not commenting publicly on precedents to defend the Court's decision while he was still on the bench. Recognizing that opposition to the Court would continue and would result from public perceptions of its decisions, he, nevertheless, exhorted his fellow citizens to heed the words of Daniel Webster, who described the Court as "one tribunal established by all, responsible to all, with power to decide for all." And Clark concluded, "If we are to have a United States of America we had best continue this safeguard to our liberties as the keystone of our governmental arch."[105]

The primary target of such criticism aimed at the Court in the 1950s and 1960s was Chief Justice Earl Warren.[106] After his retirement in 1969, he continued to speak publicly about preserving the stature of the Court and immunizing it against attacks on its power. In a speech delivered just months before his death in 1974, he commented with good humor and grace on the viciousness of salvos fired against him, his colleagues, and the institution he had led: "The Supreme Court of the United States has not been immune from the destructive cynicism of our age. No one has yet suggested that it be abolished outright, although I can attest that proposals have been made to abolish certain individual justices through the process of impeachment."[107] He remembered the attacks on the Court in 1937 resulting in FDR's unsuccessful Court-packing legislation and addressed the more recent movement in 1974 to strip the Court of some of its jurisdiction and place it in the hands of a proposed "mini-Supreme Court." He called for opposition to such a plan, which he perceived as "pulling down the pillars of the Supreme Court" and destroying "its function and its symbol as the chief architect of our constitutional way of life."[108] Furthermore, if the Court itself was to determine which part of its jurisdiction to delegate to a new court, Warren argued that it would be thrust into the political arena, where such decisions regarding jurisdiction are usually made. He urged, "The Court must be kept free from such partisan political matters. . . . [It must] retain its paramount function of preserving the constitutional rights of individuals and the primacy and uniformity of federal law."[109]

Justice Lewis Powell, named to the Court by President Richard Nixon in

1972 at the height of the post-Warren controversy, spoke in as glowing terms of his new professional home as his predecessors. He was struck by the justices' lack of informal interchange in performing their work, observing that "perhaps as much as 90 per cent of our total time, we function as nine small, independent law firms."[110] But he concluded his 1976 speech to the American Bar Association's Section of Labor Relations Law by commenting that while justices "do say in dissenting opinions some rather outrageous and unflattering things about each other, we are warm personal friends. . . . I cherish the privilege of serving on the Supreme Court of the United States."[111]

Also in 1976, Powell wrote a defense of the Court from the "myths and misconceptions" that surround it. He declared that "respect for and confidence in the Court as an institution, essential to its ultimate authority, is not enhanced either by the popular belief that we enjoy several months' vacation or by the view that we are paid for a full week's work when our duties require much less."[112] Powell described the typical work load of a justice during the weeks that the Court was in session and the summer break, attempting to convince readers that members of the Court toiled long hours during term as well as during the summer months. He also argued that clerks did not have undue influence on the decisions of the justices and that strong ideological divisions among the justices did not disrupt the harmony of the bench or the justices' "primary allegiance to our oath of office and duty as we perceive it." Moreover, to talk of "blocs" on the Court was futile because independence of thought among the justices was such a strong judicial norm that Powell remarked: "No man who wears the robe, whatever his court, is worthy of his office if he compromises his independence."[113]

During the mid-1970s, discussions raged over opening the governmental process to public examination. In the aftermath of the Watergate cover-up, so-called "sunshine laws" were passed to require numerous government institutions to maintain an open-door policy. Committee meetings in Congress, except for those addressing national security measures, were to be open to the public and television cameras. With this issue obviously preying on his mind, Justice Rehnquist, in early 1977, delivered a lecture at Washburn University entitled "Sunshine in the Third Branch." In it, he outlined the numerous reasons to continue the secret nature of the Court's conferences. He stressed that only justices participate in the meetings of the high tribunal where decisions are made regarding acceptance of appeals and case outcomes. Moreover, he worried that if Court staff, the public, and television cameras were allowed in the inner sanctum, they would irreparably damage the cordiality and collegiality of the institution. As the future chief justice expressed it, "I am not at all sure whether this cordiality would survive the opening of the Conference to the public, since I am convinced it depends in part on the fact our occasionally short tempered remarks or bits of rancorous rhetoric are kept among ourselves, and not spread upon any public record."[114] In Rehnquist's view, breaching the secrecy of the conference would inevitably damage the Court, and in the long run, the public.

It was surely not coincidental that Rehnquist just one year later found himself emphasizing the Court's harmony against journalistic perceptions of the institution as one racked by discord.[115] In addition to numerous articles in the popular press detailing the divisive voting blocs on the Court and their propensity to result in 5–4 splits in controversial cases, the Court was also portrayed as a petty, back-stabbing gathering of nine prima donnas in Woodward and Armstrong's book *The Brethren*, published in 1979.

Likewise, Justice Powell was out on the stump in 1980 again countering the "misconceptions" about the Court in remarks to the Southwestern Legal Foundation. They were published in the *New York State Bar Journal* later that year with the following editor's headnote: "Mr. Justice Powell here gives us an authentic picture of Supreme Court practices, procedures and interpersonal relationships. It provides our readers with a refreshing antidote to recent journalistic sensationalism."[116] Justice Powell repeated his previous statements, reported above, regarding the work load of the Court, the role of clerks, and the harmony among his colleagues. He ended with an additional accolade for the Court as the guarantor of "the great ideal of ordered liberty" in the United States. As a result, Powell argued, "The American people have respected the courts, and they have placed special trust and confidence in the Supreme Court. In my view, this trust has been merited. . . . The institution, nourished by its inherited traditions, is what merits respect and confidence." A closing footnote in the article cited with approbation reporter Anthony Lewis's commentary in the *New York Times*, which had asserted that the courts are "fragile. We bring [the judiciary] into the rough and tumble of politics and public gossip at our peril."[117]

By 1982, the furor over publication of *The Brethren* had begun to subside, and the next major issue on the Court's agenda was administrative in nature. With *certiorari* petitions flooding the Court and the number of opinions issued by the justices approaching the maximum level, proposals began to circulate regarding how to address the Court's work load. One plan, based on accepted procedure in the lower federal courts of appeal, suggested that the Court begin to issue more summary judgments (that is, decide cases on written briefs without a full hearing and full opinion). Justice Brennan, in an address to the Third Circuit Judicial Conference, took exception to the suggestion, arguing "that the Court's favorable image in the eyes of both bar and public rests so heavily on oral audience before us."[118]

Additionally, Brennan vehemently disagreed with those, including his "respected colleague" Justice Stevens, who were advocating the creation of another federal court, which would accept *certiorari* petitions and decide which should be granted or denied. Declaring that "the choice of issues for decision largely determines the image that the American people have of their Supreme Court," Brennan concluded dramatically that adoption of the proposed new court "would sow the seeds of destruction of the Court's stand-ing as we know it."[119]

Just two years later, Brennan, who during his 34-year tenure on the Court was a prolific speaker and writer on extra-judicial topics, proclaimed that the Court's function was not to cater to constituents but to determine what restraints might need to be placed on them. He wrote, "Independence and integrity, not popularity, must be its [the Court's] standards."[120] He wor-ried that the mystique of the judicial process was now gone and that, therefore, the Court had a greater role to play in educating the public re-garding its function and work.

Disagreeing in administrative matters as he did in jurisprudential ones with his colleague Justice Brennan, Justice Rehnquist spoke in 1986 about how the history of the Court was one of change, reform, and accommo-dation and how the proposed national court of appeals was a necessary part of the federal judiciary's evolution. He assumed that the typical lawyer, ed-itorial writer, or taxi driver perceived the Supreme Court as the "highest court in the land," and Rehnquist was not fearful that establishing another tribunal one level below the nine justices would destroy that perception.[121] Chief Justice Burger was a tireless champion of a new national court of appeals, and he advocated its adoption in numerous speeches, administrative reports, and interviews. The proposal was never adopted; and although the number of *certiorari* petitions to the Court continues to rise, the Court itself has nearly cut in half the number of cases it hears and decides each year, making its opinion work load much more manageable.

Several months before Burger retired from the Court and Rehnquist was nominated to replace him, the latter delivered an intriguing lecture on the impact of public opinion on constitutional law. Rehnquist began by recalling that he had been moved to speak on the subject after a visitor to the Court had asked him if "judges respond to public opinion." Using the Steel Sei-zure Case, which was decided during his clerkship at the Court, as an illus-tration, he argued that although judges should not "respond" to public opinion, they are inevitably "influenced" by it. He elaborated that judges read newspapers, watch newscasts, and talk to family and friends about cur-rent events. Rehnquist continued, "Somewhere 'out there'—beyond the walls of the courthouse—run currents and tides of public opinion which lap at the courthouse door. . . . This is not a case of judges 'knuckling under' to public opinion, and cravenly abandoning their oaths of office. Judges, so long as they are relatively normal human beings, can no more escape being influenced by public opinion in the long run than can people working at other jobs."[122]

Once again, Rehnquist was the voice offering a less exalted view—a more human view—of the Supreme Court, just as he had done in his 1957 mag-azine article decrying the impact of clerks' ideology on the tribunal. Some scholars and journalists had been proclaiming for years that the high tribunal was a political institution like the other two branches of government. As the preceding excerpts from judicial speeches on the Court illustrate, however, it is rare to find a member of the Court who makes such pronouncements.

The retirement of Chief Justice Burger gave his colleagues another opportunity to proclaim the unique nature of the Supreme Court in the American system of government. Justice Powell, commenting that President Nixon's desired overturning of Warren Court precedents had not occurred under Burger, declared that most judges

> try conscientiously to obey their oath of office, and to put behind them partisan and social predilections. . . . The great strength of the Supreme Court is that we have no "policy" or purpose other than "faithfully and impartially" to discharge our duties "agreeably to the Constitution and laws of the United States." . . . Commentators who expect radical changes because of personnel changes on the Court seem to overlook our fidelity to this doctrine. . . . Under our remarkable constitutional system, the Court has well discharged its responsibility to safeguard the liberties of our people.[123]

At a 1992 dedication ceremony honoring Justice Powell at his alma mater, Washington and Lee University, Chief Justice Rehnquist delivered a highly intellectual account of the Legal Realism school of jurisprudence and its belief that judges create, not find, law. According to the Legal Realists, judges base their creation of law on their own previous experiences rather than legal precedents. Recognizing that most jurists and commentators accept nearly all of Legal Realism's explanation of judicial decision-making, Rehnquist concluded, nevertheless, that the deliberative, collegial process of the Supreme Court acts as filter through which the individual contribution of a justice is strained. The process thus acts as a constraint on the creative forces of individual justices and their personal backgrounds.[124] Therefore, in recognizing Powell's confidence in this filtering mechanism, the chief justice also explicated his own belief in how the judicial process operates to counteract the human element in judging.

Rehnquist has developed into the resident Court historian on the high bench. In 1987 he published a history of the Supreme Court, which begins with a reminiscence of his clerkship at the Court with Justice Jackson in the 1950s. (Notably, it lacks any reference to his fears that his fellow clerks were dangerous leftists.) He speaks of the awe that he experienced, like the typical visitor to the Court, upon arriving at the building for his first day of work.

On the lecture circuit he is fond of delivering variations on the theme of "defining moments" in the Supreme Court's history. In these set pieces, he covers three historical attacks on the Court (Justice Samuel Chase's impeachment trial in 1805, the Radical Republicans' diminution of the Court's jurisdiction in the wake of the Civil War, and FDR's Court-packing plan in 1937). He notes that they illustrate the fact that the Court's exercise of judicial review over congressional and presidential acts, as well as state laws, is bound to sweep it into the political turmoil of its times, and he concludes that the Court "must hope that the public respect which it has accumulated over a period of years for its decisions will enable it to survive such attacks."[125]

Rehnquist's view of the Court's role in the governmental process is that of the guardian of democratic procedure and ideals, the protector of the separation of powers and federalism, which guarantee our liberties. His public comments on the more human or political traits of the Court may have been intended as a warning to the public that the tribunal is straying from what he perceives as its proper place in the American constitutional system. For example, his tirade against the leftist ideology of the clerks in 1957 admonished that they were unduly solicitous of "expansion of federal power at the expense of state power."[126]

Respect for the federal structure outlined in the U.S. Constitution continues as a favorite Rehnquistian theme in public speeches. In the fall of 1994 he spoke out against the Crime Act passed earlier that year by Congress. Avoiding judgments on specific aspects of the legislation, which he recognized had resulted from Congress's response to Americans' fear of crime, he concluded, nevertheless, that the federalization of criminal law was a dangerous precedent that ignored "the historic division between the proper business of the state courts and the proper business of the federal courts."[127]

Other justices have seemed less inclined to speak so openly and specifically regarding the Court's role as it relates to particular political issues. As new justices take their place on the high bench, they tend to continue the tradition of speaking about the Court in positive terms. Not yet on the Court one full term, in May 1994, Justice Ruth Bader Ginsburg was already delivering the rather set speech on the Court's "work ways," which described the secrecy of the conference, the important but limited role of the clerks, opinion assignment and drafting, and oral argument.[128]

Even old hands on the Court still deliver the standard, upbeat speech on the institution's strengths. Offering remarks at a civic luncheon in Palm Beach at the end of 1994, Justice John Paul Stevens said, with his typically impish, self-deprecating sense of humor, that a recent candidate for a clerkship in his chambers had asked him why he didn't resign from the Court! Stevens provided this answer to the luncheon guests:

[The Court] is a very pleasant place to work because—of course, the building is nice and the surroundings are nice and all the rest—but the people at the Supreme Court are uniformly delightful people to work with. It is really very pleasant—although you may not get this impression from our opinions—the relationship among the members of the Court is very cordial. We actually enjoy our conferences not withstanding our rather strong disagreements from time to time. On argument days and conference days usually all of us lunch together.[129]

Stevens added that he found the work of the Court very interesting, and he illustrated his point with several cases from the 1994–95 term, including the term limits case, whose majority opinion he eventually wrote.

Justice Clarence Thomas, whose speeches are often autobiographical in their themes and sometimes bitter in tone, also speaks of the pleasant atmosphere at the Court. In a 1994 speech he recalled that before his nomination to the high bench, he had not thought much about the Court as an institution, nor had he ever attended one of its oral argument sessions. He had presumed that there were warring camps and tensions on the Court. In his speech, Thomas claimed that his preconceptions of life on the Supreme Court were "far from the truth" because the institution is so civil and respectful and so dedicated to doing its best as a supreme court.[130]

The justices' frequent references to the Court's institutional and personal strengths clearly contrast with the typical stump speech of the president of the United States or a member of Congress, both of whom spend far less time discussing their respective institutions. No doubt this contrast results, in part, from the norm that justices should not discuss cases in public and should steer away from political issues (although examples exist of justices violating that unwritten rule). Traditionally, justices have viewed discussions of non-confidential Court procedure as a "safe" topic and one that audiences genuinely like to hear about from an "insider." Simply stated, presidents and members of Congress have more topics that they can and do discuss. Moreover, perhaps justices spend so much time self-justifying their institution because they know that its power and legitimacy rest precariously on public respect for the rule of law and the Court's interpretation of it. What better way to nurture that esteem than by portraying the institution as the most professional, civil, dignified, and collegial governmental body in Washington?

NOTES

1. *America and the Courts*, C-SPAN, 24 June 1995.
2. Ruth Bader Ginsburg, "Communicating and Commenting on the Court's Work," *Georgetown Law Journal* 83 (1995): 2119–20; see also Gregory Casey, "Popular Perceptions of Supreme Court Rulings," *American Politics Quarterly* 4 (January 1976): 3–45; Gerald N. Rosenberg and Christopher M. Rohrbacher, "The Changing Meanings of Supreme Court Decisions: *Carolene Products* Footnote 4 as a Political Symbol" (paper presented at the Annual Meeting of the American Political Science Association, Boston, Mass., 3–6 September 1998); and Katy J. Harriger's "Cues and Miscues in the Constitutional Dialogue," *The Review of Politics* 60 (Summer 1998): 497–524, a sophisticated analysis of the Court's communication with its "interpretive community."
3. *West Virginia State Board of Education v. Barnette*, 319 U.S. 624 (1943) (emphasis added).

4. *Richmond Newspapers, Inc. v. Virginia*, 448 U.S. 555 (1980).
5. *United States v. Curtiss-Wright Export Corp.*, 299 U.S. 304 (1936).
6. *Korematsu v. United States*, 323 U.S. 214 (1944).
7. Ibid.
8. Ibid.
9. *Cooper v. Aaron*, 358 U.S. 1 (1958).
10. Ibid.
11. Ibid.
12. Ibid.
13. Ibid.
14. Ibid.
15. *Youngstown Sheet and Tube v. Sawyer*, 343 U.S. 579 (1952).
16. Ibid.
17. Ibid.
18. *Rochin v. California*, 342 U.S. 165 (1952).
19. *Baker v. Carr*, 369 U.S. 186 (1962).
20. *Reynolds v. Sims*, 377 U.S. 533 (1964).
21. *Mapp v. Ohio*, 367 U.S. 643 (1961).
22. *Gideon v. Wainwright*, 372 U.S. 335 (1963).
23. *Miranda v. Arizona*, 384 U.S. 436 (1966).
24. *Griswold v. Connecticut*, 381 U.S. 479 (1965).
25. Ibid.
26. *Lemon v. Kurtzman*, 403 U.S. 602 (1971).
27. *Roe v. Wade*, 410 U.S. 113 (1973).
28. Ibid.
29. *San Antonio Independent School District v. Rodriguez*, 411 U.S. 1 (1973).
30. Ibid.
31. *U.S. v. Nixon*, 418 U.S. 683 (1974).
32. *National League of Cities v. Usery*, 426 U.S. 833 (1976).
33. Ibid.
34. *Craig v. Boren*, 429 U.S. 190 (1976).
35. *United Steelworkers of America v. Weber*, 443 U.S. 193 (1979).
36. *Immigration and Naturalization Service v. Chadha*, 462 U.S. 919 (1983).
37. *U.S. v. Leon*, 468 U.S. 897 (1984).
38. *Garcia v. San Antonio Metro. Transit Authority*, 469 U.S. 528 (1985).
39. Ibid.
40. *Bowers v. Hardwick*, 478 U.S. 186 (1986).
41. Henry J. Abraham and Barbara A. Perry, *Freedom and the Court: Civil Rights and Liberties in the United States* (New York: Oxford University Press, 1998), 216.
42. *Webster v. Reproductive Health Services*, 492 U.S. 490 (1989).
43. Ibid.
44. Ibid.
45. Ibid.
46. Ibid.
47. *Texas v. Johnson*, 491 U.S. 397 (1989).
48. Ibid.
49. Ibid.
50. *Lee v. Weisman*, 505 U.S. 577 (1992).

51. Ibid.

52. David J. Garrow, "Justice Souter: A Surprising Kind of Conservative," *New York Times Magazine*, 6 September 1994, 36.

53. *Planned Parenthood of Southeastern Pennsylvania v. Casey*, 505 U.S. 833 (1992).

54. Ibid.

55. Ibid.

56. Ibid.

57. Ibid.

58. Ibid. (emphasis in original).

59. *Missouri v. Jenkins*, 515 U.S. 70 (1995).

60. See Phillip J. Cooper, *Battles on the Bench: Conflict inside the Supreme Court* (Lawrence: University Press of Kansas, 1995).

61. *Romer v. Evans*, 517 U.S. 620 (1996), and *United States v. Virginia*, 518 U.S. 515 (1996).

62. Cooper, *Battles on the Bench*, 179.

63. Lewis F. Powell, Jr., "Myths and Misconceptions about the Supreme Court," *New York State Bar Journal* 48 (January 1976): 9.

64. William H. Rehnquist, " 'All Discord, Harmony Not Understood': The Performance of the Supreme Court of the United States," *Arizona Law Review* 22 (1980): 973–86.

65. Ibid., 978.

66. Ibid., 986.

67. Peter Irons and Stephanie Guitton, eds., *May It Please the Court* (New York: The New Press, 1993), xx.

68. Ibid.

69. All of the arguments described here are available on audio tape at the National Archives, in excerpted form in a set of six audio cassettes from Irons and Guitton's *May It Please the Court*, and on the Website posted by Northwestern University.

70. Irons and Guitton, *May It Please the Court*, 252.

71. Ibid., 253.

72. Ibid., 256.

73. Ibid., 25 (emphasis in original).

74. Ibid., 27.

75. Ibid., 65.

76. Ibid., 190.

77. Ibid., 192.

78. Ibid., 267.

79. Ibid., 295.

80. Ibid., 291, 296.

81. Ibid., 99.

82. Ibid., 345.

83. Ibid., 347.

84. Ibid., 346.

85. Ibid., 351.

86. Ibid., 352.

87. Ibid., 236.

88. Ibid., 237.

89. As quoted in Alan F. Westin, ed., *An Autobiography of the Supreme Court: Off the Bench Commentary by the Justices* (New York: Macmillan, 1963).

90. Ibid.

91. *The Docket Sheet of the Supreme Court of the United States* 31 (Summer 1995): 12.

92. Harold H. Burton, "The United States Supreme Court," *Women's Law Journal* 34 (Summer 1948): 4–6, 33, 43–45.

93. Ibid., 5.

94. Ibid., 45.

95. Ibid., 46.

96. Owen Roberts, "Now Is the Time: Fortifying the Supreme Court's Independence," *American Bar Association Journal* 35 (January 1949): 1.

97. As quoted in Westin, *An Autobiography of the Supreme Court*, 244.

98. William H. Rehnquist, "Who Writes Decisions of the Supreme Court?" *U.S. News and World Report*, 13 December 1957, 75.

99. Ibid.

100. Tom C. Clark, "Internal Operation of the United States Supreme Court," *Journal of the American Judicature Society* 43 (August 1959): 49.

101. Charles E. Whittaker, "The Role of the Supreme Court," *Arkansas Law Review* 17 (February 1963): 296.

102. Ibid., 300.

103. Ibid., 301.

104. Tom C. Clark, "The Court and Its Critics," *Villanova Law Review* 15 (September 1970: 521.

105. Ibid., 526.

106. Warren's colleague, Justice William O. Douglas, also found himself the target of impeachment, spearheaded by then Congressman Gerald R. Ford (R.-Mich.), in the 1960s. Douglas's liberal opinions and idiosyncratic lifestyle had prompted the investigation, which never made it out of the House of Representatives.

107. Earl Warren, "Let's Not Weaken the Supreme Court," *American Bar Association Journal* 60 (June 1974): 677.

108. Ibid., 678.

109. Ibid., 680.

110. As quoted in "What the Justices Are Saying . . .", *American Bar Association Journal* 62 (November 1976): 1454.

111. Ibid., 1455.

112. Lewis F. Powell, Jr., "Myths and Misconceptions about the Supreme Court," *New York State Bar Journal* 48 (January 1976): 8.

113. Ibid., 10.

114. William H. Rehnquist, "Sunshine in the Third Branch," *Washburn Law Journal* 16 (Spring 1977): 567.

115. William H. Rehnquist, " 'All Discord, Harmony Not Understood': The Performance of the Supreme Court of the United States," *Arizona Law Review* 22 (1980): 973–86.

116. Lewis F. Powell, Jr., "What Really Goes on at the Court," *New York State Bar Journal* 52 (October 1980): 454.

117. Ibid., 489.

118. William J. Brennan, Jr., "Some Thoughts on the Supreme Court's Work-load," *Judicature* 66 (December 1982/January 1983): 232.

119. Ibid.

120. William J. Brennan, Jr., "How Goes the Supreme Court?" *Mercer Law Review* 36 (Spring 1985): 790.

121. William H. Rehnquist, "The Changing Role of the Supreme Court," *Florida State University Law Review* 14 (Spring 1986): 1–14.

122. William H. Rehnquist, "Constitutional Law and Public Opinion," *Suffolk University Law Review* 20 (Winter 1986): 768.

123. Lewis F. Powell, Jr., "The Burger Court," *Washington and Lee Law Review* 44 (Winter 1987): 1, 10.

124. William H. Rehnquist, "Remarks on the Process of Judging," *Washington and Lee Law Review* 49 (Spring 1992): 263–70.

125. William H. Rehnquist, "The American Constitutional Experience: Remarks of the Chief Justice," *Lousiana Law Review* 54 (May 1994): 1172.

126. William H. Rehnquist, "Who Writes the Decisions of the Supreme Court?" 75.

127. William H. Rehnquist, "Convocation Address, Wake Forest University," *Wake Forest Law Review* 29 (1994): 1006.

128. Ruth Bader Ginsburg, "Remarks for the American Law Institute Annual Dinner," *St. Louis University Law Journal* 38 (Summer 1994): 881–88.

129. John Paul Stevens, C-SPAN, 28 January 1995.

130. Clarence Thomas, C-SPAN, 14 January 1995.

Chapter 4

Defrocking the Priests?
Media Presentations of the Court

Lyle Denniston, often called the "dean" of the Supreme Court press corps and one of its most accomplished reporters, has been covering the high tribunal for most of his journalistic career, which began in the late 1940s. Currently, he writes about the Court for the *Baltimore Sun*. In February 1995, Denniston appeared at a symposium jointly sponsored by the American University School of Commerce and the National Press Club that was entitled "Dialogues with the Press." Speaking to a group dominated by lawyers, he began his remarks with admiring references to iconoclastic commentator H.L. Mencken and then posed the query, "Would you want your child to become a journalist?" Before answering the question at the end of his speech, he described the core values of journalism, noting that "there is, indeed, a deep yearning in most journalists to joust with the power structure or with some elite . . . and ultimately to expose either some wrongdoing or at least someone's secret or perhaps someone's fatuousness."[1]

Denniston described Bob Woodward, who uncovered the Watergate scandal as a reporter for the *Washington Post* and a few years later exposed the Supreme Court in *The Brethren*, as the best modern example of a journalist who upholds the tradition of muckraking. Indeed, Denniston related that Woodward had recently felt stirred to report that, prior to her elevation to the Supreme Court, Ruth Bader Ginsburg had altered one of her public lectures to sound more in tune with the Clinton administration and that her husband, prominent Washington attorney Martin Ginsburg, had orchestrated her nomination behind the scenes. Denniston commented that this example illustrates the important role that journalists play in our society.

Denniston proclaimed that journalists know the difference between muckraking and mudslinging, but his concluding comments raise concerns about how the press covers the Court. Returning to his theme of whether audience members would want their children to become reporters, he warned that if one's child chose journalism as a vocation, "one day, sooner or later, your kid would heave a dead cat into some sanctuary somewhere and prove that some god was a fraud" or prove that "the hallowed wisdom" of his parents or elders "was in fact subject to doubt."[2] Denniston's remarks are revealing. Having just declared that journalists know the difference between muckraking and mudslinging, he unwittingly related that journalists engage in a variety of the latter, namely, catslinging! His metaphor is especially apt for an analysis of coverage of the Supreme Court, whose building is often compared to a religious structure or a sanctuary and whose justices maintain an image of a hallowed, priestly tribe that dispenses wisdom from Olympian heights. Obviously, the press has every right to challenge that wisdom and demystify or debunk those images. Nonetheless, to extend Denniston's own analogy, journalists should only have the right to *report* that they found a dead cat in the Supreme Court building or that one of the justices is suspected of cruelty to animals or that the Court is covering up some secret, bizarre ritual of animal sacrifice that is taking place in its sacred precincts. The press does not have the right to fling in the feline carcass in order to create a scandalous tale.

The "catslinging" mentality among some members of the press is so worrisome because the media necessarily constitute a crucial link between the Court and the public. Although slightly fewer than one million people pass through the Supreme Court's bronze doors annually, most Americans will never observe the institution on a personal visit. Their only perceptions of the Court's image result, in large part, from the print and broadcast media.

Having followed closely all events related to the tribunal in 1994–95 and having spent twelve months viewing its procedures and personalities from the inside, I was perfectly positioned to compare and contrast the precision of newspaper and television coverage with what actually occurred at the Court. Moreover, my fellowship placed me in a most propitious position for judging whether the selection of stories to report on the Court accurately reflected the whole of the 1994–95 term. As James Fallows, former Washington editor of *The Atlantic Monthly* and *U.S. News and World Report*, has written, "From the nearly infinite array of events, dramas, tragedies, and successes occurring in the world each day, newspaper editors and broadcast producers must define a tiny sample as 'the news.' "[3] Was "the news" reported on the Court in 1994–95 representative of the whole body of the tribunal's work and the justices who produced it? Before turning to that question, some historical context is necessary.

THE MEDIA AS "JUNKYARD DOGS"

Political scientist Larry Sabato has concluded that journalists, who once fulfilled their constitutional duty as "watchdogs" of government, have transformed themselves into vicious "junkyard dogs" in the post-Watergate era. As another commentator has described the modern press, "Ingrained cynicism rather than knee-jerk liberalism is the media's real bias."[4] The media have also been accused by James Fallows of "concentrating on conflict and spectacle, building up celebrities and tearing them down, presenting a crisis or issue with the volume turned all the way up, only to drop that issue and turn to the next emergency."[5] The media's preoccupation with conflict often results in their transforming stories on politics and the judiciary into athletic contests. Winners and losers in the political and judicial arenas splash across the headlines and are forgotten as quickly as the ephemeral score in a ball game.

Besides the media's attachment to cynicism, conflict, and athletic analogies, another major theme of post-Watergate journalism is the desire to eliminate any distinctions between the private and public realms, especially for public figures. Ironically, in an era that saw the Supreme Court create a zone of privacy to protect access to contraceptives and abortions, and in a time when we often hear people refer to their "right" to undertake virtually any kind of activity in private, the media have blurred all lines between public and private undertakings. From television talk shows, where individuals discuss openly and in minute detail some of those very intimate activities they believe they have the right to engage in, to reports by and on public officials' most private actions, the media have come a long way from the "gentlemen's agreements" in the Roosevelt and Kennedy administrations when the press agreed not to report presidential peccadillos or even ill health.

Pulitzer Prize–winning presidential biographer Doris Kearns Goodwin has questioned the wisdom of the media's erasure of the line between politicians' public and private lives. In fact, in 1976 Goodwin squarely faced this dilemma when she interviewed presidential candidate Jimmy Carter. To a question about his morality, Carter responded that he often felt guilty for lusting "in his heart" for women other than his wife. Goodwin discussed the comment with her husband, Richard, a former aide to JFK, and decided to forego placing the Carter "mea culpa" in her article. Nevertheless, a few days later, Carter made the same remark during an interview for *Playboy* magazine, which most assuredly included the comment in its feature on the presidential candidate. Thus, candidates and officeholders have often violated their own privacy by offering too much information about themselves. President Clinton's 1993 answer to an MTV audience member's question about what kind of underwear he prefers (he responded "briefs") is another example of how far we have come in the media age to destroying whatever dignity public officials and their institutions previously maintained. (Of course, Clinton's own sexual behavior would ultimately erode further the stateliness of the presidential office.) Goodwin has urged politicians "to have a sense of guarding their dignity, especially the president. I mean, no one would have ever thought of asking FDR about his underwear—whether he wore boxers or briefs—and he certainly would have never answered."⁶

Goodwin also noted that although Americans may seem to desire intimate knowledge of their leaders, which they might miss if they were denied access to it, the net gain could be an increase in respect for public officials and a concomitant increase in their ability to govern. She also pointed to the example of Jackie Kennedy, "who went to extremes to keep her life private. In the end, everyone [was] saying, even people in the press, 'Oh, I admire her so much because she wouldn't let us talk to her.' Perhaps she could get away with it because she wasn't running for office—but it shows the other side is out there." Only a future president with "utter self-confidence" comparable to FDR's will have the security to draw the line with the press and say, "These are legitimate issues of public concern, and these are private matters."⁷

Cokie Roberts, longtime NPR commentator and ABC correspondent, disagrees with the Goodwin approach. In a July 1995 presentation to a Capitol Hill audience, she argued that because Americans vote "for the person" in deciding between presidential candidates (as opposed to issue-based voting, which she claimed governs Senate races), "anything is fair game" for journalistic investigation. She thus draws the line differently for the president or presidential candidates in determining what knowledge voters should have about occupants of the White House. She goes beyond the standard, advocated by some, that a president's private life should only be investigated and reported if it impinges on his public duties. Roberts does admit, however, that "the press makes it harder" for presidents to be reelected because "every foible is examined, reexamined, and highlighted."⁸

Another development in modern media coverage of the government is the C-SPAN phenomenon of gavel-to-gavel broadcasts of Congress. When William Cohen announced his retirement from the Senate in 1996, he cited the impact of such coverage on the institution, which he was leaving prematurely. His musings, so pertinent to how overexposure of the Supreme Court could damage the tribunal, are worth quoting at length. Cohen described the classic "club" atmosphere of the Senate when he arrived on the scene in 1978, but he noted that

television has transformed the situation. . . . When the lights are on, it is theater. And I think we have evolved into more performing rather than deliberating and working things out in an intimate atmosphere. You see the positive benefits of people really seeing what's taking place, seeing their government in action. On the other hand, there is less willingness to drop one's rigid position to find some kind of a common ground. *The sense of majesty and mystique has been stripped away from Congress as a result of C-SPAN.* [emphasis added] Most people feel, "Hey, wait a minute, he doesn't know any more about the issues than I do. So why should we defer to *his* judgment?"⁹ (Cohen's emphasis)

C-SPAN, which does indeed perform an invaluable educational function, can also defend itself by pointing out that it simply broadcasts what occurs on the floor of the Senate and House of Representatives. If Congress members are hams and cannot help performing for cameras, that's their own fault. Moreover, Congress is its own worst enemy when it reveals its arcane mores and procedures to viewers. Indeed, political scientists John Hibbing and Elizabeth Theiss-Morse have concluded that by displaying the less edifying elements of democracy, Congress has become "public enemy" #1 among the American electorate.[10]

A segment on media coverage of government institutions would not be complete without at least a brief mention of the flood of references to the courts, the judicial process, and the media that resulted from the first O.J. Simpson trial. Although the U.S. Supreme Court had no involvement in the case, lessons from the Simpson media event loomed large in both the public consciousness and the minds of federal judges. Many of the visitors I briefed at the Court in 1994–95—both Americans and foreigners—wanted to know about the trial and if the case would ever reach the highest court in the land. It is highly likely that federal judges were influenced by the spectacle of the Simpson trial coverage in their September 1994 vote to end an experiment on the use of television cameras in federal courts. In March 1996, five months after the verdict in the Simpson criminal case when some of the furor over his acquittal had died down, these same federal judges voted to reinstate cameras in federal courts of appeals (not federal trial courts or the Supreme Court) at the discretion of each appellate judge.

The day after the Simpson jury in the criminal case acquitted the former football star, national newspapers ran stories on the impact of the trial on the American justice system and the role of the media. Two former state judges, Andrew Napolitano of New Jersey and Richard Neely of West Virginia, came to opposite conclusions regarding cameras in the courtroom. Napolitano focused on the salutary function of cameras that allow the "public to view, up front and close, the least understood branch of government. Whether the public liked what it saw or not, the result of this can only be positive: An understanding that the search for truth is tedious; a realization that trials, which need not be perfect, must nevertheless be fair; and a perception that the criminal justice system, like virtually every aspect of American society, has warts that can be addressed only after careful observation."[11]

In contrast, Neely argued that the media's financial concerns force them to place entertainment ahead of information, with negative results for how the press covers the courts. He minced no words; "cameras must be banned from *all* courts, both criminal and civil." The former judge, now a practicing attorney, then made a surprising admission: "Whenever I get in front of the camera, even if for a fleeting moment, I change like Mr. Hyde from lawyer to carnival barker." He concluded, "Much to the consternation of television executives, human nature exerts natural limits on freedom of the press, which is the real lesson of the O.J. trial."[12]

While many postmortems on the Simpson case concentrated on the putative impact of media on the trial, some centered on how the "trial of the century" may have forever changed the media. Many Americans made the trial a part of their daily lives. (There were even bizarre stories of people who did nothing but watch the trial and who worried about how their lives could go on once a verdict was rendered.) An average of 2.3 million households watched the trial's coverage every weekday from noon to 8 p.m. During the same time period one year earlier, CNN had averaged 470,000 households tuned in to its programming.[13]

The Simpson case discovered a public interest in the judicial process and nurtured it. The Court TV network had been covering state judicial proceedings long before O.J. Simpson went on trial, but new television programming geared toward public interest in the law has developed in the wake of the Simpson case. Roger Cossack and Greta Van Susteren, CNN's commentators throughout the trial, now have their own daily program on the network, *Burden of Proof*, which covers current legal issues in a 30-minute format. CNN's executive vice president Ed Turner has concluded, "The public has become far more educated about the way the judicial system works. . . . The public has come to realize that they have a right to see what one-third of their government is doing."[14]

But Pearl Stewart, former editor of the *Oakland Tribune*, sounded the alarm for future coverage of the courts in the aftermath of the O.J. circus: "The overkill, the extensive publicity surrounding this case went too far. If we continue to do our jobs based on what there's an appetite for, then every paper will be the *National Enquirer*, the *Globe* and the *Star*."[15] Even more striking, coming from a journalist, is her suggestion that although the media have the constitutional right to publish and broadcast virtually anything they wish, they should not be guided solely by the public's seemingly insatiable appetite for sensationalism. Sadly, as long as catering to such appetites increases the number of media consumers and, in turn, advertising revenues for media outlets, the welfare of American institutions and their processes is unlikely to be the abiding concern of journalism.

MEDIA COVERAGE OF THE SUPREME COURT IN THE MODERN ERA: HELPING OR HURTING THE COURT'S IMAGE?

Despite the media excesses surrounding the Lindburgh kidnaping case, scandal and sensationalism were much less a part of public affairs media coverage in the 1930s. Journalists of the period have been characterized as "lapdogs," whose docile nature and generally even-tempered approach informed their reporting.[16] The *Literary Digest* article, discussed in Chapter

1, was hardly an example of hard-hitting, investigative journalism. Although the article described the ideologies and personalities of each of the justices who sat on the bench in 1934, it used adjectives like "majestic," "half-deified," and "awe-inspiring," to describe the Court and its members.

Nevertheless, the journalistic world did display some cynicism toward the Court's actions. The socialistic *New Republic* had supported the philosophy of the New Deal, and the journal attacked as a "legal fiction" the image of the justices as dispassionate, neutral arbiters of constitutional law. The leftist periodical viewed the justices as just nine more players in the economic policy-making process.

As noted earlier, the most scathing onslaught against the Court came from Drew Pearson and Robert Allen's book *The Nine Old Men*. Attacking both the Court's decisions against the New Deal and its new building, the book, which was excerpted in newspapers throughout the country, unleashed a scathing volley of viciously snide comments. Fortunately for the Court's image, the visceral attack from Pearson and Allen made few dents in the institution's overall reputation.

Evidence of strong media support for the Supreme Court came in the form of widespread journalistic opposition to Roosevelt's plan to pack the tribunal in 1937. Although it is difficult to sort out support for the Court as an individual institution from broader public backing of the American constitutional system, embodying the rule of law and an independent judiciary, it is clear that with few exceptions the media bolstered rather than weakened the Court's image.

In the 1940s the Court's image was less exalted by the press. This fact is reflected in the reporting of a wound inflicted on the Court by its own hand. The Supreme Court, like other institutions, has made errors. Some, like the *Dred Scott* decision, have been worse than others, but the Court has always eventually regained its legitimacy by realigning itself with America's revered constitutional system. The decade following the Depression witnessed an interpersonal squabble among the justices that broke into the open, resulting in negative publicity. The root cause of the dissension on the bench was a personal, professional, and jurisprudential feud between Justices Hugo Black and Robert Jackson. In a 1980 lecture, then Justice William Rehnquist cited a 1946 *New York Times* article that focused on the Supreme Court's inner turmoil. The *Times* had written on the occasion of Fred Vinson's appointment to chief justice in 1946:

As it is told in the cocktail parties and congressional corridors, personal antagonisms were never more accentuated among the black-robed Justices than in the term now closing. The hidden fires . . . are smoldering in the closed conference room, so it is said. . . . Further than that, Washington hears more about what goes on inside the court than formerly. Once upon a time, and that was back in the days when the New Deal began, the conferences were shrouded in mystery. So were the persons of the

Justices to a large degree. The austere court judges of that period seemed to live much apart from the passing world. Now the scene has altered. Even though still men of eminence, the jurists do not instill the old awe.[17]

Maintaining the "old awe" was nearly impossible when Justice Jackson, who had only exacerbated the situation by leaving the Court shorthanded while he served as the United States' chief prosecutor at the Nuremberg Trials, went public with his unhappiness over the Court's feuding. He coveted, and believed he had been promised, the chief justiceship, but Justice Black might have resigned had President Truman carried out FDR's putative promise to Jackson. Thus, Truman nominated his friend Vinson, thinking (mistakenly) that with his warmth and charm he could bring peace to the dueling justices. Only divine intervention accomplished this feat when Jackson went to his grave in 1954.

By that time the Supreme Court had started down a road which would lead it into the public consciousness through its cases rather than its personnel. Although the media cannot report on all Supreme Court cases, they do provide coverage of those judicial decisions that they deem most important. Not surprisingly, *Brown v. Board of Education* was one such case; after its momentous announcement, long-term media coverage of school desegregation increased by half. The Court's controversial ruling in the 1962 case of *Engel v. Vitale*, which struck down state-sponsored prayer in public schools, prompted a similar increase in media coverage of church–state issues. *Texas v. Johnson*, the 1989 case that invalidated state ordinances barring flag desecration (in this instance, flag burning), generated an identical proliferation of media attention to freedom of speech issues. These three particular cases spurred such long-term change in media coverage of their respective issues because the decisions all ran counter to prevailing public opinion.[18]

Beginning with *Roe v. Wade* in 1973, which polarized public opinion by reinforcing and strengthening people's previous positions on terminating a pregnancy,[19] abortion has often been the leading issue covered by media reporting on the Court. From 1976 to 1981, it was the one controversy most likely emphasized in televised Supreme Court stories. Every such decision handed down by the justices during that five-year interval was reported on by at least one of the three major networks.[20]

During the 1989–90 term alone, abortion was still the legal issue that garnered the most attention from ABC, CBS, and NBC. Only the so-called right-to-die case, *Cruzan v. Director, Missouri Dept. of Health*, received more instances of coverage (fourteen) than the term's most reported abortion case, *Hodgson v. Minnesota* (which had eleven stories devoted to it on the networks). A similar case involving the question of parental notification of minors seeking to abort their pregnancies was covered in six network news stories. *U.S. v. Eichman*, another flag-burning case—this one striking down *federal* statutes against desecrating the flag, was covered by nine different news segments on the network broadcasts. Another 1989 term case, *Metro Broadcasting v. FCC*, in which a narrow Brennan-led majority approved the use of affirmative action in awarding broadcast licenses, received network attention in four news stories. This figure pales in comparison to the amount of network television coverage devoted to the original affirmative action case of *Regents of the University of California v. Allan Bakke*, whose oral argument and decision alone were reported in 37 news stories.[21]

Interestingly, a 1989–90 case that created a major stir (including an eventual overturning by Congress in the Religious Freedom Restoration Act of 1993, which itself was declared unconstitutional by the Court in 1997), *Oregon Employment Division v. Smith*, merited a relatively small number of stories (four) from the network news.[22] The Court's 1990 decision had approved the state's policy of declaring peyote a controlled substance, despite liturgical use of the hallucinogenic drug by American Indians.

The year after the Court handed down its landmark 1978 decision in *Bakke*, a landmark book about the tribunal hit the market. *The Brethren*, coauthored by Bob Woodward and Scott Armstrong, was journalistic, not scholarly, in its tone and methodology, which partially accounted for its popularity. Accessible to the general reader, it became a best-seller. In some ways it was a less snide version of its predecessor *The Nine Old Men*. Yet instead of being a polemic against the Court, *The Brethren* ostensibly was an attempt by its authors to introduce readers to the judicial process as carried out by the highest court in the land. Where the Woodward/Armstrong work paralleled the Pearson/Allen book was in its effort to peek behind the velvet curtains in order to provide a sense of the inside story of the Court.

Woodward, who claims that Justice Potter Stewart outlined the book for him and that four other justices cooperated in the enterprise, believed that because the Court makes decisions affecting the country, someone needed to examine the institution more closely than had ever been done previously. Not surprisingly, given his role in uncovering the Watergate scandal, Woodward has asserted that the public cannot know too much about how the government operates. In addition to the purported participation of some justices in *The Brethren*, the authors relied heavily on interviews with law clerks to learn more about the Court behind the scenes. Some of the anecdotes reported in the book are reminiscent of the passage from the *New York Times*, cited previously, regarding the interpersonal squabbles on the Court in 1946. For example, Woodward and Armstrong portray Chief Justice Warren Burger as a petty, weak leader of the Court; such a portrayal may not have been far from the truth, for by most accounts Burger lived up (or down) to those adjectives. What also disturbed admirers of the Court was *The Brethren*'s descriptions of strategizing among the justices, whereby coalition builders, such as Justice Brennan, reportedly took advantage of the human frailties of colleagues, notably Justice Blackmun, to achieve the magic figure of five needed to win a case.

The Court, as well as its supporters, were enraged over the portrayal of the institution. One of the major criticisms of *The Brethren* was, and remains, that the book relied too heavily on anecdotal evidence from the law clerks, whose notorious egos may not have made them the most dependable sources. At the very least, Chief Justice Burger was shocked and incensed by the breach of confidentiality, especially among the clerks. The Court might well have had the same reaction to the 1998 publication *Closed Chambers: The First Eyewitness Account of the Epic Struggles Inside the Supreme Court.* Written by Edward Lazarus, a law clerk to Justice Harry Blackmun in 1988–89, the book accuses the justices of petty political and ideological manipulation of case outcomes. The book's sensational title alone put most reviewers on alert that Lazarus might be seeking his proverbial "fifteen minutes of fame." Despite a grain of truth in some of Lazarus's observations, reviews accused him of everything from egotism to alleged violation of federal laws for taking documents from the Court.

Throughout the post-1937 period, the Court would occasionally splash across the headlines and news broadcasts for matters related to judicial appointments. One of the most publicity-drenched nominations was President Lyndon Johnson's promotion of Associate Justice Abe Fortas to chief justice in 1968. Conservative senators blocked the appointment and discovered, in the meantime, improprieties in Fortas's finances that ultimately prompted his resignation from the bench in 1969.

In more recent years, the failed nominations of Robert Bork (voted down by a hostile Senate opposed to his conservative jurisprudence) and Douglas Ginsburg (withdrawn by President Ronald Reagan when the press discovered that the nominee had smoked marijuana with his students while a law professor) have drawn attention to the Court. Yet these abortive nominations may have stirred more negative publicity for the nominating president, the Senate, and the unsuccessful candidates than for the Supreme Court itself.

The same cannot be said for the Clarence Thomas nomination. The televised gavel-to-gavel coverage of the Senate hearings to investigate the sexual harassment charges leveled against Thomas by then University of Oklahoma Law Professor Anita Hill did irreparable damage to Thomas's reputation and indirectly to the Court's image. His reticence and sometimes presumed inattention on the bench do nothing to salvage his reputation. At most, Thomas asks several questions at oral argument per term. He traces his reticence to advice imparted by his grandparents: "My grandmother told me, 'You can't talk and listen at the same time.' If I wanted to talk a lot, I'd be on the other side of the bench."[23] Although past luminaries on the bench, like Justice Brennan, did not pose numerous oral argument queries, Thomas seems especially isolated in his muteness because the current bench is composed of eight other vocal participants in oral sessions. His silence during oral argument contrasts sharply with his propensity to speak bluntly outside the Court about the origins of his conservative philosophy and the pain that he has suffered at the hands of liberal critics, particularly those in the black community. Visitors to the Court, particularly American audiences, typically inquire about Thomas. If they have attended oral argument, they want to know why Thomas did not ask questions or why he appeared to be daydreaming or even dozing. Rightly or wrongly, the media coverage surrounding the Thomas nomination and his highly publicized speaking engagements may have wrought damage on the high court that will last as least as long as he remains on the bench, which Thomas has vowed to do for decades to come.

MEDIA VERSUS THE COURT (1994–95)

A statistical profile of the *Washington Post*'s coverage of the Court for September 1994 through August 1995 shows that the paper devoted almost 90 stories to cases before the Court. Nine stories reported primarily on cases that had been denied by the Court, seventeen news items featured previews on cases that had just been accepted or were about to be argued at the Court, sixteen articles recounted the oral argument of cases, and forty-seven pieces discussed the outcome of cases decided by the justices.

In other categories, the *Post* covered justices of the Supreme Court in 22 stories. Former Chief Justice Warren Burger's death in June 1995 prompted six of those twenty-two stories on members of the Court. The *Washington Post* included nine stories on the Court as an institution. For example, stories appeared on the Court's annual Christmas party, anecdotes about amusing occurrences at the Court, how the justices have to solidify five votes in order to win a case, and how the 1994–95 term showed indications of the Court's giving more deference to state prerogatives over federal power. The miscellaneous category contained seven stories, which covered the issue of cameras in the courtroom, the chief justice's annual year-end report, and topics related to the federal judiciary as a whole (such as how to apply antidiscrimination laws to employees of the federal courts).

Both the *Post* and the *New York Times* place their primary emphasis in Supreme Court coverage on the outcomes of cases. Each of them reported on approximately half of the fewer than 100 cases that the Court hands down each year. One pronounced difference in their coverage, however, is that the *Post* devotes more stories to the justices themselves. Many of the *Post*'s and *Times*'s Supreme Court articles are carried by local and regional newspapers throughout the country.

New York Times reporter Linda Greenhouse, a 1998 Pulitzer Prize winner for her stories about the Supreme Court, has expertly covered the tribunal for some 20 years. Her news articles on cases are models of cogency, accuracy, and balance. She likes to speculate on the justices' strategies that underlie votes and opinion-writing, but she is not subsumed by that intriguing subject. Instead, she speculates insightfully on what the opinions reveal about how decisions and opinions were hammered out, and then devotes her stories to sorting out the often complex strands of cases and their possible effects. Her occasional features on the Court read more like scholarly treatises. For instance, her May 1995 piece on the "Constitution-in-exile," a phrase she borrowed from federal Judge Douglas H. Ginsburg (the abortive Reagan nominee to the Supreme Court), was a sophisticated analysis of constitutional principles that may be resurrected as the Court becomes more deferential to state prerogatives—a position it had discarded in the 1930s. Greenhouse seems far less seduced by human interest stories on the justices, although she was as intrigued by Chief Justice Rehnquist's gold stripes as the rest of the American media. Her feature on the alteration of the chief's robe included an excerpt from the pertinent Gilbert and Sullivan play.

Greenhouse's counterpart at the *Washington Post*, Joan Biskupic, has reported on the Supreme Court for her paper for about seven years. Before that, she covered the institution for *Congressional Quarterly*. Biskupic understands that reporters have to interpret cases themselves because no one plays the role of explaining decisions at the Court. She has admitted that such self-interpretation is difficult because even lower court judges occasionally do not understand the Supreme Court's rulings. She therefore relies on law professors and lawyers who follow or argue the cases to assist her in interpreting decisions.[24]

Biskupic seems partial to lighter features on justices and their personalities. At the beginning of the 1994 term, she prepared a lengthy article on each justice's defining character traits and his or her personal likes and dislikes. She also authored an anecdotal column on comedic moments at the Court. One amusing exchange, which occurred at an oral argument in the fall of 1994, was Justice David Souter's attempt to question a counsel about the "flaw" in his argument. It was a reasonable question to be sure—except that with Souter's New Hampshire accent, the question asked for the "floor" in the attorney's contention. The baffled counsel paused and then wisely asked for a clarification on Souter's question regarding the "floor" in his position. The justice realized the source of confusion and then sheepishly apologized for his "regional accent," which prompted laughter from those assembled in the courtroom.

Unlike the *Post* and the *Times*, C-SPAN's broadcasts on the Court's 1994–95 term did not emphasize case outcomes. Instead, C-SPAN devotes more airtime to previews and coverage of oral argument day for important cases. The nature of television at least partially dictates the network's agenda. C-SPAN's *America and the Courts* series cannot really cover case outcomes because there is nothing for the network to film. Its cameras cannot be present in the Court's chamber when cases are announced. Rarely are the parties present on opinion days so they are not available for comment on camera. Justices do not interpret the decisions for public consumption nor do any other officers of the Court.

But preview and oral argument coverage is much more productive for C-SPAN. In previewing cases coming before the Supreme Court, the network often gathers the two attorneys in the case who will argue it before the justices, or counsel for interest groups that have submitted *amicus* briefs in the case sometimes appear. *America and the Courts* also features journalists who cover the Court and scholars who specialize in constitutional issues. After cases have been argued, C-SPAN cameras can capture the excitement of the day by photographing the traditional press conference on the Court's front plaza in which the arguing counsel and other interested parties in the cases are free to make statements and take questions.

The most frequent subject for C-SPAN broadcasts on *America and the Courts* is the justices themselves. In 1994–95 alone, the network covered speeches and public appearances by every current justice (except Scalia, who refuses to appear on television) and retired Justice Harry Blackmun. The network also reran a 1986 interview taped with Chief Justice Burger after his retirement, on the occasion of his death in June 1995.

To accompany its *America and the Courts* series, C-SPAN has produced, in cooperation with the American Bar Association, a 52-page guide to the history and procedures of the Supreme Court (available to viewers for a modest $8.95). The booklet provides a public service by introducing interested C-SPAN viewers to the Court in a succinct, lively, readable format. In addition, and more pertinent to my argument regarding the Court's image in the American mind, the guide treats the institution like a unique branch of government, which occupies a temple-like structure, is served by dignified and honorable justices, and is wedded to principle, tradition, and the rule of law that assures, in the words of the booklet's title, "justice for all."

In 1994–95 the media covered one retirement from and one appointment to the Supreme Court. Justice Harry Blackmun announced his retirement in April 1994; President Clinton named his successor, Stephen Breyer, the next month. Coverage of the events in the *Washington Post, New York Times,* and the broadcast medium was similar. Most reports portrayed Blackmun as a compassionate, sweet, gentle man who, ironically, given his placid nature, was perceived as responsible for the firestorm of controversy surrounding *Roe v. Wade,* whose majority opinion he authored. Repeatedly, the news accounts portrayed him as modest, unassuming, grandfatherly, humorous, humble, bookish, and diligent. His former clerks, who were interviewed on the air and for newspaper stories, were understandably eager to paint such a favorable impression of their beloved mentor. (For many years, morning visitors to the Court could see Justice Blackmun huddled together with his young clerks at a cafeteria table during breakfast, seemingly having a delightful time and often discussing baseball.)

Likewise, praise for President Clinton's choice of federal Judge Breyer of the First Circuit Court of Appeals was almost equally effusive and positive. In addition to covering his superb academic and professional credentials, a typical paragraph from the *Washington Post*'s feature on him enthused, "He is a gourmet cook, a bird watcher, an avid reader, a serious student of philosophy, father of three children, a judge who still teaches at Harvard Law School, a speed typist and chronic worrier given to nervous pacing. At 55, he is teaching himself Spanish, taking the language tapes with him as he exercises in the morning. He is an unpretentious millionaire who mows his own lawn, a man who takes delight from ideas and their application."[25] Even a feature on his wife, Joanna, a staff psychologist at Boston's Dana-Farber Cancer Institute, was unabashedly laudatory.[26]

Stories on Cases. Media coverage of the Court's 1994–95 cases was typical in its emphasis on issue areas that resonate with the general public. Thus, Greenhouse's and Biskupic's previews of the term summarized cases on racial and gender discrimination, freedom of speech, the death penalty, and questions related to basic government structure, rules, and power (like term limits for members of the U.S. House and Senate and Congress's authority to restrict possession of guns near schools). C-SPAN also focused on the term limits case in its preview show and presented a spokesperson for each side on whether states can limit the terms served by their members of Congress. Labeling cases as "landmarks" at the outset of the Court's term is problematic for journalists because the justices have only selected half of their caseload for the term before they meet for their opening oral argument on the first Monday in October. Moreover, Chief Justice Rehnquist and Justice Thomas have both accused the press of ignoring genuinely precedent-setting cases in less glamorous areas like banking, taxation, and administrative law.

By the time the Court hands down the cases with the most public interest, usually in the last few weeks of the term, the press knows which decisions to showcase. Then the problem for journalists is analyzing numerous complex decisions in literally a few hours in order to make press deadlines, and persuading editors to devote the necessary space or airtime to afford thorough coverage of the outcomes. Nevertheless, coverage of the denouement of landmark, or otherwise highly publicized, decisions is generally thorough, accurate, and balanced in national publications like the *Post* and *Times*. The three major television networks are deprived of videotape of the Court's announcement of decisions; in addition, by virtue of their news program formats, they usually devote less than several minutes to cases. CNN's *Headline News* offers just what the name suggests on Supreme Court decisions, but has the option of providing lengthier coverage on its *Burden of Proof.*

June 12, 1995, was illustrative of news coverage at the end of the Court's term. That day the floodgates opened on the backlog of cases awaiting decision before the justices' summer recess. The justices announced eight rulings, the most important of which were *Adarand v. Peña* and *Missouri v. Jenkins*, two closely monitored decisions on race. The *Washington Post* banner headline the next day said it all: "Court Toughens Standard for Federal Affirmative Action." Biskupic's article on the 5–4 *Adarand* decision was commendable for sorting through the complexities of Justice O'Connor's majority opinion and explaining its technicalities in a manner comprehensible to the average reader. (She avoided the mistake made by a *Time* magazine reporter, appearing on PBS's *Washington Week in Review*, who stated that the Court had struck down the affirmative action plan at issue in *Adarand*.) Biskupic observed that the ruling, which required that judges apply "strict scrutiny" to federal affirmative action programs, jeopardized all such programs. The decision returned the program at issue to the lower court for adjudication using the "strict scrutiny" standard. Moreover, *Adarand* overturned a 1990 precedent framed by retired Justice Brennan, signaling an ideological shift on the high court.[27]

According to Biskupic, the shift was also evident in the *Jenkins* case. In that decision, the justices ruled by another 5–4 vote that a federal judge had improperly attempted to integrate the public schools of Kansas City, Missouri, by ordering massive expenditures in order to attract students from surrounding suburbs. Biskupic also added a portion of Justice Thomas's stunningly emotive concurring opinion, which took the Kansas City plan to task for trying to attract white students in order to improve urban schools. Wrote Thomas: "It never ceases to amaze me that the courts are so willing to assume that anything that is predominantly black must be inferior."[28] A separate article by two of Biskupic's colleagues at the *Post* focused on the political ramifications of the two rulings.[29]

Greenhouse folded more of the political implications of the *Adarand* ruling into her lead article on the case, declaring that the decision was "likely to fuel rather than resolve the debate over affirmative action," and noting that "the Supreme Court today cast doubt on the constitutionality of Federal programs that award benefits on the basis of race." She elaborated: "By refusing to foreclose affirmative action as a constitutional option, the Court has done little to relieve President Clinton, as well as other elected officials now confronting the issue, of the need to make and defend their own policy choices."[30] Eventually, President Clinton would announce cutbacks in, but not elimination of, federal affirmative action programs.

Greenhouse reflected more detail from the Court's majority opinion in *Jenkins*, and she also quoted directly from Thomas's bitter concurrence.[31] In addition, the *Times* ran a separate article labeled "Reaction," in which another of the paper's reporters described responses to the *Adarand* decision among interest groups on both sides of the issue and within the Clinton administration.[32]

The *Post* and *Times* had their editorials ready to publish the day after *Adarand* and *Jenkins* came down. The *Post* was far less chagrined over the two rulings, saying simply that "a sharply divided Supreme Court is demonstrating the difficulty the entire government is having with the future of affirmative action programs."[33] The paper did not see the two decisions as marking the end of an era but rather signaling the need to find alternatives to traditional policies to remedy racial discrimination. The *Times*'s position was much more pointed, announcing: "The Supreme Court, a place where minorities once looked for racial justice, did what it could yesterday to halt the progress its own decisions once sparked." The New York paper angrily labeled Justices O'Connor, Scalia, Thomas, and Kennedy, along with Chief Justice Rehnquist, a "constitutional wrecking crew" because their majority opinions limited remedial programs that address the history of segregation in this country.[34] For those who believe that the *Times* and *Post* are cut from the same ideological cloth, these editorials from the two papers reveal marked differences in their responses to two controversial Supreme Court rulings.

Subsequent news analyses of *Adarand* speculated about the ramifications of the decision along practical, political, and strategic lines. Justice Ginsburg and James Fallows have both criticized the press for spending too much time engaging in such activity, but the articles that appeared in the *Post* and the *Times* were certainly moderate and informative in theorizing about the impact of *Adarand* on businesses, presidential politics, and public opinion.[35]

Predictably, George Will was less than pleased with the compromise ruling penned by Justice O'Connor's controlling opinion in *Adarand*. He argued that the Court "would have made significant history" if Justice Scalia's concurrence, arguing that the government can *never* justify racial discrimination against whites as a remedy for past discrimination against minorities, would have set the precedent in the case.[36] On the other hand, William Raspberry, a more liberal columnist, pointed out the irony of Justices O'Connor and Thomas voting against affirmative action, when they both had benefitted from it in their elevation to the nation's highest court; and Thomas had advanced throughout his academic and professional career because of racial preference policies.[37]

Conservative commentator Charles Krauthammer took yet another approach to the case, arguing that *Adarand* was relatively insignificant because the Supreme Court would no longer be the major battleground for affirmative action cases. Rather, Krauthammer argued, "it is best for democracy—indeed it is best for conservatism—that such revolutionary decisions be made not by nine wise (wo)men in black robes but by the people, in Congress and in their legislatures."[38] In Krauthammer's view, nine justices in black robes, wise though they may be, are the antithesis of democracy by the people. Indeed, the unelected federal judiciary has often been portrayed as "undemocratic," but history demonstrates that the Supreme Court breathed life into constitutional guarantees of rights to minorities and women, whose voices had been excluded from electoral politics or so diluted as to be ineffectual.

The most provocative decision of the 1994–95 term produced equally divergent editorial reaction, but news coverage of it was accurate, if slightly sensational. Announced on April 26, 1995, *U.S. v. Lopez*, in which the justices, by a close 5–4 vote, struck down the Gun-Free School Zones Act as overstepping Congress's power to regulate interstate commerce, marked a departure from nearly 60 years of the Court's jurisprudence. From the time of the announcement of the decision until the next week, the newspapers and airwaves were filled with stories on *Lopez*. Greenhouse was most dramatic in her lead, "The Supreme Court today dealt a stinging blow to the Federal Government's ability to move into the realm of local law enforcement."[39]

Biskupic raised the political relevance of the justices' decision, writing that "the Court added its voice to the nation's increasingly volatile debate over the size and roles of the federal government. . . . The decision immediately acquired extra resonance because of the Oklahoma City bombing," after which the president and Republican leaders had called for more investigative powers for the federal government.[40] In a follow-up article the next day, Biskupic included responses from a host of experts in the field, who called the *Lopez* decision "breathtaking and historic."[41]

The *Washington Post*, in a short editorial published two days after announcement of the *Lopez* decision, agreed with the Court's majority that Congress had not met the standard of proving that the guns it intended to ban from zones around schools had any relation to interstate commerce. Rather than assuming "the-sky-is-falling" approach, the *Post* reasoned that the *Lopez* opinion did not foreshadow a "fundamental restructuring of federal-state relations."[42]

On the other hand, the *New York Times* waited another day to ponder the case and then issued a longer and more strident response to *Lopez*. It declared that the Court had "taken an unfortunate historical turn and needlessly questioned previously settled law." The *Times* accused the justices of crippling Congress's efforts to address a national problem as they had done in the early days of the New Deal, and concluded that "to strip Congress of the power to function is a throwback to the misguided rulings of earlier times."[43]

In reporting another landmark ruling, the term limits case (*U.S. Term Limits v. Thornton*), the mainstream press once more provided eye-catching headlines and informative coverage. The *Washington Post* ran a banner headline on its front page to signal the importance of the decision, which by a 5–4 vote struck down laws limiting the terms of members of Congress from 23 states.

The *Post* ran short summaries of Justice Stevens's 61-page majority opinion and Justice Thomas's 88-page dissent. In addition, the front-page story above the fold contained pithy quotations from Stevens and Thomas under a photograph of each justice. The Stevens position for the majority read, "Permitting individual States to formulate diverse qualifications for their representatives would result in a patchwork of state qualifications, undermining the uniformity and the national character that the Framers envisioned and sought to ensure." For the dissenting justices, Thomas's excerpt stated, "The Constitution is simply silent on this question. And where the Constitution is silent, it raises no bar to action by the states or the people."[44] Both quotes were perceptive and representative choices for conveying the heart of each position to *Post* readers. The paper also published a separate story on responses from members of Congress to the decision.[45]

One of the Court's last decisions in 1994–95 garnered the most sensational headlines from the front page to the sports page. With two frail members of the Court's old liberal bloc (Justices Harry Blackmun and William Brennan) looking on wanly from the audience, the justices had announced their decision in *Vernonia School District v. Acton*. By a 6–3 vote the Court upheld the Oregon school district's policy of random urinalysis drug testing for middle or high school student athletes. Biskupic's narrative on the decision noted that the Court's ruling "could touch the lives of millions of schoolchildren." At the heart of Justice Scalia's majority opinion was the argument that students are children who do not enjoy the same rights as adults and who are committed to the custody of school officials acting in the place of parents. Moreover, Scalia's opinion for the Court returned to the issue raised at oral argument—that drug testing cannot be considered a violation of student athletes' rights of privacy when they have no expectation of privacy in school locker rooms and restrooms. As Scalia succinctly expressed it, "School sports are not for the bashful."[46] The *Post* also carried a brief excerpt of the majority's opinion and an article reporting that the Court's ruling had strong support from high school athletes in the Washington area. Nevertheless, the *Post*'s editorial on the case sided with Justice O'Connor's reasoning in dissent, which argued that all searches are intrusive, especially those that involve the person, as opposed to homes, papers, or personal effects. The newspaper maintained that millions of students should not be exposed to such intrusive measures when the vast majority of them are innocent of wrongdoing.

As she often does, Greenhouse focused on the historical and strategic oddities of the case, observing that for the first time the Supreme Court had upheld random drug testing. She also reported that the voting line-up in the decision was "unusual," with conservative and liberal justices mixed on each side of the case.[47] The *Times* included lengthier excerpts from the majority and minority opinions. Like the *Post*, the *Times* reported that local high school athletes, their parents, officials, and coaches endorsed the Court's ruling. Unlike the *Post*'s perspective, however, the *Times* wrote that educators predicted that practical considerations would prevent widespread testing of student athletes. The *Times* editors agreed with those at the *Post* that the Supreme Court had erred in permitting what the *Times* called "a needless and dangerous relaxation of the Fourth Amendment's safeguard against unreasonable searches."[48] In its sports section, the *New York Times* carried another editorial questioning the constitutionality of the kind of drug testing upheld by the Court in *Vernonia*.[49]

Covering Oral Arguments. Although headlines and stories on Supreme Court decisions may occasionally reflect modern media sensationalism and even hysteria, oral arguments at the Court are more likely to provide grist for the mills of journalists seeking the proverbial "Man Bites Dog" story. *Vernonia*, brought by fifteen-year-old aspiring football player James Acton, was one such case. During the oral argument of Acton's case, Chief Justice Rehnquist opened the way for some locker-room humor with his reasoning that urinalysis is hardly a violation of privacy when boys' locker rooms are rarely private, with their rows of open urinals and "guys walking around naked." Justice Breyer added that he did not think that providing a urine sample was necessarily an intrusion on privacy because urination is a fact of life; or, as Breyer put it (betraying a male perception), "It isn't really a tremendously private thing." The attorney for James Acton had to concede that everyone urinates. Then, visibly nervous over the tough questioning he was facing, the advocate also conceded, "In fact, I might do so here!" That line brought down the house. Of course, Joan Biskupic reported the exchange word for word in her article on the oral argument in the next day's *Post*. She correctly observed that "the talk in the stately courtroom, ringed in red velvet and white marble, was decidedly unceremonious."[50] Biskupic's inclination to report the humorous dialogue is understandable; nevertheless, if the Court's oral arguments were televised, undoubtedly such atypical comments would be the only sound bite from the dialogue included on the evening news.

Another jocular story derived from oral argument appeared in the press in January 1995. Although Joan Biskupic waited until February to report the event in a longer feature, Lyle Denniston published an unusually funny exchange among the justices the day after it happened. In the case of *Florida Bar Association v. Went For It Inc.*, the Court faced the question of whether Florida could impose a 30-day waiting period on letter-writing by lawyers who attempt to solicit business from accident victims or their survivors. Impropriety among attorneys is a rather embarrassing issue to bring before a panel of nine justices, but the Florida case represented a First Amendment challenge to the state's ban, which the Supreme Court chose to decide.

Justice O'Connor, who eventually would write for the Court in its 5–4 ruling upholding the Florida ban, was obviously contemptuous of the unfortunately named Went For It, Inc., at oral argument. Her voice dripped with sarcasm when she addressed the company's attorney about exactly what his client was going for. His response was that the company finds the names of accident victims and furnishes them to lawyers.

Denniston reported in the *Baltimore Sun* that Chief Justice Rehnquist "asked [Florida's attorney general] in mock seriousness whether it was 're-ally a terribly legitimate state goal to protect the appearance of the profession' from the 'ambulance chaser' image." Interestingly, the lawyer answered that even the Supreme Court was careful to protect its own image by having the justices wear black robes (this was just a week before the chief justice altered his own robe), maintaining a dress code for attorneys who argue before it, and sitting ceremoniously in a "magnificent building."

Comparing the next segment of the oral argument to a *Saturday Night Live* script, Denniston reported that after the chief justice asked the Went For It attorney if the state should try to clean up the image of lawyers, Justice Stevens interjected, "Maybe the state could pass a statute that you can't say unnice things about lawyers." Justice Ginsburg: "Or a law that you can't read Dickens or Shakespeare." Justice Souter: "Or not admit greedy people to the practice of the law." Justice Scalia: "I'm glad I never passed through the practice of law before I got where I am!" Justice Breyer: "It might have helped you, actually."[51] Here were the justices of the Supreme Court exchanging lawyer jokes and engaging in comedic one-upmanship. Although the audience in the courtroom that day enjoyed the exchange, it is worrisome that these types of *Saturday Night Live* skits might impair the image of the Court, particularly when they are bound to be reported in the media and likely would be showcased if video cameras were ever allowed to film oral argument.

Linda Greenhouse, a superb analyst of the Court's behind-the-scenes maneuvering, detected some intriguing machinations in the Court's final vote tally in *Went For It*. By studying each opinion carefully, Greenhouse concluded that Justice Breyer may have abandoned an initial majority to strike down the Florida ban and that the most junior justice then joined a four-person faction led by Justice O'Connor to form a new majority that upheld the ban.[52] One might argue that Greenhouse's propensity to comment on the Court's private struggles to fashion a majority diminishes the institution's image in the public mind. There is always that possibility in any report that emphasizes the human characteristics of the justices. Yet Greenhouse presents her articles in straightforward, objective prose, which avoids the elements of yellow journalism. Moreover, if she ferrets out her suppositions from inside sources, she never indicates as much; thus, her speculations seemingly appear as the result of someone who has done her homework in reading opinions and who has been at the Court long enough to be able to make educated guesses about how majorities were formed.

Another example of lifting oral argument occurrences out of context and overemphasizing them is the predictable reporting of Justice Thomas's rare questions during these sessions. In coverage of a November 1994 case, Biskupic took the opportunity to comment that Thomas, who had not asked a question in oral argument for over a year, finally posed a query to one of the counsel. The occasion was memorable, as indicated by the reaction of the law clerks, who practically fell out of their seats when the unfamiliar voice came over the Court's P.A. system. Although the case in which Thomas spoke had a rather narrow reach (it involved the constitutionality of a law forbidding federal workers from accepting honoraria for speeches and articles unrelated to their government work), Biskupic gave it more coverage than the *Lopez* case argued the same day; she devoted a mere one paragraph to oral argument of what would become one of the most significant cases of the term and the past 60 years.[53]

Despite the media's tendency to scour oral argument sessions for atypical and/or humorous events (which are becoming more typical with wits like Justice Scalia on the bench), journalists tend to provide adequate summaries of the dialogues that occur between justices and counsel at these fascinating public spectacles. In fact, argument sessions demonstrate one of the main differences between procedural norms in the Supreme Court and in Congress. Although the latter receives kudos in the media for being open to cameras, the Court on oral argument days is about as open as an institution can be—except for the cameras, of course. Because everyone works under one roof at the Court—unlike in Congress or the presidency—the whole building takes on an air of excitement before such major arguments. Spectators gather in long lines on the front plaza, arguing attorneys huddle nervously with friends and colleagues on the steps before their final informational briefing with the clerk of the Court in the Lawyers' Lounge, Court police stand watchfully at their posts as security increases on argument days, and other personnel in the building run through their precision routines to see that the session proceeds without a hitch. If the case is highly controversial, protestors may gather on the front plaza to picket, and they will be joined by the media, attorneys, and interest group advocates attending the post-argument news conferences. Biskupic captured some of this drama and excitement in her articles on the term limits oral argument; the *Post* published a photograph of picketers outside the Court.[54] C-SPAN was able to portray the atmosphere outside the Court that day most accurately with its cameras trained on the parade of senators, representatives, attorneys, and interest group members who were all too happy to oblige reporters waiting to solicit the perfect sound bite.[55]

Indeed, the exterior scenes after oral arguments can offer quite a contrast to the quiet dignity of the actual courtroom drama. For example, the impromptu press conference on the Court's front plaza after argument in the case of *U.S. v. X-citement Video*, which questioned the interpretation of a federal child pornography statute, took on a circus atmosphere as reporters jostled for position and interrupted each other's questions. Pete Williams, NBC's Supreme Court correspondent, interjected, in the midst of the comments of one of the attorneys in the case, that he should not use technical words like "scienter" (even though that term, meaning "to act knowingly," was crucial to the statute's interpretation) because "stations all over America will turn off." Williams also truncated a fellow reporter's inquiry about "strict liability" with the observation that CNN viewers will understand its meaning, but NBC viewers would not.[56] It is rare that we have the opportunity to watch the dumbing down of the news by the American media before our very eyes.

Deciding Not to Decide. With over 7,000 appeals arriving at its doorstep every year (and acceptance of fewer than 100 annually), one of the most important duties of the Supreme Court is determining which cases to reject. In addition, the Court receives emergency appeals in death penalty cases (usually as the time of execution draws ominously near) and in other time-sensitive legal disputes (like the Watergate controversy, national strikes in essential industries, and even the Clinton sex scandal). Obviously, the media cannot report all denials of appeal; but when they do so, short broadcast sound bites sometimes encourage the misperception that the Supreme Court has made a substantive decision. In fact, such a denial simply leaves intact the lower court's ruling.

The print medium has the space to feature more details about denied appeals in cases that capture readers' interest—though, once more, a fine line exists between simply reporting such details and sensationalizing a case. Two instances from the 1994–95 term are illustrative. The first was the Court's denial of the application for a stay of execution in the case of one Jesse DeWayne Jacobs, convicted of murder by the state of Texas and sentenced to die on January 4, 1995. The story burst on the national scene when the Court voted 6–3 against Jacobs's appeal of his impending execution. In a rare dissent from such a denial of appeal, Justice Stevens argued that "at a minimum" Jacobs's death sentence should be stayed. Even the Vatican newspaper *L'Observatore Romano* commented on the case, writing that the execution was "monstrous and absurd"; it compared the Supreme Court to Pontius Pilate, who washed his hands of Christ's case before turning him over to the Jews for crucifixion.

The outrage over the Jacobs case was understandable. Authorities in Texas had retreated from their original position that Jacobs had been the trigger-man in a plot with his sister to kill her rival in a love triangle. In the sister's subsequent trial, prosecutors decided that *she* actually pulled the trigger and that Jacobs was an accomplice. Yet when the Supreme Court denied Jacobs's appeal, his death sentence went forward as scheduled. The next day *Washington Post* columnist Richard Cohen analyzed the decision of the Court's majority, which apparently saw no matter of law to dispute in this case: "A jury had made its decision, and even if it had been given information by the prosecution that was later contradicted, it could not be overruled. This [Supreme C]ourt prefers to deal with law. It has little interest in justice."[57] Two weeks later, Nat Hentoff wrote in the *Washington Post* that the Supreme Court had "appallingly" failed the defendant in the Jacobs case and that the Court "had diminished itself."[58] Although several journalists and scholars have argued in recent years that the Supreme Court's sharply diminished case output and its efforts to remain aloof from the policy process have removed it from center stage of the American governmental system, the conflict over a murder case from Texas proves that at any moment the Court's actions (or inaction) can catapult it to the forefront of American consciousness via the media.

Another emergency appeal that garnered brief but poignant coverage was the so-called "Baby Richard" case. The *Post* and the *Times* reported that by a vote of 7–2 the justices refused to delay an Illinois court order transferring custody of the three-year-old child from his adoptive parents to his biological father. Justice O'Connor wrote, in a dissent from the Supreme Court's denial, that the case involved "wrenching factual circumstances."[59] Indeed, these custody cases capture headlines around the country as they make their way through the courts. Like so many issues, they eventually arrive at the highest court in the land, which is reluctant to intervene in state decisions over child custody. Yet the Court's Public Information Office often receives numerous telephone calls from the public urging the Court to rule on the merits of these touching cases. The PIO has noted, however, that the justices are not swayed by such appeals from public opinion.

Of course, *acceptance* of cases can prompt headlines, too. In February 1995 the Supreme Court announced that it would hear during its next term a Colorado gay rights case that raised the question of whether the state's constitutional amendment, barring all local measures protecting homosexuals against discrimination, violated the U.S. Constitution's guarantee of equal protection of the law. Both the *Post* and the *Times* noted that this case of *Romer v. Evans* would offer the Court the first opportunity to rule on gay rights in a decade.[60] Paul Barrett's *Wall Street Journal* article on the granting of *certiorari* in *Romer* focused more on the potential political fallout from the decision, noting that the anticipated ruling in the case would come in 1996, "practically guaranteeing that it will become an issue in the presidential election campaign."[61] In its landmark 1996 decision, the Court struck down the Colorado amendment that barred protective legislation for gays.

If the Court accepts an appeal early enough in its term, the case will be argued and decided before the justices adjourn for the summer. In such circumstances, the media are likely to report in more detail on the granting of *certiorari*, as they did in 1994 with acceptance of a majority-minority district case from Louisiana. The consolidated cases of *Louisiana v. Hays* and *U.S. v. Hays* would, as Biskupic wrote in her *Washington Post* article, "test the constitutionality of congressional districts that were drawn to consolidate racial minorities and enhance their political power." Quoting from two spokespersons on opposite sides of the case, the *Post* article captured the essence of the debate. The attorney representing the Louisiana voters who had brought suit in the case against the black-majority district commented, "The civil rights movement was about bringing people together. What's happening now is that we are balkanizing our society by carving up congressional districts based on race." On the other side, a member of the NAACP Legal Defense and Educational Fund countered, "The question is whether there will be any—or hardly any as there are now—blacks in Congress."[62] C-SPAN also covered the Court's acceptance of this potential landmark case with spokespersons from both sides of the dispute. At first, the guests wanted to cut immediately to the heart of the substantive issue in the case, but the moderator wisely kept bringing them back to procedural matters before returning to the merits of the case.[63] The public affairs network performs a public service by informing viewers of how the Supreme Court operates as well as about cases and issues that come before it. Ultimately, the Court dismissed the *Hays* case because the Louisiana voters bringing the suit did not live in the challenged district and, therefore, lacked standing. The justices split narrowly in a Georgia reapportionment case heard the same day, ruling that when race was *the* "predominant factor" in establishing legislative districts, they should be presumed unconstitutional.[64]

Covering the Justices. After reports on Supreme Court cases, the next largest category of media stories on the high tribunal is devoted to the justices who sit on its bench. In the print medium, many of these stories take the form of lengthy feature profiles of the justices' biographies, personalities, professional lives, and jurisprudence. A superb analysis of Justice David Souter appeared in the *New York Times* one week before the opening of the Court's 1994–95 term. The lengthy piece, which served as the cover story of the weekly magazine section and which included numerous photographs, was contributed by Pulitzer Prize winning author and professor, David J. Garrow, who had just published a book on the right of privacy and *Roe v. Wade.* The article provided an important update to that story—a description of Souter's crucial role in the 1992 abortion case of *Planned Parenthood of Southeastern Pennsylvania v. Casey.*[65] Overall, the piece was a highly flattering portrait of Souter as a self-confident yet humble justice who is both witty and highly intellectual and who absolutely reveres the Court on which he now serves.

Joan Biskupic has developed an expertise in profiling members of the current Court. In 1994–95 alone, she published in the *Washington Post* short personality profiles of all nine justices and then later contributed lengthy analyses of Rehnquist, Ginsburg, Kennedy, O'Connor, and Stevens. The brief profiles provided a short paragraph on, and photos of, each justice. The information offered was strictly trivial, but accurate, and contributed to her concerted effort to humanize the Court and make it familiar and accessible to the American public. She reported that Rehnquist likes to lead singa-longs at Court parties, Stevens always sports a bow tie, O'Connor takes her clerks whitewater rafting, Scalia loathes the media but is charming at social events, Kennedy is a dogged inquisitor during oral arguments and adores Shakespeare, Souter is "Mr. Congeniality," Thomas loves cigars and drives a Corvette, Ginsburg is sometimes shy off the bench and wears her hair pulled back and tied with a bow, and Breyer frames his questions with prefatory material before asking them.[66]

Biskupic's lengthier feature on Chief Justice Rehnquist was utterly reliable in its portrayal of his personal traits and his leadership style on the bench. She noted that in oral argument he is "bristly." An upcoming session would prove that label all too true. The February 1995 exchange between the chief and an embarrassingly underprepared attorney, Robert Moxley, occurred in the vaccine liability case of *Shalala v. Whitecotten*. Moxley, representing the family of a young girl allegedly injured by a vaccine, had responded inconsistently to the same question addressed to him by several different justices. Finally, an exasperated Rehnquist blurted out, "How can you stand up there at the rostrum and give these totally inconsistent answers?"

Moxley's response, "I'm sorry, Your Honor," only further infuriated the chief justice, who chastised him with, "Well you should be." Moxley tried to placate the seething chief by saying, "I don't mean to confuse the Court." Rehnquist, all the more enraged, pounced on the wilting counsel, "Well you . . . haven't confused us so much as just made us gravely wonder . . . how well-prepared you are for this argument." As Moxley attempted to extricate himself from the hole he had dug, Rehnquist abruptly and angrily declared, "Your time has expired." Tony Mauro later reported that Moxley's earthy description of how it felt to be publicly humiliated at the Supreme Court was, "I felt like I dropped out of a tall cow's ass."[67] Not surprisingly, the justices eventually voted 9–0 against Moxley's weakly argued position.

Biskupic also wrote about Rehnquist that "in opinions, he is terse and unyielding. And in conference, his no-nonsense timetable leaves little room for serious discussion of cases. Yet, privately Rehnquist gives other justices more room for dissent than did his immediate predecessors. He does not twist arms to get votes or punish those who go against him. Liberal justices who opposed him philosophically praise him for not manipulating case assignments or getting crafty with vote tallies as Chief Justice Warren E. Burger did."[68] Here, too, Biskupic seems to have hit the right note. If Rehnquist runs the Court's conferences the way he efficiently guides the Judicial Conference (whose meetings I attended), there is certainly no time allowed for meandering conversations or grandstanding by colleagues. Yet the chief has written on the important role of dissent on the bench (as reported in Chapter 3), and he played that role to the hilt in the 1970s when he was known as the "Lone Ranger" for his solo dissents. Despite his perceived ideological rigidity, he allows others to display equally strong jurisprudential convictions—even when they run counter to his.

As Justice Stevens approached his seventy-fifth birthday in April of 1995, Biskupic produced in equally precise portrayal of the Supreme Court's oldest justice. Often described as "quirky" for his solitary opinions and their unconventional legal reasoning, Stevens (appointed in 1975 by President Gerald Ford) was enjoying his new status on the bench as second in length of tenure only to the chief justice. He "drafts his own opinions, down to the footnotes, rather than rely on his law clerks for the task as other justices do." After discussing his jurisprudence on such visible and controversial issues as prisoner rights, death penalty, abortion, free speech, and religion, Biskupic remarked, quite correctly, that Stevens is "self-effacing" in asking questions of attorneys arguing before the Court. He often prefaces his query with, "Excuse me, there's one thing that puzzles me." But one advocate who has been on the receiving end of Stevens's gentle approach commented that his seeming deference usually hides a razor-sharp, and often novel, line of inquiry. The attorney recalled, "As he begins to ask his question, you can hear the saw going into the floor around you." Biskupic hit the right note with this piece, which combined a sufficient amount of substantive analysis about Stevens's unique jurisprudence with a sense of his personality and style.[69]

Biskupic's feature on Ruth Bader Ginsburg in April 1995 seemed slightly less insightful than her articles on Rehnquist and Stevens, perhaps because Ginsburg's tenure on the Court has been much shorter or because she is more enigmatic. For example, Ginsburg is quite shy, introverted, and retiring in social settings if she does not know those in attendance; yet she is very warm and caring toward people with whom she is familiar. Her jurisprudence is also difficult to label because it does not necessarily reveal the passion of her advocacy that she exhibits in speaking off the bench. Moreover, like O'Connor, Ginsburg portrays an older version of feminism that is not altogether in step with newer varieties. Both women, for example, fight for gender equality based on the similarities (not differences) between men and women. The *Post* article on Ginsburg claimed that she was using her position on the Court to advocate her "feminist message" in a way that no previous justice had done.[70] Perhaps no other justices have spoken so frequently on feminism, for obvious reasons, but many of her colleagues, both past and current, have lectured authoritatively on a wide array of their pet subjects (as Chapter 3 revealed).

In contrast, a televised profile of Ginsburg in late 1994 was more complete in its coverage of her life, personality, and observations from the highest bench in the land. The broadcast on ABC's *Prime Time Live* focused on Ginsburg's impressive law school and professional careers in which she overcame the handicaps of being female in the male-dominated world of law. As a law professor and attorney for the ACLU's Women's Rights Project, she successfully argued five out of six cases for gender equality before the high court on which she now sits. Filmed in her distinctly feminine chambers, with their bright, modern decor, Justice Ginsburg spoke admiringly of her colleagues, "We have heated discussions, but not what one would regard as angry arguments. This place specializes in reason. And we reason together." Asked to comment on media reports of differences between her and Justice O'Connor, Ginsburg graciously replied that she and her only female colleague "had the kind of relationship that sisters would have that don't always agree." To a question about whether Justice O'Connor reportedly was angry with Ginsburg for interrupting her at oral arguments, the second woman justice answered rather impatiently that such a story "would never have been noticed if there were two guys [interrupting each other]." Despite raising these somewhat negative issues, the ABC story was clearly laudatory right down to Diane Sawyer's report that Ginsburg is so disciplined that she takes a flashlight to the movies so that she can read her mail.[71]

As the Court neared the end of its 1994–95 term and the press awaited the most contentious decisions, Biskupic produced two separate analyses on Justices O'Connor and Kennedy and how one or the other often provides the crucial fifth vote in closely decided cases. Biskupic maintained that Justice O'Connor was especially skilled at fashioning compromise opinions on which a majority can agree, and, for that reason, the chief justice often assigns her particularly troublesome decisions, such as in the affirmative action realm. Biskupic also correctly noted that Scalia seldom writes the majority opinion in narrowly decided cases because his bold assertions alienate colleagues from his position. The article was insightful regarding opinion-writing strategies on the Court, as well as informative for general readers who simply wanted to know more about the Court's procedures.[72]

In the Kennedy feature, Biskupic was correct in arguing that even more than O'Connor, Kennedy has cast the most dispositive votes in recent important cases. According to one of his former clerks, "Justice Kennedy is a very sophisticated man who knows that whatever a Supreme Court justice does, somebody will criticize him or her for it. That doesn't influence his decisions." Another former clerk to Kennedy explained that his ex-boss takes to heart "the notion that a judge is supposed to be doing something other than giving vent to his personal philosophy." Biskupic, whose article was accompanied by an informative list of previous cases in which Kennedy had provided the fifth vote, suggested that the justice "promotes the image of doing the right thing, of having the weight of the world on his shoulders." Prior to announcing his crucial vote in the 1992 Pennsylvania abortion case, he excused himself from a reporter, saying, "I need to brood. . . . It's a moment of quiet around here to search your soul and your conscience."[73]

Biskupic demonstrably took a more positive view of the Kennedy and O'Connor swing votes, but critics sometimes decry their "fence-sitting" in important cases. Jeffrey Rosen, *The New Republic*'s Supreme Court commentator, described O'Connor's "conflicted" approach to closely decided cases in 1994–95 and labeled some of her opinions as "anxious." He reported that the first draft of her concurring opinion in the 5–4 Georgia racial gerrymandering case was "uncharacteristically, in her own hand."[74] While Linda Greenhouse writes equally intriguing articles about the justices' jockeying for position in closely decided cases, she does so as a responsible news reporter without violating confidences or relying unduly on inside sources. In contrast, *The New Republic* commentary may have utilized sources (possibly law clerks) feeding confidential information from behind closed doors. Moreover, too much emphasis on 5–4 votes threatens to dilute the judiciary's legitimacy by highlighting the ideological factions into which the Court sometimes divides. (Yet close to one-half of the justices' decisions are unanimous.) As James Fallows has warned, "Legal correspondents live for the cliffhanger, 5–4 split decisions from the Supreme Court, which can be analyzed to show who is the swing vote, which group of justices is acting as a team, which president has gotten the best and worst value out of his appointees, and how the next split decision will go."[75]

As the Court's terms draw to a close in late spring, and the institution is thrust into the news with announcements of final decisions, C-SPAN simultaneously covers justices' speeches at commencement exercises around the country. In 1995, Justice Kennedy presented, without notes, an eloquent appeal to the assembled graduates of McGeorge Law School to reinject civility into public discourse. Delivered just several weeks after the Oklahoma City bombing, Kennedy's remarks were especially weighty.[76]

On a less edifying note, Justice Thomas gave his standard "life is unfair" stump speech, which seemed especially out of place at a commencement exercise for Louisiana State University Law School graduates. He related to the students that he felt like giving up "a thousand times a day" as he experienced life's disappointments and frustrations. The most positive aphorism that he offered the newly minted law grads was a bitter, "Never quit, ever." He continued as if he were preparing troops for battle, "Prefer to die standing up—never quit. Quitting is suicide. Victimization is enslavement." Ironically, Justice Thomas is noted among Court employees as an upbeat, warm individual, and occasionally he displays these traits in public. He has spoken graciously on C-SPAN of his colleagues on the bench and how cordially they welcomed him to the Court in 1991.[77]

Similarly, Chief Justice Rehnquist delivered a canned speech to the audience at the Valparaiso Law School in June 1995, but unlike his colleague Justice Thomas, the chief presented an avuncular, inspirational address on using time wisely and productively in both professional and personal pursuits.[78]

Retired Justice Blackmun was equally inspirational, with just a bit of his characteristic melancholia thrown in, during his 1995 commencement speech at George Washington Law School. He encouraged the students to find heroes who embodied the traits of true professionals, especially integrity and commitment to hard work. Blackmun spoke of his allegiance to the Supreme Court. "Even though it has caused me great pain at times and its status has been shaken somewhat, [it] is a heroic institution." More upbeat than Justice Thomas, Blackmun simply urged, "The world is out there; take it as it comes." He ended on his usual ironic note, telling the graduates that if they ever needed encouragement they should go to a trial and "if those two old goats that are trying the case can make a practice out of law, so can you. Good luck, all of you!"[79] Thus, other than Justice Thomas's rather stinging remarks at LSU, the spring 1995 speeches delivered by the justices of the high court and televised on cable television were generally motivational, stately, and befitting the black robes that they wear on the bench and at academic exercises.

A sad, symbol-laden event in media coverage of the Court and its justices in 1995 was the death of former Chief Justice Warren Burger in June. His demise of congestive heart failure at age 87 was hardly unexpected, but it taxed journalists and the Court alike when he succumbed on the Sunday before the final six cases of the term were handed down. It was as if the old chief—ever aware of the symbols of office and always theatrical in his bearing—planned a grand exit for himself to coincide with the last week of the term. During the one week when the media and the public are most focused on the Supreme Court, Burger would have a final opportunity to capture public attention. Still, reviews of him in death were as mixed as they had been in life: news and editorials cited his looking and sounding as if Central Casting had sent him to play the role of chief justice, praised his talents in judicial administration and his courageous opinion against President Nixon (his appointing president) in the Watergate tapes case, and condemned his light intellect and ineffective leadership of the Court. C-SPAN provided the last words on his long life with broadcast of a taped 1986 interview of Burger in which he vowed to keep the Court's oral arguments off-limits to cameras. Justice O'Connor's televised eulogy to her former colleague, who, she recalled, had chivalrously taken her arm to guide her down the front steps of the Court after her 1981 innauguration as its first female member, ended with a touching encomium from the poet Longfellow: " 'The heights, by great men reached and kept, were not attained by sudden flight. But they, while their companions slept, were toiling upward in the night.' I am sure that [Chief Justice Burger] is now, once again, toiling upward in the night to make even heaven a better place."[80]

"Accentuate the Positive, Eliminate the Negative"? Despite the positive coverage of the Court's pomp and circumstance and the generally balanced representation of its decisions, mitigated by the occasional focus on the trivial or atypical event at the high tribunal, the Supreme Court did not emerge completely unscathed by negative media attention in 1994–95.

Given the circumstances under which Justice Thomas arrived at the Court, he may likely attract negative publicity for the rest of his tenure. All media outlets hurried to report yet another unfavorable book about him that was published in the fall of 1994.[81] As publicity over the book increased, Thomas held an extraordinary meeting at the Court, during which he met with invited black journalists and other African-American opinion leaders. The gathering was front-page news in the *Washington Post*; Joan Biskupic reported that Thomas responded to questions from his visitors about his votes by declaring: "I am not an Uncle Tom." He added defiantly, "I'm going to be here for 40 years. For those who don't like it, get over it." Even self-described liberals at the meeting were quoted as saying they were "very moved" by some of Thomas's statements and were impressed just to meet with him at the Court.[82] The setting and its symbolism are powerfully persuasive.

The closest thing to a scandal involving the Court in 1995 began with an investigation by the *Minneapolis-St. Paul Star Tribune* into the Devitt Distinguished Service to Justice Award, a $15,000 prize established in 1982 and awarded to an outstanding federal judge. (Reuters news service picked up the story and wired it around the country.) At least seven Supreme Court justices had served on the selection committee for the award; they included sitting Justices O'Connor, Stevens, Scalia, and Kennedy and retired Justices Powell, White, and Brennan. West Publishing, based in Minnesota, reportedly provided funds to the justices to travel to exotic and luxurious locales ostensibly to work on selecting the Devitt recipient each year. To make matters worse, the Minneapolis newspaper discovered that former Justice Lewis Powell had specifically asked West Publishing to schedule the meetings in such resort destinations as Hawaii, Palm Beach, and the Virgin Islands. West was also accused of providing gifts, such as law books and entertainment, to judges attending legal conferences at the very time that the publishing company was defending its business practices in courts throughout the country. The media rightly reported such a story after getting a whiff of possible impropriety. The lesson for federal judges is that they must be scrupulously careful in their relations with outside parties lest they damage irreparably the public respect that they have earned over two centuries of the judiciary's existence.

Coincidentally, in the very week that the Devitt Award stories appeared, Justices Kennedy and Souter made their annual appearance before the House Subcommittee on Appropriations to provide testimony on the Supreme Court's budget requests for the coming year and to answer questions. This now-yearly ritual provides a unique opportunity to watch members of the Court and Congress interact directly and personally, without the constraints of the judicial process. The members of the House have a chance to pose policy questions to sitting justices who generally feel free to answer because they are members of the Court for life. The Congress has another crack at the members of the Court, and the justices can speak much more freely than at their own confirmation hearings.[83]

At the March 8, 1995, appearance of Kennedy and Souter before the House committee, they were asked about the West Publishing affair. Representative Taylor, chair of the committee, began his question by saying that "we all know [about] sensationalism in the press," but he asked if Kennedy or Souter would care to comment on the story that had appeared in the *Washington Post*. Kennedy, the Devitt Committee's chairman, responded that the Devitt Award was named for "one of the great judges in the United States system" and that it was "given to an outstanding judge every year." He then compared the West Publishing Company's travel reimbursements to a bar association picking up the tab for a justice's travel to a meeting to deliver a speech. Kennedy concluded that the Devitt Award inspires judges.[84]

Justice Souter added that he had never served on the Devitt Committee, but he emphasized that any litigation that had come before the Supreme Court involving West Publishing Company had never received any special treatment because of the award. Souter's response was particularly effective because he seemed so indignant that anyone would presume impropriety on the part of his colleagues. The House members asked no further questions on the subject. C-SPAN aired the justices' testimony on March 11, 1995. Two months later the press announced that West Publishing had turned over the selection of the Devitt Award winner to the American Judicature Society—a private organization devoted to promoting the effective administration of justice.[85]

Other stories about the Court are less scandalous but merely focus on justices' rare, and innocuous, gaffes in the courtroom. In the first decision he reported from the bench during his initial term at the Court, Justice Breyer failed to announce that there were two dissents in the case. After concluding the professorial synopsis of his majority opinion in a case arising out of an extermination company's termite contract, he sat silently until Justice Thomas and the chief justice stage-whispered, "the dissents." A bit startled, Breyer smiled sheepishly and replied, "Oh, there was a dissent [actually two] as well."

A more serious story on supposed discord at the Court was Joan Biskupic's feature that questioned the propriety of the tribunal's annual Christmas party for staff and their families. The *Post*'s article quoted unnamed former law clerks who thought that a giant, decorated fir tree in the Court's Great Hall, seasonal delicacies, and the singing of Christmas carols led by the chief justice all violated the spirit of religious neutrality (if not the Court's own jurisprudence on holiday displays) required of the highest court in the land.[86]

Not surprisingly, the media reserve some of their most venomous criticism for the debate over cameras and secrecy at the Supreme Court. In September 1994 the Judicial Conference (the policy-making body of the federal judiciary, chaired by the chief justice, and consisting of lower federal court judges from around the country) decided to end an experiment that had allowed television cameras to cover civil (not criminal) cases, at the judge's discretion, in two federal courts of appeals and six federal district courts. The Conference bars the press from its meetings so subsequent media stories on actions taken there provide insight on how journalists cover secret judicial gatherings. Linda Greenhouse's article in the *New York Times* was strictly factual in its coverage, with the story's narrative based on information provided by a spokesperson for the Conference, a staff member of the Administrative Office of the U.S. Courts.[87]

Joan Biskupic's approach was slightly more sensational in tone and its visual impact, which resulted from two photographs surrounding the story. One was a picture of Court TV coverage of a trial, and the other was a photo of O.J. Simpson with one of his attorneys. In addition to reporting the vote of the Judicial Conference on the cameras experiment, Biskupic also commented on the possible impact of the Simpson trial on the debate over television coverage of judicial proceedings. She included quotations from advocates of allowing cameras in courtrooms, including the founder and chief executive officer of Court TV.[88]

To the trade papers that cater to attorneys, Tony Mauro, who writes for the *Legal Times* and *USA Today*, contributed a much more scathing report on the Judicial Conference's vote. The headline of his *Legal Times* commentary was "Camera Debate Was Sloppy and Shallow." Included with the story was a photo of the chief justice with the caption, "William Rehnquist sat by as judges made a visceral decision." Because Mauro was denied access to the meeting, along with the rest of the press, he had to cobble together impressions gleaned from those who had witnessed the debate. He took the opportunity to opine that if the meetings were open to the public and the press, he doubted if the discussions would have been so "sloppy." Moreover, he claimed that an unidentified member of the Conference had commented on the influence of the Simpson case on the judges' vote, saying that although the trial had not been mentioned at the meeting, it was " 'Topic A in the hallways' before and after, . . . and often cited as proof positive for keeping cameras out." Among other fellow advocates of cameras in courtrooms, Mauro quoted David Bartlett of the Radio-Television News Directors Association, who once inelegantly commented that the only decision that judges should be allowed to make about broadcasters in court is "whether we pee in the punch bowl."[89]

Mauro took his position to the airwaves in a September 24, 1994, appearance on C-SPAN's *America and the Courts*, in which he described the Judicial Conference decision on cameras in federal courtrooms. He also seized another opportunity to complain about the press's lack of access to the Conference meetings. Always balanced in its presentations, C-SPAN included in the debate David Reiser of the Public Defenders Service, who is opposed to television coverage of court proceedings because of fear of intimidation of witnesses and jurors, concern over misuse of media by judges (especially those at the state level who are elected to office), and worry about media abuse of the right to edit taped courtroom events.

Media coverage of the Supreme Court of the United States thus runs the gamut from mean-spirited commentaries (as represented by Tony Mauro and, to some extent, by Jeffrey Rosen), to less sensational but more human-interest articles (as portrayed in some of Joan Biskupic's work), to highly intellectual features and news pieces that focus on jurisprudential strategies (as evident in Linda Greenhouse's contributions), to scrupulously balanced reports of cases and the institution without any framing by reporters or editors (as broadcast through the unique cable television medium of C-SPAN).

The Supreme Court has thus far escaped the brunt of modern media sensationalism, unlike the presidency and Congress. The tribunal's propitious fate results from its majestic images and symbols that have endured in tandem with the rule of law and the Constitution in this country, the usually irreproachable personal and professional conduct of its members, and the traditions of the institution that have successfully limited overexposure or unbecoming portrayals in the press.

NOTES

1. C-SPAN, 25 February 1995.
2. Ibid.
3. James Fallows, *Breaking the News: How the Media Undermine American Democracy* (New York: Pantheon Books, 1996), 260.
4. Thomas E. Patterson, "Bad News, Period," *PS: Political Science and Politics* 29 (March 1996): 17.
5. Fallows, *Breaking the News*, 267.
6. Doris Kearns Goodwin, "Of Privacy and the Press: The Dilemma of Modern Politics," *Los Angeles Times*, 23 October 1994, M3.
7. Ibid.
8. Cokie Roberts, talk to Capitol Hill interns, Washington, D.C., 28 July 1995.
9. "The So-Long Senators: For Bill Cohen, a Midlife Correction," *Washington Post*, 26 January 1996, F1, F2.
10. John Hibbing and Elizabeth Theiss-Morse, *Congress as Public Enemy: Public Attitudes Toward American Political Institutions* (New York: Cambridge University Press, 1995).
11. "Was Justice Served?" *Wall Street Journal*, 4 October 1995, 12.
12. Ibid. (Neely's emphasis).
13. "Trial Rewrites Media's Rules on Coverage," *USA Today*, 4 October 1995, 5B.
14. Ibid.
15. Ibid.

16. See Larry J. Sabato, *Feeding Frenzy: How Attack Journalism Has Transformed American Politics*, updated ed. (New York: Macmillan/The Free Press, 1993).

17. As quoted in William H. Rehnquist, " 'All Discord, Harmony Not Understood': The Performance of the Supreme Court of the United States," *Arizona Law Review* 22 (1980): 973.

18. John R. Bohte, Roy B. Flemming, and B. Dan Wood, "The Supreme Court, the Media, and Legal Change: A Reassessment of Rosenberg's *Hollow Hope*" (paper presented at the Annual Meeting of the American Political Science Association, Chicago, Ill., September 1995), 25 and passim.

19. Charles H. Franklin and Liane C. Kosaki, "Republican Schoolmaster: The U.S. Supreme Court, Public Opinion, and Abortion," *American Political Science Review* 83 (1989): 751–71, as cited in Bohte et al., "The Supreme Court," 3.

20. Ethan Katsh, "The Supreme Court Beat: How Television Covers the U.S. Supreme Court," *Judicature* 67 (June–July 1983): 10.

21. Elliot E. Slotnick and Jennifer A. Segal, "Television News and the Supreme Court" (paper presented at the Annual Meeting of the American Political Science Association, Chicago, Ill., September 1992); Elliot Slotnick, "Television News and the Supreme Court: A Case Study," *Judicature* 77 (July–August 1993): 21–33; and Elliot E. Slotnick and Jennifer A. Segal, *Television News and the Supreme Court: All the News That's Fit to Air?* (New York: Cambridge University Press, 1998).

22. Ibid.

23. Joseph Neff, "Thomas Stands Firm in His Beliefs," *Raleigh News and Observer*, November 1994, 3A.

24. Joan Biskupic, *America and the Courts*, C-SPAN, 8 October 1994.

25. Malcolm Gladwell, "Judge Breyer's Life Fashioned Like His Courthouse: Creating Something Practical from Life in the Law," *Washington Post*, 26 June 1994, A1, A18.

26. Lloyd Grove, "The Courtship of Joanna Breyer: The Nominee's Blue-Blooded Wife Is No Stranger to High Places," *Washington Post*, 11 July 1994, B1, B2.

27. Joan Biskupic, "Court Toughens . . .", *Washington Post*, 13 June 1995, A1.

28. Joan Biskupic, "Desegregation Remedies Rejected," *Washington Post*, 13 June 1995, A1.

29. John F. Harris and Kevin Merida, "Ruling May Sharpen Debate on Preference Policies," *Washington Post*, 13 June 1995, A6.

30. Linda Greenhouse, "By 5:4, Justices Cast Doubts on U.S. Programs That Give Preferences Based on Race," *New York Times*, 13 June 1995, A1.

31. Linda Greenhouse, "Justices Say Lower Courts Erred in Orders in Desegregation Case," *New York Times*, 13 June 1995, A1.

32. Tamar Lewin, "5–4 Decision Buoys; For Others It's a Setback," *New York Times*, 13 June 1995, D5.

33. "The Future of Affirmative Action," *Washington Post*, 13 June 1995, A20.

34. "A Sad Day for Racial Justice," *New York Times*, 13 June 1995, A24.

35. See Peter Behr, "A Rush to the Defense of Affirmative Action," *Washington Post*, 14 June 1995, A1; John F. Harris, "For Clinton, a Challenge of Balance," *Washington Post*, 14 June 1995, A1; and Linda Greenhouse, "In Step on Racial Policy," *New York Times*, 14 June 1995, A5.

36. George Will, "Affirmative Action: The Court's Murky Ruling," *Washington Post*, 14 June 1995, A24.

37. William Raspberry, "... And Americans' Ambivalence," *Washington Post*, 14 June 1995, A24.

38. Charles Krauthammer, "Affirmative Action: Settle It Out of Court," *Washington Post*, 16 June 1995, A25.

39. Linda Greenhouse, "High Court Kills Law Banning Guns in a School Zone," *New York Times*, 27 April 1995, A1.

40. Joan Biskupic, "Ban on Guns Near Schools Is Rejected," *Washington Post*, 27 April 1995, A1.

41. Joan Biskupic, "Court Signals Sharp Shift on Congressional Powers," *Washington Post*, 28 April 1995, A3.

42. "Federalism and Guns in Schools," *Washington Post*, 28 April 1995, A26.

43. "The High Court Loses Restraint," *New York Times*, 29 April 1995, A22.

44. Joan Biskupic, "Congressional Term Limits Struck Down," *Washington Post*, 23 May 1995, A1.

45. Kenneth J. Cooper and Helen Dewar, "Ruling Isn't End of Fight, Term Limits Backers Vow," *Washington Post*, 23 May 1995, A2.

46. Joan Biskupic, "Court Allows Drug Tests," *Washington Post*, 27 June 1995, A1.

47. Linda Greenhouse, "High Court Upholds Drug Tests for Some Public School Athletes," *New York Times*, 27 June 1995, A5.

48. "Unwarranted Student Drug Testing," *New York Times*, 28 June 1995, A18.

49. Ira Berkow, "No Cause, No Testing for Drugs," *New York Times*, 28 June 1995, B9.

50. Joan Biskupic, "Supreme Court Looks Into the Locker Room," *Washington Post*, 29 March 1995, A9.

51. Lyle Denniston, "Justices Poke Fun at Legal Profession's Poor Image," *Baltimore Sun*, 12 January 1995, A14.

52. Linda Greenhouse, "High Court Backs Florida Restriction on Solicitation of Accident Victims by Lawyers," *New York Times*, 22 June 1995, A22; Greenhouse, "At the Bar," *New York Times*, 23 June 1995, A23.

53. Joan Biskupic, "Justices Question Honoraria Ban," *Washington Post*, 9 November 1994, A4.

54. Joan Biskupic, "Justices Skeptical of State Restrictions," *Washington Post*, 30 November 1994, A1.

55. *America and the Courts*, C-SPAN, 3 December 1994.

56. Ibid.

57. Richard Cohen, "Justice Derailed," *Washington Post*, 5 January 1995, A27.

58. Nat Hentoff, "The Court Has Diminished Itself," *Washington Post*, 14 January 1995, A25.

59. Edward Walsh, "Justices Refuse to Delay Transfer of 'Baby Richard,'" *Washington Post*, 14 February 1995, A3; "Supreme Court Refuses to Halt Custody Switch," *New York Times*, 14 February 1995, A11.

60. Joan Biskupic, "Court to Consider Colorado's Attempt to Negate Local Gay Rights Laws," *Washington Post*, 22 February 1995, A15; Linda Greenhouse, "Supreme Court to Rule on Anti-Gay Rights Law in Colorado," *New York Times*, 22 February 1995, A11.

61. Paul Barrett, "High Court to Decide Whether States May Ban Laws Protecting Homosexuals," *Wall Street Journal,* 22 February 1995, A4.

62. Joan Biskupic, "High Court to Rule on Race-Based Congressional Districts," *Washington Post,* 10 December 1994, A3.

63. *America and the Courts,* C-SPAN, 17 December 1994.

64. *Miller v. Johnson,* 515 U.S. 900 (1995).

65. David J. Garrow, "Justice Souter: A Surprising Kind of Conservative," *New York Times Magazine,* 25 September 1994, 36; see description of *Casey* in Chapter 3.

66. Joan Biskupic, "Behind the Robes, Songs and Whitewater Rafting," *Washington Post,* 20 October 1994, 19.

67. Tony Mauro, "Invoking the Wrath of Rehnquist," *Legal Times,* March 1995.

68. Joan Biskupic, "The Mysterious Mr. Rehnquist: Where Is the Chief Justice Going and Who Will Follow?" *Washington Post,* 25 September 1994, C1.

69. Joan Biskupic, "At Long Last, Seniority," *Washington Post,* 20 March 1995, A15.

70. Joan Biskupic, "High Court Justice with a Cause," *Washington Post,* 17 April 1995, A1.

71. *Prime Time Live,* ABC, 29 December 1994.

72. Joan Biskupic, "As Deadline Nears, Court Leaders Pin Hopes on 'Holding 5,' " *Washington Post,* 7 June 1995, A19.

73. Joan Biskupic, "When Court Is Split, Kennedy Rules," *Washington Post,* 11 June 1995, A14.

74. Jeffrey Rosen, "The Color-Blind Court," *The New Republic,* 31 July 1995, 19–25.

75. Fallows, *Breaking the News,* 164.

76. Anthony Kennedy, *America and the Courts,* C-SPAN, May 1995.

77. Clarence Thomas, *America and the Courts,* C-SPAN, May 1995.

78. William Rehnquist, *America and the Courts,* C-SPAN, 17 June 1995.

79. Harry Blackmun, *America and the Courts,* C-SPAN, 24 June 1995.

80. "Burger, Praised as a 'Graceful Patriot,' Is Buried," *New York Times,* 30 June 1995, D17.

81. Jane Mayer and Jill Abramson, *Strange Justice: The Selling of Clarence Thomas* (New York: Plume, 1994).

82. Joan Biskupic, " 'I Am Not an Uncle Tom,' Thomas Says at Meeting," *Washington Post,* 28 October 1994, A1.

83. Harvey Rishikoff and Barbara Perry, " 'Separateness but Interdependence, Autonomy but Reciprocity': A First Look at Federal Judges' Appearances before Legislative Committees," *Mercer Law Review* 46 (1995): 667–95.

84. *America and the Courts,* C-SPAN, 11 March 1995.

85. "A Retreat for West Publishing," *The Hill,* 10 May 1995, 6.

86. Joan Biskupic, *Washington Post,* 15 December 1994, 10.

87. Linda Greenhouse, "U.S. Judges Vote Down TV in Courts: 3-Year Experiment to End on Dec. 31," *New York Times,* 21 September 1994, A18.

88. Joan Biskupic, "Federal Court Camera Ban Continued: Panel of Top U.S. Judges Breaks from Trend Taken By Majority of the States," *Washington Post,* 21 September 1994, A3.

89. Tony Mauro, "Camera Debate Was Sloppy and Shallow," *Legal Times,* 26 September 1994, 10.

Chapter 5

"Do the Justices Wear Clothes?" Public Perceptions of the Court

Justice Sandra Day O'Connor, the first woman to sit on the Supreme Court of the United State and the most readily identifiable of the nine justices, has become an international icon. She is much in demand as a speaker and has now delivered addresses in each of the 50 states and in many countries around the world. Several years ago the Indian Supreme Court visited their U.S. counterpart, and the sari-clad, deferential wives of the Indian jurists surrounded Justice O'Connor to tell her animatedly what a heroine she is to them. O'Connor's husband reports that at a lecture stop in snowy North Dakota, citizens turned out in force to see the renowned justice, and parents brought their children up to her after she spoke so that she could touch them. This "laying on of hands" apparently has a transitive property, too. On the front plaza one evening, an officer of the Court encountered a couple of tourists, who asked if he worked with Sandra Day O'Connor. When he responded that he did, the woman in the pair reached out and grasped the officer's arm. She seemed to want to touch someone who knew the first female justice on the Supreme Court. These accounts may demonstrate the public's admiration for Sandra Day O'Connor more than its love for the institution she serves, but people frequently express other manifestations of respect for the Court itself.

Individuals often display nearly childlike excitement when they come to the nation's highest court. Even Senator Orrin Hatch (R.-Utah), chair of the Senate Judiciary Committee, was uncharacteristically bubbly when he appeared on C-SPAN's *Washington Journal* program, which was devoted one summer morning in 1995 to the Supreme Court. After viewers had been treated to a tour of the Court, a network correspondent asked Hatch if there was a room in the Court building that he liked in particular. Hatch effused, "Frankly, everything about the Court is historic and terrific. I like all of the rooms, but I've been invited into the chief justice's chambers from time to time, and that's always a great thrill!"[1] This warm exclamation came from a man whose steely cross-examination of Anita Hill in 1991 sliced through her testimony by displaying his incredulity and contempt over her accusations that Clarence Thomas had once discussed "pubic hair" on Coke cans and his favorite porn star "Long Dong Silver," with her. Moreover, as a member of the legislative branch, constitutionally designed to check the judiciary, Hatch was less than adversarial in his display of enthusiasm over the Court's aura. Obviously, even the most experienced Washington politicians are not immune to the institution's ambiance.

Still, not all observers of the Court are as favorably inclined toward the bench as are O'Connor's fans and the senator from Utah. On the same program where Hatch appeared in July 1995 to talk about his impressions of the Court, C-SPAN took phone calls from viewers for the senator and several other guests that day. Not one was positive; each complained about something that the Court was doing or not doing on a particular issue of interest to the caller. The Court's Public Information Office has noted that many of the calls they receive run along similar lines. The most obvious demonstration of public dissatisfaction with the Court occurs every January when thousands of pro-life demonstrators gather around the building to shout their protests over the 1973 *Roe v. Wade* ruling. Yet pro-choice advocates always counterdemonstrate in support of the Court's precedents upholding access to abortion.

This analysis focuses more on public attitudes toward the Supreme Court as an institution than on public opinion regarding particular judicial issues—though the two undoubtedly are related.[2] Public respect for the presidency and the Congress as institutions has diminished, in part, because of the problematic behavior of individual presidents and members of Congress and the widespread coverage of them in the media, whereas the generally honorable dispositions of justices and their limited appearances in the media have helped to preserve the luster of the jewel in the crown of the nation's judiciary.

THE NINE JUSTICES OR THE THREE STOOGES?

Impressions are mixed regarding public awareness of the Supreme Court. One school of thought argues that there has been a demonstrable growth in the "popularization of the American judiciary" as a whole. According to Professor Ronald K.L. Collins, the plethora of recently published biographies of judges and justices is indicative of this phenomenon. Alex Wohl, a lawyer and frequent contributor to the *American Bar Association Journal*, believes that the escalating media coverage of retirements from, and appointments to, the U.S. Supreme Court has contributed to the expanding image of the institution in the public consciousness. Mark Tushnet, who has written a two-volume authorized biography of Thurgood Marshall, agrees. He maintains that increased public attention to recent Supreme Court confirmation hearings has resulted, as least partially, in growing public interest in federal judges and their lives. Likewise, the authorized biographer of Justice Brennan, Stephen Wermiel, has argued that "public consciousness of the importance and influence of the Supreme Court that began to be heightened in the Warren Court years has grown into a fuller appreciation of the role the Court plays in our society as well as an accompanying interest in the members of the Court."[3]

Aside from decisions that have a direct impact on Americans, in subtle and indirect ways, the Supreme Court has been woven into the fabric of American life. The exclamation, "I'm gonna take this case all the way to the Supreme Court," is as ubiquitous in American society as the emblematic facade of the Court's building. CNN's *Burden of Proof*, for example, uses a portrait of the Court as the program's logo.

Nevertheless, public opinion polls show a troubling lack of attention to, and knowledge of, details regarding the Supreme Court among Americans. At the end of 1995 the Times Mirror Center for the People and the Press released a report indicating that only one in four Americans pays very close attention to most news. A survey of 75,000 people questioned in 54 national surveys between 1989 and 1995 yielded an "interest index" of 480 stories for a database. Almost half of the public paid little or no attention to any one of the news stories. For the period covered, the most-followed news stories included the Challenger explosion in 1986 (80 percent followed closely), the 1989 San Francisco earthquake (73 percent), the Rodney King beating verdict and subsequent riots in 1992 (70 percent), and the 1987 story of the little girl who fell down a well in Texas (69 percent). Not quite 30 percent of the public followed reports about the economy, major Supreme Court rulings, race and gender issues, and landmark scientific events. The least-followed stories were the break-up of Woody Allen and Mia Farrow (3 percent), the civil war in Cambodia (4 percent), scandals involving the British royal family (5 percent), and conflict in the former Yugoslavia (5 percent).[4]

The *Washington Post* took great delight in reporting in the fall of 1995 that another poll indicated that Americans were woefully ignorant of the justices who serve on the Supreme Court of the United States. Crowed the Washington paper, "More than half of all Americans can't name a single justice" on the Court. The statistics, from a survey of 1,200 randomly selected adults conducted by a research company in Arlington, Virginia, demonstrated that 55 percent could not name even one member of the high tribunal. Sixteen percent could name only one justice, 11 percent could name two, and 17 percent could name three. The same article noted with gleeful sarcasm that more Americans could identify the character names of the Three Stooges! In fact, the poll showed that 59 percent could name three (of the five [actually, it was six]) members of the slapstick comedy trio. Only 13 percent could not name one Stooge.[5]

The *Post*'s Court reporter, Joan Biskupic, had some more fun with the same poll statistics a few days later. She began with tongue in cheek: "Supreme Court justices often protest that they speak as a court, not as individuals. They try to avoid press attention and as much as possible sheathe their personalities in black robes. Well, it's working." She then provided the telling data: only 1 percent of respondents in the poll could name Justice Stevens or Justice Breyer. Four percent could identify Justice Kennedy and Justice Souter as members of the nation's highest court. Justice Scalia was named by just 6 percent of the respondents, while Justice Ginsburg was identified by 7 percent. Despite his position as the highest ranking jurist in the land, only 8 percent could name Chief Justice Rehnquist. Not surprisingly, Clarence Thomas was identified by 30 percent of those polled, and Sandra Day O'Connor was the most recognized member of the Court at 31 percent.[6] Despite Biskupic's ironic observation about the individual anonymity of the justices, the poll data illustrate that the members of the high court have indeed been successful in deflecting the ever-present glare of public curiosity. That fact only increases the probability that the Court can maintain its symbols and images of dignity, when all about them in Washington are losing theirs.

Chief Justice Rehnquist never polled higher than 9 percent in recognition polls taken before his stint as presiding officer in the 1999 Clinton impeachment trial. He achieved that figure in a 1989 survey. In contrast, the same poll revealed that 54 percent of the respondents could name Judge Wapner, then the presiding jurist on the popular television show *The People's Court.*[7] Still, the chief justice faired better in the 1989 poll than he did in the 1995 results reported above or a more extensive poll, sponsored by the *Washington Post*/Kaiser Family Foundation/Harvard University Survey Project, released early in 1996. Again, Rehnquist was identified as the chief justice of the U.S. Supreme Court by only 6 percent of randomly selected Americans. By comparison, 60 percent could name the vice president of the United States, 53 percent the speaker of the U.S. House of Representatives, and 34 percent the majority leader of the U.S. Senate. The question that solicited the highest percentage of correct responses (86 percent) was the one asking respondents to name "who was president when the Watergate scandal took place."[8] Notably, over half or 54 percent of those polled selected correctly "the Supreme Court" from a multiple choice set of answers to the question, "As far as you know, who has the FINAL responsibility to decide if a law is constitutional or not?"[9] In terms of the power and prestige of the Court, it is more important that a majority of people know about, and presumably accept, the institution's exercise of judicial review than remember the name of the chief justice.

PUBLIC CONFIDENCE IN THE GOVERNMENT AND ITS INSTITUTIONS

It is instructive to compare public attitudes toward the Court with citizen trust in the government as a whole and the presidency and Congress in particular. Newspapers and textbooks are filled with opinion data and commentaries that often reflect and bemoan the startling increase in public mistrust in the federal government. In fact, the massive 1995 survey sponsored by the *Washington Post*, the Kaiser Family Foundation, and Harvard was completely devoted to solving the question that became the title of the resulting report, "Why Don't Americans Trust the Government?"

To begin, the survey asked, "How much of the time do you trust the government in Washington to do the right thing?" Only 4 percent responded, "Just about always"; 21 percent said, "Most of the time"; the vast majority (71 percent) answered, "Only some of the time"; and 4 percent responded, "None of the time." Thus, only one-quarter said that they trusted the national government to do the right thing just about always or most of the time. In contrast, when the same question was posed in 1958, over three-quarters of those polled expressed trust in the national government to do the right thing nearly always or most of the time; trust continued at that level until 1964, when it began to decline precipitously. Mistrust of the federal government reached a 30-year low in 1995.[10] In fact, the line indicating public trust in the national government plummets steeply between 1964 and 1980, rises markedly in the early 1980s, levels off during that decade, but began its most recent drop at the end of the 1980s. Commentaries on the period from 1964 to 1980 suggest that President Kennedy's assassination, disillusionment over the Vietnam War, and the Watergate scandal are logical explanations for the country's disenchantment with government and politics.[11] The rise in public confidence in the national government in the early 1980s may have resulted from renewed optimism during the Reagan era, when the nation was told by its perennially sunny president that it was "morning again in America" and that we would once more be the "shining city on a hill" for all the world to see and admire.

To tease out more specific reasons why the majority of Americans do not trust the federal government, the 1995 Harvard survey posed the open-ended question, "What is the MAIN reason you don't trust the federal government?" Respondents' reasons for lack of trust in the government very often involved the perceived behavior of politicians: They are not honest, they lie, they don't give all the facts, they are corrupt, they support special interest groups, they don't represent the interest of the people, they don't listen to the public, they don't care about the middle class, they are influenced by money, and they don't accomplish anything.[12] Note that when people are mentioned as the source of mistrust, they are "politicians," not judges or justices, and it is unlikely that Americans consider federal jurists to be politicians in the generic sense of that word. Not surprisingly, then, the U.S. Supreme Court has almost always scored higher than either of the other two "political" branches of government in surveys measuring Americans' confidence level in the institutions or the people who run them.

The Harris Survey began in 1966 to measure citizen confidence in officials who lead various institutions in America. In 1966, 50 percent of those polled had "a great deal of confidence" in the people running the Supreme Court as compared with 42 percent for Congress and 41 percent for the federal executive branch. The military and higher education, scoring 61 percent each, and major companies at 55 percent, garnered more confidence from the respondents than the Supreme Court. Still, the high tribunal outpaced not only Congress and the executive branch but organized religion (41 percent), the press (29 percent), and organized labor (22 percent) in terms of confidence in the people leading these institutions. By 1979 and 1981 the Harris Poll's identical question reflected a precipitous drop in public confidence for all the institutions included in the survey. The Supreme Court declined to 28 percent in 1979 and 29 percent in 1981 but was still ahead of Congress (18 percent in 1979 and 16 percent in 1981) and the executive branch (17 percent in 1979 and 24 percent in 1981). In 1984, as trust levels in government rose, the Court scored a 35 percent confidence rating, compared to 28 percent for Congress. (The executive branch was not included in the survey that year.)[13]

During the same period, the Gallup Poll also measured public confidence in the Supreme Court, with slightly different wording for the standard question. Between 1963 and 1973, the query asked, "In general, what kind of rating would you give the Supreme Court—excellent, good, fair, or poor?" After 1975, Gallup posed the question, "Would you tell me how much confidence you have in the Supreme Court: a great deal, quite a lot, some, or very little." The questions were not included in the poll every year, but the responses categorized as "excellent" or "a great deal" of confidence in the Supreme Court ranged from a low of 33 percent responding as such in 1969 to a high of 56 percent in 1988. In fact, from 1985 through 1988, the Court enjoyed a streak of responses above 50 percent expressing "a great deal" of confidence in the tribunal. As noted, this time period corresponds with the temporary increase in overall public confidence in the government's likelihood of doing the right thing.

When the slide in public trust in the government as a whole reached a low point in the 1995 *Post*/Kaiser/Harvard survey, so did the public's confidence level in the Supreme Court, particularly in the category of "a great deal" of confidence in the institution. The tribunal scored only 13 percent at that level. Still, it once again outdistanced the Congress (4 percent) and "the Clinton Administration" (9 percent). (The survey offered no explanation of why it named the president rather than using the general category of "the presidency" or "the executive branch.") Moreover, in the highest category of confidence, the Court outscored large business corporations and the news media, both of whom earned a mere 6 percent in the highest category of public trust. Only the military, at 32 percent, and medicine, at 24 percent, scored higher than the Court in that column. In the category of "quite a lot" of confidence, 26 percent of the respondents listed the Supreme Court. There, too, it outpaced the Congress (10 percent) and the Clinton administration (16 percent). Forty-one percent of those polled said that they had at least "some confidence" in the Court; Congress received the same score in that category. President Clinton's administration elicited a rating of 36 percent. In the "very little" confidence column, the Court received just 16 percent, the president 33 percent, Congress 41 percent. Combining confidence levels above the "very little" category indicates 80 percent for the Court, 61 percent for the Clinton administration, and 55 percent for Congress. The same combinations show 92 percent for the military and 88 percent for medicine.[14]

With a booming economy, and relative tranquility in the world, American trust in the federal government began to inch up in 1997 (despite scandalous stories swirling around the Clinton White House). According to a survey conducted by the Pew Research Center for the People, trust in Washington moved from 21 percent in 1994 to 38 percent in late 1997.[15] Even Congress, long a scapegoat for disgruntled American voters, improved its job approval rating to 47 percent by early 1998.[16] Later in 1998, however, Congress's handling of the Clinton impeachment investigation diluted those poll numbers. Citizens polled by the Gallup organization in 1997 showed a slight increase in those responding that they had a "great deal" of confidence and trust in the judicial branch headed by the Supreme Court; the figure stood at 19 percent. Fifty-two percent said they had a "fair amount" of confidence and trust in the judicial branch. Comparable figures for the executive branch headed by the president were 13 percent and 49 percent; for the legislative branch made up of the House and Senate, the numbers were 6 percent and 48 percent. Again, the highest two categories of confidence levels combined to place the judiciary at the apex of the poll among the three branches.[17]

Since at least the 1950s, political scientists have tried to disprove previous theories that the public revered and even deified the Supreme Court. In the 1960s and 1970s scholars reported that Americans possessed "only a relatively shallow reservoir of knowledge about or affect toward the Court."[18] But in the 1980s more nuanced studies of the dynamics of public opinion on the Court over time admitted that political scientists had "oversold" their "pessimistic view of the public evaluations of the Court." Although individual citizens may "evince little or no knowledge of or concern for the Court," aggregate "shifts in public confidence in the Court" reflect rational and calculated responses "to events on the political landscape and to actions taken by the Court."[19]

It makes sense, then, that as mistrust in the federal government expanded, the confidence level in the Supreme Court dropped. Political scientist Thomas Marshall has argued that even though the Court continues to earn higher levels of confidence from the people than do Congress and the president, "only a third to half of Americans have held clearly favorable views of the Court." He forms that conclusion by comparing statistics for people who give the Court "excellent" or "good" marks to those who award it labels of "fair" or "poor."[20] But adding the categories above "poor" produces a higher score for positive (or at least not negative) perceptions.

In the *Post*/Kaiser/Harvard poll, merging the categories measuring confidence to include "a great deal," "quite a lot," and "some," shows the Court with a score in the 80 percent range, compared to 61 percent for the Clinton administration and 55 percent for Congress. Nonetheless, the Court should be concerned that, like all institutions, it has lost most of its points in the "great deal" of confidence range. Undoubtedly, this fact is partially a result of mistrustful public attitudes in general. Yet Chapter 3 cautions that increasing public sniping among the justices in opinions and on the lecture circuit, as well as the controversy that continues to swirl around Justice Thomas, could also harm the Court's image.

Many scholars consider the Court's typical ranking above the president and Congress too lightly. Why does the Court always outstrip the other two branches in public regard for it and its work? Modern political science attempts to debunk the explanation identified by jurists, journalists, and scholars like Jerome Frank, Max Lerner, and Edward Corwin, that the Court's image of impartial and wise judges, arrayed in black robes, ensconced in the marble palace, holds a powerful sway over the public mind. (For the record, Frank and Lerner derided the explanation as myth; Corwin celebrated it as reality.) Or as government professor Alan Westin expressed it in the 1950s, despite periodic attacks on the high tribunal (including the one he was witnessing in the aftermath of *Brown*), "residual Court-worship" and "judge-worship" exist in the American population.[21] Undoubtedly, the Court's symbols and images, which bolster the residual worshipful attitude in the population, combined with the relative isolation of the institution and its members, *have* allowed it to preserve a public aura of mythic proportions.

"THIS MIGHT BE A STUPID QUESTION, BUT . . ."

The old aphorism that the only "stupid question" is the one not asked might have to be amended for the queries that are sometimes raised regarding the Supreme Court. My favorite—one that I fielded from a college student—is "Do the justices wear clothes?" In answering the inquiry, I correctly presumed that the young man was asking about what the justices wear when they are not on the bench in their judicial robes. Generally, however, the questions posed during my briefings were more sophisticated.

I usually spoke to groups that had specifically requested meetings with the Court's judicial fellow, so my audiences were self-screened to some extent. Their curiosity typically related to procedural aspects of the Court's work, qualifications and personalities of the justices and law clerks, and historical conflicts among the three branches of the federal government. Foreign audiences often expressed interest in interinstitutional relations, undoubtedly because they hailed from countries where such relations were highly conflictual, and there was no final arbiter accepted by a majority of the people or those in power.

The most frequently asked questions at my briefings included the following:

- What are the backgrounds and previous experience of the justices?
- What are the roles of the president and Congress in selecting justices?
- How does the Supreme Court operate with the other two branches in the system of checks and balances?
- What is the procedure for selecting cases for review? What happens to cases that are denied review?
- How are the law clerks selected? What is their role?
- What are oral arguments like?
- How do the justices decide the cases heard on review? How is opinion writing divided among the justices?

The Supreme Court's interns, who deliver most of the lectures to visiting tourists, have heard a more varied mix of questions. Among the more peculiar were whether the justices talk to each other, whether there have ever been any assassinations in the courtroom, what does the crank on the lectern in the courtroom do, and which justice will be conducting the lecture? Sometimes a query will reveal a remarkable lack of information on the part of the questioner, such as when one asked why the courtroom looked so different from when the Clarence Thomas confirmation hearings were held there.

For the most part, however, many of the general public's questions were similar to the ones my more select audiences asked, namely, inquiries that were strictly informational and often requested explanations of the Court's rather arcane procedures. These included:

- How is the chief justice different from the other eight justices? How is the chief selected?
- Do all of the justices have to be present to hear a case? What happens if there is a tie vote?
- What are the qualifications/credentials of the justices?

- What happens to cases that are not accepted for review? Do all of the justices read all of the petitions?
- What do the law clerks do and how long do they serve?
- How long after oral arguments are opinions released?

Other questions fielded by the interns from their general audiences fell more into the realm of "trivial pursuit," such as: what is the salary of the justices, what is the average age of the justices, have there always been nine justices, do the justices' families and friends come very often to the Court, and what is behind the curtain in the courtroom? Still others were tinged with controversy or had a slight edge to them. They included, what do the justices do in July, August, and September when no public sessions are held; why is Moses depicted in the Courtroom; and what are the political preferences of the justices (which are more conservative, which are more liberal)?

Questions that come to the Court's Public Information Office, most likely by phone or mail, are sometimes crankier or even cynical. The difference in their tone may result from the fact that the questions that the interns and I heard were from people who, for the most part, wanted to be at the Court and felt generally positive about the experience. Although they could have expressed their upset with or dislike of the institution and its decisions, they rarely chose to do so. On the other hand, it appears that citizens view the Public Information Office as if it were the Court's ombudsman who listens and responds to their complaints. This phenomenon could also be part of the larger syndrome whereby the American citizenry voices its irritation at the federal government through direct communications with the institutions of power. Whatever the cause, the PIO has received questions such as:

- What can I do if I don't like a Supreme Court opinion?
- I'd like to tell the Supreme Court how I feel about an issue. How do I go about it?
- How do I get my case before the Supreme Court?
- The Supreme Court won't hear my case and won't tell me why. What can I do?
- My town has a law against _____ , and I think it's unconstitutional. What can I do?
- The Constitution says the Supreme Court's jurisdiction applies to "cases and controversies" arising under the Constitution and federal law. How come it can find a state law, such as the death penalty, unconstitutional?
- How are justices selected? Why are there nine? How do I work to remove one with whom I disagree?
- Why isn't there television in the courtroom?

On the opposite side of the street from the Court, the U.S. Senate Historical Office distributes a pamphlet to hand to visitors in the Senate chamber. Entitled "Frequently Asked Questions About the United States Senate Chamber," it reflects inquiries similar in tone to the various questions directed to Supreme Court personnel. Half of the dozen questions presented ask for basic facts about when a senator comes to the floor, when does he or she speak, who presides, what is a quorum call, and who are the other people on the floor of the Senate? The other half dozen queries are of the crabby variety (though less weighty than those the Supreme Court hears), specifically, why are reading and writing prohibited, why must calculators be checked, why can't I see my senator from my seat, why are the admission lines so long, and why are passes required? Indeed, the American public can sometimes be a disagreeable lot—and more so when they have been standing in long lines during steamy Washington summers. In addition, everything from the U.S. Constitution to talk radio encourages them to express their unhappiness.

In light of this verity, visitors to the Court are strikingly well behaved, mannerly, and deferential. Of course, in their excitement, tourists, especially schoolchildren, can be rather loud, but most exhibit at least minimal respect, if not awe, for the place and what it represents. The typical scene in the courtroom just before oral argument when the police officers calm the spectators and a reverential silence descends over the crowd, seems to indicate that the visitors have a sense that they are now in the inner sanctum and are about to witness an exceptional ceremony—one that they have not grown familiar with or contemptuous of by tuning in to television.

Not to denigrate the Court's aura, but it is reminiscent of the atmosphere surrounding the Wizard in the classic film *The Wizard of Oz*. In the movie, as Dorothy and her companions approach both the entrance to the Emerald City and the Wizard's inner sanctum, they are stopped by a guard, not unlike the police who patrol the entrances to the Supreme Court and its chamber. Once they are granted an audience with the Wizard, they quake before the "great and powerful Oz," whose amplified voice, enlarged image, mysterious curtains, and shooting flames render them nearly speechless. The Scarecrow steps forward and tentatively addresses the Wizard as, "Your honor," then "Your excellency." The Cowardly Lion, who hoped to attain courage from the Wizard, tries to ask for his gift and faints in his tracks. All the while, the Wizard shouts insults at the awestruck supplicants. The scene recalls Chief Justice Rehnquist's wrathful display directed at an unprepared attorney in the 1995 *Whitecotton* case described in Chapter 4. At the very least, most attorneys are noticeably jittery as they step before the Supreme Court for oral argument, and some have been known to faint. As noted, tourists often ask Court interns "What's behind the curtain?" In *The Wizard of Oz*, when Toto the dog pulls back the draperies surrounding the Wizard's light and sound machine, revealing him as a mere mortal, he exclaims, "Pay no attention to the man behind the curtain!" In the land of Oz and high tribunals, mystery equals power.

THE "PEOPLE'S COURT"?

Of the approximately 3,000 people I formally briefed during my twelve months at the Court, about one-third were American audiences and the balance consisted of foreign visitors. Our discussions, which usually began with my brief overview of how the Court operates, followed by a question and answer period, revealed in vivid detail what was on the minds of these visitors regarding the United States' highest tribunal. All groups, both foreign and domestic, usually began with the types of procedural questions previously illustrated. American audiences, which consisted of teachers, students, and business executives typically asked more personal inquiries about the justices themselves. Sometimes they just seemed curious about the personalities of these judges who do not parade before the media. Other times, Americans wanted to know if and how the justices' demeanors influenced decision-making on the Court. Because of the publicity that Justice Thomas has received, both before and since his elevation to the bench, many visitors asked about him. If they had been to oral argument, they would ask why he did not pose questions to the counsel or why he seemed uninterested in the proceedings. Visitors assumed from his lack of participation that he is a "loner," and some would ask about his relations with his colleagues.

Other questions about the personal attributes of justices were more substantive in nature. A particularly lively and knowledgeable group of secondary school teachers wanted to know about the religious affiliation of the Court's members. Two Jewish teachers in the group commented that the appointment of Ruth Bader Ginsburg to the Supreme Court—its first Jewish member since Abe Fortas resigned in 1969 over questionable business arrangements—had been a happy event for their co-religionists. They were also pleased that Stephen Breyer, the current Court's second Jewish justice, had been named to the tribunal. Perhaps with Fortas's resignation in mind, one of the teachers in another group asked whether justices take honoraria and/or do consulting. Afterward, an individual teacher approached me to ask if *The Brethren* had painted an accurate picture of the Supreme Court. He wanted to know if the clerks really have as much power as the book portrayed and if Chief Justice Burger was as bad as the book indicated. He also wondered out loud whether I was cynical about the Court, either from having read Woodward and Armstrong's work or from my own experiences as a Fellow. I could honestly report that neither had made me a cynic regarding the Supreme Court—though *The Brethren* had made me rather skeptical about investigative journalists and Supreme Court clerks.

Students seemed especially prone to ask about the latter, perhaps because so many of them have read *The Brethren* and because numerous students are law school bound and aspire to a clerkship at the Supreme Court. Many asked about the clerks' influence on judicial opinions. Students also commonly wanted to know about the impact of outside forces on the Court's decisions; for example, they often asked about the influence of public opinion on justices. One especially thoughtful young man was obviously trying to sort out the age-old conundrum of how the Court can decide basic questions of politics when it theoretically is a non-political institution. The perceptive undergraduate asked, if the justices are supposed to be above politics, why were they deciding the term-limits case and the racial reapportionment decisions in the 1994–95 term?

Some of the students' queries fell into the old Art Linkletter (now Bill Cosby) "kids say the darndest things" category. These young visitors to the Court simply wanted to learn more about the justices' lives. If adolescents ask about what kind of underwear the president prefers, they surely want to know some personal data about the members of the Court. One student asked me, "What are the justices like around the building?" Another, the same one who asked about their clothing, wanted to know if they drive their own cars. Still another asked if the justices talk to people at parties.

My most interesting encounter with students came when I was asked to be prepared for a briefing of a large group of high schoolers who were in Washington for a law seminar. They were to meet with Justice Scalia, and I was to be on hand if he cut short his presentation. Scalia graciously spoke to, and took questions from, the eager students for nearly an hour, and I had no desire to follow the master showman of the current Court. The justice's briefing for the students was a firsthand experience for them in learning the symbols and images of the Supreme Court. The "audience" with Scalia took place in the courtroom itself, which was the only chamber that could accommodate the 300 students. When the justice entered, the students stood and applauded. He immediately chided them, "When a judge enters this room, we stand but do not clap." He then schooled them in his "textualist" and "originalist" approach to constitutional interpretation, which, he always emphasizes, eschews his own personal vision of how the Constitution should be interpreted in favor of the original meaning of its text. As nervous and highly deferential students trooped to the microphones to pose their questions to the intimidating, yet jovial, Scalia, he often responded that he could not answer those queries that related to issues that might come before the Court. He sidestepped inquiries about abortion, California's Proposition 187 (regarding state policies toward immigrants), and privacy in cyberspace.

Scalia revealed his humorous and human side when a student asked his reaction to the man who claims to have invented the intermittent windshield wiper and who has prolonged litigation over its patent. The disappointed inventor/litigant failed to have his case accepted by the high court, which, the student reported, he called "a joke." Scalia's response was, "Did he really? I'm sure he's not the first person to think that!"

The students' admiration for the justice was clear. They asked him for the secret of his success and seemed genuinely compelled by his answer that hard work is necessary to search for answers in one's chosen profession. He commented that the search in law was not always fun, but it was always interesting and challenging. For a generation that must often be entertained in order to learn, the justice's lesson was an important one.

During my year at the Court, four large groups of business executives and MBA students requested briefings. They had come to Washington, D.C. to learn about the political system and institutions of government from a perspective "inside the Beltway." The groups were mature and knowledgeable, and they contributed unique vantage points, resulting from their business backgrounds. In contrast, most of the students and teachers I spoke to were in a law-related curriculum, so they came to the Court with certain premises (usually positive) about the judicial process.

The business executives were more confrontational, and their questions often revealed negative assumptions about the Supreme Court and its members. One minority female executive was quite hostile about the routine work of the Court. She maintained that nine justices could not possibly give proper review to the over 7,000 petitions that pour into the Court annually. Moreover, she asserted that the justices were public figures who should submit to television coverage. She also argued that the Supreme Court "makes policy" even when it denies review of a case.

From a different group of executives came a more general question that teachers had posed to me: Was I disillusioned by anything I had seen during my tenure at the Court? It was always fascinating to me that some Americans assumed that there just had to be some activity occurring in the hidden corridors of power, to which they thought I now had accesss, that would make us all cynical about the institution. Having become skeptics regarding the president and Congress, some Americans have the Court next on their list of government institutions that they should now mistrust. Although the last 30 years have witnessed an increase in public disillusionment for the reasons listed earlier in this chapter, Americans are congenitally skeptical of power, so their negative questions were not surprising.

My answer to the cynicism question always had two parts. First, I simply never heard or saw anything of the sort the audiences seemed to want to know, and certainly nothing that disillusioned me, about the institution. Edward Lazarus, author of *Closed Chambers*, worked very closely with his justice (Harry Blackmun) and fellow clerks. He obviously had a different experience from mine. Yet so much of his criticism of the Court and its inner deliberations resulted from his premises about, and interpretations of, the Court's work—all of which are, at the very least, debatable. If nothing else, the Court's four new members (Souter, Thomas, Ginsburg, and Breyer), who took their seats after Lazarus's clerkship, have very different work habits from those criticized in *Closed Chambers*. Second, I told the visitors that in my 20-year observation of the Court before I came to work for it, my interviews with justices for research in the 1980s, and my work in 1994–95 revealed nothing that made me lose faith in the Supreme Court or its members. The Court does not have to spend time hiding wrongdoing, since it rarely exists, but it does devote itself to trying to do the right thing in terms of its public service. It knows that the American people may not always agree with its decisions, so it must protect the symbols and images of its power. That is why even the Devitt Award "mini-scandal," described in Chapter 4, was a concern. Any taint of impropriety could damage the tribunal's prestige.

Another question from a business executive was particularly worrisome. Although it was posed lightheartedly, it presented a potential problem for the Court's image. The executive asked why the chief justice had added stripes to his judicial robe. I could only respond with the official pronouncements that had appeared in the media at the time, namely, that the chief had admired similar decorations on the lord chancellor's robe in a Gilbert and Sullivan play. Rehnquist himself later commented that the media paid so much attention to the story because the Court is such a slow news beat. In part, that is true. In addition, the media love to report departures from the norm, especially from the tradition-bound uniformity of the Supreme Court. The robe's alteration was not unimportant, however. Part of the Court's imagery is to portray the chief justice as the "first among equals," whose vote carries no greater weight than his colleagues. The uniformity of the Court's actions as an institution has been symbolized, from early in its history, by the similarity and simplicity of the justices' robes. Moreover, when Rehnquist wore his striped robe to the Clinton impeachment trial in 1999, comedian Jay Leno compared the chief's attire to that of the late flamboyant pianist Liberace—known for the sequins and feather boas he modeled at his Las Vegas performances.

On a more substantive plane, the business executives struggled, like other visitors to the Supreme Court, to square the image of the institution as being above politics with their knowledge that politics constantly swirls around the tribunal's decisions. One asked if politics influenced the Court and whether the institution affected politics. Another distinguished between politics "inside and outside" the Court and asked if either or both had an impact on the justices' rulings. Some of the executives' inquiries linked both power and politics. They wanted to know if the Court could simply take a case without its being appealed to it. They brought the president into the equation by questioning, "Don't presidents try to pack the Court?" One executive wanted to know what happens when the justices declare a law unconstitutional; is the law immediately void or does it have to be formally repealed?

Finally, the executives raised several issues that were particularly related to their business concerns. They asked how the justices decide economic issues. They also wondered about the problem of downsizing in the private sector and if the concept had reached the Court via its own budget. One executive wanted to know if the justices, especially the older ones, kept up with new computer technology and developments, like the Internet. Aside from these factual questions, and the usual inquiries about procedures, the business executives and MBA students were slightly more curious about differences between their perceptions of image and reality regarding the Supreme Court than were teachers and students to whom I spoke.

Letters to the Supreme Court also present a mixed bag of attitudes toward the institution. Generally, they reflect the positive image of the Court reflected in public surveys. Aside from threatening letters sent by crackpots, citizen correspondence falls into several categories: students at every level of education asking for research assistance; citizens of all ages offering their advice to justices on how to vote on particular issues or cases, or expressing disagreement with a past decision; requests for souvenirs and memorabilia (e.g., Constitutions, signed photographs, and autographs); and pleas for help with personal legal problems. Although some of the missives display a lack of knowledge about the Court and the judicial process (for example, ignorance of the fact that justices do not consult public opinion in rendering judgments and do not dispense legal advice or make decisions outside the bounds of properly framed cases), most of them evince respect for the Court's power and expertise.[22]

INNOCENTS FROM ABROAD

With the exception of a few highly skeptical, occasionally hostile, foreign visitors, audiences from abroad that I briefed were noticably admiring of the Supreme Court and genuinely desirous of information on how it seemingly functioned so successfully in the American system of checks and balances. Most of the foreigners to whom I spoke (sometimes one-to-one, sometimes in large groups) consisted of judges, lawyers, prosecutors, justice ministry officials and court administrators, legislators and politicians, journalists, and scholars and academics. Miscellaneous positions represented included a Belgian cabinet secretary, a Mexican police official, Canadian Parliament interns, a member of the Eritrean Constitutional Commission, and several clerics from Turkmenistan. Some of the visitors understood English; most required translation to their native language by interpreters. Whether the briefings were in English or required translation, I followed the same practice as with the American audiences of presenting a brief overview of the Court's procedures and work load, followed by a dialogue of questions and answers. Frequently, a group's escorts would request in advance that I address issues of particular interest to the group. The vast majority of these foreign visitors to the Court had been invited by the U.S. Information Agency (USIA), who then contracted with private educational consulting firms in Washington, D.C. for provision of travel arrangements, programs, and interpreters.

Many of the foreign visitors expressed to me how impressed they were with the physical beauty and majesty of the Supreme Court building and the courtroom. Others, a Japanese judge and an Italian diplomat, were stunned at the number of American tourists they saw visiting the building. The Italian commented that the average citizen in his country would have no interest in visiting courts in Italy. As I escorted the Japanese judge through the building, an older American woman approached me and began to engage us in a monologue about her admiration for the late Justice William O. Douglas. She told us of her concern during his career over his numerous marriages and her fear that they had harmed his reputation. When we could extricate ourselves from the enthusiastic Douglas admirer, we visited the Court's Gift Shop and viewed the display of justices' photographs available for sale. The Japanese judge remarked on the contrast with her own country where, she noted, the general public would have little if any interest in the judiciary and certainly not enough to warrant purchasing pictures of judges.

Not surprisingly, most foreign judges inquired about subjects related to their counterparts on the U.S. Supreme Court. Several women judges from Senegal asked if American justices were allowed to belong to political parties and vote; Senegalese jurists were forbidden to maintain partisan affiliations or cast ballots. (In order to preserve his partisan neutrality, the late Justice Lewis F. Powell, Jr., voluntarily declined to vote in elections after assuming his seat on the Court in 1972.) The judges from Senegal also commented favorably on the U.S. Supreme Court's diversity, with its two women, a black, and an Italian. In contrast, a Zimbabwean judge worried about the socioeconomic homogeneity of the justices and wondered if both the judges and their clerks were too elitist. (On the opening day of the Court's 1998–99 term, the NAACP staged a protest on the front plaza against the dearth of minority and women law clerks.) Likewise, judges from Benin, Mali, and Gabon wanted to know if the "underprivileged" had ever served on the high court. (In the 1996 case of *Romer v. Evans*, in which the Supreme Court struck down a Colorado constitutional amendment prohibiting the creation of "special rights" for gays, Justice Scalia's dissent accused the Court's majority of representing an elitist mentality that was out of step with society's mainstream views on homosexuality. He again applied the elitist label to the majority in his *VMI* dissent.)

The judges from Benin and Mali also were concerned about why judicial nominees in America were so closely examined regarding their personal lives. With Clarence Thomas in mind, they declared that a nominee's relationships with women did not matter and should not be investigated. Yet other judges, like those from Thailand, worried about corrupt behavior of justices once on the bench, and they wanted information about the impeachment and removal process. A particularly well-informed group of justices from the Costa Rican Supreme Court asked about the extra-judicial activities of

American justices. They had heard about the Warren Commission and wanted to know if Chief Justice Earl Warren's service as chair of the committee that investigated the assassination of President Kennedy was typical.

Many of the questions related to the procedure and power of the Court, but the foreigners seemed most intrigued by the U.S. Supreme Court's power of judicial review and how it had been exercised over the other two branches of the federal government as well as state and local actions. The visitors would often ask for historical examples of how the Court had reined in the power of Congress and/or the president. Several foreigners were familiar with the story of Watergate and the Supreme Court's ruling against President Nixon in the tapes case. A group of Russian judicial administrators asked if the Court could overrule the legislative or executive branch at will. They wondered if the president had control over the justices he had appointed and whether a president could send in troops to stop the Supreme Court from acting. A group of Haitian officials asked how the Supreme Court settles disputes between the president and Congress. Obviously, the content of questions was often directly related to the experiences of the visitors in their own countries.

The tone of inquires was also linked to a foreign visitor's background. My most hostile encounter came from two Kazakhstani judges who maintained vociferously that when the U.S. Supreme Court rejected the vast majority of petitions it received, particularly from prisoners, it meant that all of those petitioners' rights were being denied. I attributed the hostility of the question to the fact that residents of the Central Asian Republics would have been exposed both to an unjust Soviet legal system for years, as well as anti-American propaganda from the Communists for an equivalent period of time. Both factors made it difficult for the Kazakhstani visitors to judge the American judicial system with anything approaching objectivity. When one of the disgruntled judges approached me after the briefing, I thought it was to apologize for his rather rude outburst. Instead, through an interpreter, he asserted that he was right because the United States did not have a "real democracy."

Two different groups of Chinese scholars who were doing research in the United States also presented concerns about the Supreme Court's role in the American system. They were more interested in how the representative branches of government checked the Court rather than the converse. A rather insistent Chinese professor asserted that the justices should *not* have life tenure; he advocated term limits for all American government officials. One of the few women among the Chinese academics timidly asked about the role of women on the Supreme Court. She also told me after the briefing how much it meant to her that a woman had spoken to her group.

Understandably, the members of foreign parliaments and politicians from abroad were most interested in political issues that reached the Court. A frequent topic of questions from parliamentarians and prosecutors was the death penalty. They often compared procedures in our respective countries, especially those that attempted to afford due process to those receiving capital punishment. A Montenegrin politician, who was a member of the opposition party in that troubled part of the world, wanted to know about protection of individual liberties in the United States. He specifically asked about the issue of flag burning, in addition to the death penalty. Before he left my office, he wrote in English (although an interpreter had translated the entire briefing) on a slip of paper, "No rule of law," to describe the difficult state of affairs in his region. As a member of the opposition, his freedom of speech had been denied by the ruling party in Montenegro. Several visitors asked about the abortion issue, including a Catholic Italian parliamentarian, who put the question directly to Justice Scalia. The Italian presumed that Scalia's antiabortion jurisprudence resulted from his own Catholic affiliation. The justice assured the visiting parliamentarian that his position on abortion derived solely from the original meaning of the Constitution and its amendments.

Journalists also inquired consistently about politics and the Court. More generally, they wanted to know if political lobbying could influence the judiciary as it does the other two branches. Specifically, they asked about the death penalty, race relations, term limits, gays in the military, and Miranda rights. A group of Russian reporters had heard about Clarence Thomas and the issue of sexual harassment and wanted to know about the controversy.

Foreign lawyers had a marked propensity to ask about the Supreme Court's image among the American public. A Peruvian attorney, for example, was interested in how the judiciary in the United States had developed images and symbols that contributed to the people's respect for the Court. His question was purely practical because he wanted to know how South American judiciaries could attain similar respect, which they currently do not enjoy. Occasionally, some visitors (including a Mexican court official) were so admiring of the Supreme Court that they could not comprehend that it had any weaknesses. Nevertheless, fearing the impact of the O.J. Simpson trial and the infamous McDonald's hot coffee litigation on the image of the American legal system, an exceedingly bright Nigerian lawyer, who practices in the United Kingdom, asked for my perceptions of how these actions might damage the judicial process and Americans' visions of it.

Sources of the foreign visitors' information about the U.S. Supreme Court were indeed varied. For two groups it was American popular culture. A Middle Eastern contingent knew about the Warren Commission from the Oliver Stone film *JFK* on the Kennedy assassination. A Mexican social science professor's vision of the Court came from another movie, *The Pelican Brief,* based on the novel by John Grisham. The story centers on the mysterious murder of two fictitious Supreme Court justices, one of whom is strangled as he watches a pornographic film in a gay movie house in Washington, D.C. The professor's question to me was whether the story was "true to life?"

Without a doubt, the most colorful, and in some ways memorable, group consisted of three clerics from Turkmenistan. Two were Moslem holy men and one was a Russian Orthodox priest. They arrived in full clerical and national regalia—complete with a black cassock, biretta, and large gold cross for the priest, and white knee-length vests and tall lambs wool hats for the Moslems. They constituted a committee in their country to help establish and maintain religious freedom; therefore, they were particularly interested in the school prayer issue in the United States and why it was such a "hot issue" (according to the interpreter's translation). Although I had attempted to provide a background lecture on religious freedom and the separation of church and state in this country, it was difficult to explain the nuances of this complex field of history and jurisprudence in a short talk and through a translation from English to Russian.

Despite all of the barriers formed by language, religion, politics, nationality, race, and gender, each briefing convinced me that a genuine exchange of information and opinions had occurred. From Mongolia to Mali, from Costa Rica to Kazakhstan, over 2,000 visitors from nearly 80 countries had come to the Supreme Court and heard a judicial fellow briefing in 1994–95. Even given the fact that most of them were chosen by the USIA to come to the United States to learn more about American-style democracy, there was near-universal admiration for the U.S. judiciary. Obviously, not all foreign visitors were convinced that this was the system for them or even for the United States. Nonetheless, the high regard for the Supreme Court and the federal judiciary as a whole expressed by the foreign visitors proved that the prestige of the priestly tribe has spread far beyond the nation's borders. As Justice Tom Clark observed almost 30 years ago, the U.S. Supreme Court has become a "world exemplar" of law.

NOTES

1. *Washington Journal,* C-SPAN, 28 July 1995.

2. See Gregory Caldeira's initial seminal work, cited in the bibliography, followed by his subsequent refinements, "Neither the Purse Nor the Sword: Dynamic of Public Confidence in the Supreme Court," *American Political Science Review* 80 (1986): 1209–26.

3. Alexander Wohl, "Read All about Them: Supreme Court Justices Have Become Popular Subjects for Biographers," *American Bar Association Journal* (May 1995): 45, 48.

4. Darlene Superville, "What's New?" *Louisville Courier-Journal,* 30 December 1995, A2.

5. Richard Morin, "A Nation of Stooges," *Washington Post,* 8 October 1995, C5.

6. Joan Biskupic, "Has the Court Lost Its Appeal?" *Washington Post*, 12 October 1995, A23.

7. Lee Epstein et al., *The Supreme Court Compendium: Data, Decisions, and Developments* (Washington, D.C.: Congressional Quarterly Press, 1994), 609.

8. *Washington Post/* Kaiser Family Foundation/Harvard University Survey Project, "Why Don't Americans Trust the Government?", 10; Richard Morin, "Who's in Control? Many Don't Know or Care," *Washington Post*, 29 January 1996, A6.

9. "Why Don't Americans Trust the Government?", 11.

10. Ibid., 3; Richard Morin and Dan Balz, "Americans Losing Trust in Each Other and Institutions," *Washington Post*, 28 January 1996, A6.

11. Liz Spayd, "Welcome to the State of Paranoia," *Washington Post*, 23 July 1996, A1–A2.

12. "Why Don't Americans Trust the Government?", 11–12.

13. As reported in James Q. Wilson, *American Government: Institutions and Policies* (Lexington, Mass.: D.C. Heath and Co., 1992).

14. "Why Don't Americans Trust the Government?", 3; for similar results on public regard for the Court, see also John M. Scheb II and William Lyons, "Public Holds U.S. Supreme Court in High Regard," *Judicature* 77 (March–April 1994): 273–74, and J. Scheb and W. Lyons, "Public Perception of the Supreme Court in the 1990s," *Judicature* 82 (September–October 1998): 66–69.

15. David S. Broder, "Trust in Government Edges Up," *Washington Post*, 10 March 1998, A15.

16. Richard Morin and Claudia Deane, "Poll Shows Americans More Satisfied with U.S.," *Washington Post*, 21 January 1998, A6.

17. "Gallup Puts Judiciary at Top of Poll," *The Third Branch* 29 (November 1997): 7.

18. As reported in Caldeira, "Neither the Purse Nor the Sword," 1209–26.

19. Ibid., 1223–24.

20. Thomas R. Marshall, *Public Opinion and the Supreme Court* (Boston: Unwin Hyman, 1989), 141.

21. Alan F. Westin, "When the Public Judges the Court," *New York Times Magazine*, 31 May 1959, 42.

22. See John W. Johnson, " 'Dear Mr. Justice': Public Correspondence with Members of the Supreme Court," *Journal of Supreme Court History* II (1997): 101–12.

Conclusion: "God Save This Honorable Court!"

Chapter 2 describes how the Supreme Court Historical Society and Street Law, Inc. have sponsored the Supreme Court Institute for Teachers each summer since 1995, in order to provide educators with an "inside" view of the Supreme Court that will allow them to teach about it and the law more knowledgeably. Participants are expected to return to their schools and districts and provide similar training for their colleagues. Street Law calculates that the annual seminar allows them to reach indirectly thousands of students and teachers around the country.

This new means of spreading the word about the Supreme Court of the United States is obviously an important conduit for transmitting the tribunal's image to an audience of high school students that typically has not had broad exposure to the topic. Just what do the teachers learn about the highest court in the land? After the opening sessions of their institute, which consists of a presentation on Supreme Court statistics, and talks with lawyers who have served as clerks at the Court and who have argued before it, there is a session on using documentary evidence and the Internet to teach about the Court, and a lively panel on the politics of judicial appointments.

The teachers then have a tour by the Senate curator of the restored old Supreme Court chamber on the lower level of the Capitol building. Although the room is small, it has been authentically furnished to reflect the style of the early nineteenth century. Only the Marshall and Taney Courts occupied it. The curator comments about the chamber's original reputation as a "potato hole" because of its basement location and rather dark, dank atmosphere. Then the teachers move up one floor to the restored Senate chamber, used by the upper house until 1860, where the teachers have a chance to view what was the Court's home from 1860 to 1935. The group next convenes across the street at the modern Supreme Court building for a VIP tour and a discussion with the Marshal of the Court Dale Bosley, a meticulous but unassuming man, retired from a brilliant military career as a Navy Seal. The marshal's office is responsible for the security and maintenance of the Court. What a contrast for the teachers to see the three successive venues of the Supreme Court, starting with the small "potato hole," moving up to the larger former Senate chamber in the Capitol, and then out to its present separate home in a magnificent setting.

The next two days are devoted to learning about current cases before the Court; the seminar includes a moot court (in 1998 on *NEA v. Finley*, the case involving criteria for government funding of controversial art). The teachers also have a session with a reporter who covers the Court. They thus view the Court from a wide variety of perspectives: legal, historical, political, and journalistic.

Their exposure to the tribunal at the end of the seminar is firsthand. They attend an opinion session of the Supreme Court, at which the justices hand down decisions. The teachers' excitement is palpable. Many have been to the Court previously, but they are delighted to return and see the justices in the flesh. That fact is even more obvious when the Institute is hosted at the Supreme Court for an evening reception. The mood is electric as the teachers mill about the softly lit conference room waiting for the guest of honor, Justice Sandra Day O'Connor, to arrive. Each summer she attends, accompanied by her husband, and they graciously greet the guests for some time. One teacher, who was among the first to meet Justice O'Connor at the 1996 reception, practically swooned as she walked away from her judicial hero and exclaimed, "I can now die a happy woman!"

The individual conversations are topped only by Justice O'Connor's poignant remarks to the teachers. She praises them for their work and describes her own educational experience with inspirational mentors. Her personal comments to the teachers move some of them to tears. She tells them how important they are to their students and how many successful people often cite those who taught them, more often than their own families, as the source of their inspiration. In a country that grants very little prestige or monetary reward to its educators, O'Connor's words themselves are an inspiration. Justice Ruth Bader Ginsburg spoke at one of the receptions in 1998, and she, too, charmed the teachers, who gave the second female justice to serve on the Supreme Court rave reviews.

HOW OPEN SHOULD THE SUPREME COURT BE TO THE PUBLIC?

Undoubtedly, if the Supreme Court could offer such a memorable experience to all members of the public, it might do so to guarantee its exalted image across the land. Of course, bringing the entire American populace to

Washington for a reception at the Court is impossible, so the question re-mains: Who will have access to the highest court in the land and under what conditions? (The question refers to non-adjudicative admittance as opposed to litigational access, which is established by the rules and customs of the American judicial process.) The media can provide the broadest view of the Supreme Court for the public; therefore, the issue of journalistic access has dominated the debate. Not surprisingly, the two major participants in the discussion have been reporters and the justices themselves.

U.S.A. Today and *Legal Times* correspondent Tony Mauro has maintained a constant drum beat for wider access of the media to the Supreme Court of the United States. Specifically, he maintains that the Court must allow cameras to record its oral argument sessions. His contention is based on the general proposition that a constitutionally protected free press and the hal-lowed concept of open government positively require the Court to allow cameras in its chamber. He uses the flap over the release of the Thurgood Marshall papers as support for his position, arguing that the documents actually "ennobled the Court by making it clear to the public that each decision is preceded by careful, if not tortured, deliberation."[1] Mauro be-lieves that the Court could actually come out a winner in the public mind if its public work during oral argument was televised. In Mauro's view, the admittance of TV cameras would allow more precise coverage of the Court. Whether the justices would have to suffer greater recognition or loss of privacy, or whether they would present a positive or negative image of them-selves as individuals, is of no concern to Mauro. He believes that televising the Court's proceedings is part of an inexorable movement in the infor-mation age. He concludes, "The Supreme Court is neither well served by being, nor is it entitled to be, an exception to that trend."[2]

The guru of televised government broadcasts, Brian Lamb, the founding director of C-SPAN, longs for the day when the Supreme Court will allow his public affairs network to cover oral arguments from gavel to gavel. Be-cause of his network's policy of providing complete coverage, without an-alytical intrusion, he believes that if TV can broadcast the Supreme Court usefully, it will be C-SPAN that can offer such salutary programming to the public.

For some justices the issue of *complete* coverage of oral arguments, versus *edited* versions, like those that would be presented on short news broadcasts, is paramount. Ruth Bader Ginsburg, for example, has said on many occa-sions that she worries about distortions that might occur through the sound-bite problem.[3] Mauro takes her to task for what he declares is an unconstitutional intrusion into the editorial prerogatives of the broadcast medium.

By definition, the sound-bite matter does not apply to print journalism, but as was noted in Chapter 4, Justice Ginsburg has criticized Court re-porters for other sins, which she categorized in a 1995 speech and subsequent articles. She accused the press of occasionally failing to report genuinely important decisions or reporting them with too much emphasis on what they divine as the practical effects of the case, which may not even be discernable in the slow-moving judicial process. Ginsburg also criticized reporters for sometimes making too much of the Court's denials of *certiorari* by reporting the case as if the high court had actually decided it, when what it really did was decide *not* to decide it on its substantive merits, leaving intact the lower court's ruling.[4]

Chief Justice Rehnquist has commented similarly in public remarks that the press often misportrays the Court's work to readers and viewers by simply exaggerating the importance of some decisions and neglecting other truly important ones. In a speech to the Fourth Circuit Judicial Conference in 1994, for example, he argued that the press tends to exaggerate First Amendment cases. He agreed that First Amendment principles are important to the country, but not every decision that relates to them is ipso facto significant. The chief justice asserted that cases relating to other topics may well be more important if they contain new interpretations of statutory law or the Constitution.[5]

Justice Clarence Thomas, understandably no admirer of the media, has also commented that they too often fail to cover truly significant cases or report them as "garbage cases." In a spring 1994 address at Ohio Northern University, he cited decisions related to the Constitution's commerce clause that he thought were important but that the media found boring. Instead, he said, they tend to focus on emotional issues such as abortion. Consequently, Thomas said, "I don't read the paper often."[6]

Justice Stevens has made more veiled comments criticizing how the press covers the Supreme Court. More than ten years ago he noted that at the beginning of the 1985 term, the press made no remarks on the fiftieth anniversary of the Supreme Court building, which Chief Justice Burger had commemorated with a special ceremony. On the other hand, at least one television network commentator reported that the justices had returned to the bench "after completing their three-month vacation." Like professors who bristle when asked what they do while they are "off" during the summer, Stevens explained before a meeting of the Chicago Chapter of the Federal Bar Association that justices really do conduct Court business even during the months when they are not in session. One task they undertake is to speak to judicial conferences or other professional associations, but Stevens took a swipe at the press when he observed that they report critical remarks that a justice might make about the Court at such meetings but ignore the same arguments maintained in a dissenting opinion from the bench.[7]

Print journalists themselves have complained about the editorial constraints on their ability to report more fully on the work of the Supreme Court. Even Linda Greenhouse, whose *New York Times* gives some of the most comprehensive and perceptive coverage of the Court in the nation, has identified the problem. She once commented that her editors and colleagues simply want to know "what's the story at the Supreme Court?" In other words, "what did the Court do?"[8] Greenhouse may be given 1,200 words in which to write a "round-up" story on the Court, but her colleagues at other newspapers are given considerably less—and some merely recount the Associated Press wire service reports. As Frank Murray, Supreme Court correspondent for the *Washington Times,* has described the problem, editors will run a headline story on a public policy issue when it is debated in Congress or signed into law by the president, but they may devote only a brief story to the same policy when the Supreme Court addresses it. Murray believes that because editors may fail to see the politics involved in Court decisions, they tend to give them short shrift.[9]

Neither Greenhouse nor Murray is likely to change the editorial blind spots and column-inch limitations under which they labor. Greenhouse, however, has suggested how the Supreme Court could make the journalist's job of reporting accurately on the Court easier. She proposed once to Chief Justice Rehnquist that the Court could spread out the announcement of decisions at the end of the term so that she and her colleagues would not have to report on sometimes up to nine cases for one edition of the newspaper. Rehnquist's response? "Why don't you save some for the next day?"[10] This was hardly an indication that the chief justice was truly attuned to, and sympathetic with, the plight of the modern-day print reporter who must fight to make news sound fresh in an old-fashioned 24-hour news cycle, while CNN updates its televised stories every fifteen minutes and the Internet offers instantaneous reports.

Greenhouse and her colleagues who cover the Court also have inquired whether the transcripts of oral argument could be made available on a same-day basis, which the transcription company had indicated was now possible with new technology. The journalists' request was denied summarily by the chief justice, forcing them to continue with the current system, which makes the transcripts available two weeks after oral arguments when they are absolutely useless to reporters who need to report accurately the next day on what was said in the courtroom. As Greenhouse concluded, she is not asking for radical changes in the relationship between the Supreme Court and the press. In fact, she has so learned to accommodate the status quo that she does not begrudge the lack of access to justices because she never has to worry about having such access to sources withdrawn. Nevertheless, what she reasonably would like to see is some dialogue between the Court and the press on how they can improve the flow of accurate and prompt information to the public.

Although her suggestions thus far have not been accepted by the current chief justice, they may be someday by a different Court. In any event, Greenhouse's requests may stand more chance of approval than the demand for television camera coverage of oral arguments. Justice John Paul Stevens commented that he has been a minority of one (not an unusual position for him on the Court), since Justice Brennan retired, in supporting TV cameras in the courtroom. He would like to see the high court at least experiment with television, especially for important cases. Stevens believes that such exposure might even engender more respect for the Court among the public. Still, the Court's eldest member acknowledges the arguments against television coverage. The oral argument is an institution that functions smoothly now, and he worries that television might introduce unforeseen problems into the process. For example, Stevens notes that his confirmation hearings in 1975 were not televised, and he emphasizes the alteration in senators' behavior after such hearings were routinely televised. If nothing else, they were prone to make lengthier statements and ask repetitious and redundant questions in order to have more air time to impress the constituents back home. As Stevens has said about oral argument, "If it ain't broke, don't fix it." He also recognizes that it is easier to be an anonymous justice than a television celebrity.[11]

Even if a majority of the Court favored televising oral argument, it would be very difficult to change the current system without the chief justice's support. Rehnquist, in a 1992 interview, noted that a majority has never voted to televise the sessions during his tenure or his predecessor's. The current chief justice added, "And certainly the people who want radio and television coverage have good arguments on their side, but we simply have decided to leave matters as they were."[12]

Some justices have commented in their confirmation hearings that they would not mind the televising of oral argument sessions. Even Justice Thomas, in his pre–Anita Hill hearings in 1991, stated, "I have no objection beyond a concern that the cameras be as unobtrusive as possible. . . . It's good for the American public to see what's going on in there."[13] Justice Stevens, however, did not count Thomas as a supporter of cameras in the courtroom since he has been on the bench. In Ruth Bader Ginsburg's 1993 confirmation hearings, she responded to a question on the issue by saying, "I don't see any problem with having proceedings televised. I think it would be good for the public."[14] Nevertheless, as previously noted, she has more recently focused on the problems inherent in the editing of televised oral argument. The inevitability of distortion through sound-biting makes her dubious regarding the adoption of cameras in the courtroom.

David Souter, during his statements before the Senate Judiciary Committee's confirmation hearings for his 1990 nomination to the U.S. Supreme Court, gave a somewhat ambiguous response to the question about allowing cameras to film the justices. He observed, "If the cameras are unobtrusive and are not making sound that is distracting, that's one thing. There is still a risk . . . cameras which are obtrusive to oral argument so that they really do distract your attention. That is something that has to be avoided. . . . There's no question there's value there."[15]

By 1993, however, Justice Souter had clearly settled on the negative side of whether to allow cameras to film oral argument. He commented that the New Hampshire Supreme Court, on which he had previously served, allowed televising of its sessions; he remembered that he had deliberately avoided asking certain questions because he thought they would be misunderstood by the public to whom they would be broadcast. Souter also appreciated his relative anonymity, which he said he had nearly regained after the burst of publicity surrounding his nomination three years earlier.[16]

Souter's position has solidified even more in the interim. In March 1996 he and Justice Kennedy testified before a House of Representatives subcommittee on the Court's annual budget. At the end of the hearing, they were asked their views on televising judicial actions at the trial and appellate levels, and even at the Supreme Court. Justice Kennedy began by citing the truism that "TV is part of the environment we live in. It is hard to excise it." He added, however, that he was not in favor of televising Supreme Court oral arguments and would never support the change as long as even one justice objected. Justice Souter seemed to relish the moment he was asked to add his views on the subject. With no hesitation, he declared, "The day you see a camera in our courtroom, it's gonna roll over my dead body!"[17]

His colleague Justice Antonin Scalia has been equally adamant about banning cameras from the courtroom. To an audience of foreign correspondents visiting the Court in 1994, he asserted that judges should not become media stars because it is not in the Anglo-Saxon tradition for judges to "thrust themselves into the limelight." Thus, he said, "you won't see me on television."[18] He does lectures and speaking engagements around the country but refuses to allow them to the televised. Scalia, like several of his colleagues, seems to treasure his anonymity, too; he told the story of how a motel clerk out West asked him if he pronounced his name like the Supreme Court justice. The acerbic jurist said he could barely refrain from blurting at the clerk, "How many Antonin Scalias are there?"[19]

It is clear that Scalia is unlikely to change his mind on this issue. In contrast, Justice O'Connor, who, because of her celebrity as the first woman justice, has been one of the most visible of the justices, seems more open-minded on the subject. At the eighth Circuit Judicial Conference in 1993, she responded to a question from the audience as follows: "I do not think that I want to force any of my colleagues who have strongly opposing views to subject themselves to media coverage, and unless there's pretty strong consensus among the nine that it should be done, I would not be one to vote for a change. And if there is a strong consensus that we should go that route and virtual unanimity on the subject, then I'll go along. But I think it's going to be awhile."[20] Undoubtedly, she is correct.

The justice who was most devoted to the idea of opening the Supreme

Court to television cameras was William Brennan. Before his retirement in 1990, he commented, "Ours is a public proceeding. And there is no reason in my judgment why only those who can gain entrance to the courtroom should be able to witness the proceedings."[21] At an informal discussion in 1994, he said about cameras in the courtroom, "I'm all for it! Always have been!" Asked how to get the other justices to join his position, Brennan replied, "Give them some sense!"[22]

Another retiree, Justice Byron White, at the same eighth Circuit Judicial Conference attended by Justice O'Connor in 1993, recalled that he had always voted against bringing cameras into oral argument. White added: "I just don't think it would contribute a whole lot to our proceedings, and I'm not sure that it would be so educational to the public. That's been the view of the majority of the justices so far but it's certainly not unanimous. . . . I wouldn't be a bit surprised if sooner or later the court will be made up of justices who say, 'What was wrong with those old guys anyway?' "[23]

THE IMPACT OF MORE OPENNESS ON THE COURT'S SYMBOLS, IMAGES, AND LEGITIMACY

Despite a spate of younger appointees over the past decade, members of the Supreme Court, like all mortals, inexorably continue to age. It is possible that several of its oldest members—Chief Justice Rehnquist, Justice Stevens, and Justice O'Connor—could retire in the next few years. Would the influx of new justices sway the Court to a new posture regarding televising of its oral argument sessions? The institution is so tradition-bound that it is difficult to envision the overturning of its own ban on cameras.

When first considering this question in earnest during the controversies over the Marshall papers and the Irons tapes, I passionately believed, as Justice Brennan did and Tony Mauro does, that such public proceedings must be open to television. I also thought that such coverage would provide the general public, and particularly students at all educational levels, with a unique tool for learning about the judicial process and the Supreme Court's role in it.

After several more years of contemplating the issue, I have reached the opposite conclusion. My year at the Court was not one of co-option or "going native," as political scientists describe bureaucrats who thoroughly embrace the parochial interests of their respective agencies. Rather, my fellowship in Washington, D.C., and additional years of observing the intriguing dance of the government, public, and media, convinced me that the image of the Supreme Court of the United States is indeed unique and well worth preserving. Despite modern political science literature and popular treatises that try to convince them otherwise, most Americans do not view the highest court in the land as just another political institution, populated by political animals, making political judgments. Two judicial giants of the twentieth century delineated the distinguishing features of the judicial (as opposed to the political) process. Justice Benjamin Cardozo admitted that all humans "may try to see things as objectively as we please. None the less, we can never see them with any eyes except our own." Yet he argued that judges are guided by precedent, logic, history, and standards of justice in making their decisions.[24] His intellectual equal, Justice Louis Brandeis, drafted a litany of standards in *Ashwander v. Tennessee*[25] that restrain judges from becoming "knight-errants." Professor Henry Abraham labels these standards the "taught tradition of the law" and codifies them in his "sixteen maxims of judicial self-restraint."[26]

Linda Greenhouse explains the phenomenon expertly for general audiences: "While the justices naturally draw on their own values and perspectives in approaching cases, most of them, most of the time, act not as politicians but as judges, working within the constraints of precedent and of the judicial enterprise to give judicial answers to the problems that people bring to the Court." Greenhouse believes that justices avoid what she calls "low" politics, correctly explaining that they engage in "high" politics,[27] which one might define as determining answers to questions regarding the most basic of our political arrangements—federalism, separation of powers, checks and balances, and civil rights and liberties. ←

Originally set forth in our fundamental law—the Constitution—these arrangements require periodic interpretation, and once the Supreme Court established itself as the final arbiter in such disputes, it had bound itself firmly with that document and the symbol and substance of the American democratic regime. A comparative experience I had in Jerusalem in 1996 provided several new insights on this subject. Scholars have not been able to explain the rather high levels of public confidence in the law in Israel— even among Palestinians. After touring the new Israeli Supreme Court building in West Jerusalem, I understood once more how symbolism can ← in part, help to create positive images and legitimacy for the law. The Israeli Court's modern architecture, which is so different from the Greek classical form of the U.S. Supreme Court's edifice, brilliantly encapsulates the religious history of the City of David by using native Jerusalem limestone to create walls and symbols of the town's holy sites. Moreover, the architects innovatively created entrances for natural light, which imitates the yellow glow that radiates from the Jerusalem skyline at dawn and dusk. Through geometric shapes, such as a straight line representing truth, and the use of water in exterior courtyards, the designers borrowed sentiments from the psalms, which state, "Truth will go forth from the earth," and "Justice will be reflected from the sky."[28] Israeli history and religion are embodied in the highest court of that country in an effort to tie law and justice to higher and more profound sources.

Ironically, Ahron Barak, president (or chief justice) of the Supreme Court of Israel, has argued that judging is "subjective,"[29] and that there is not one answer to every legal question. His position runs counter to the very symbols of his own court, such as the straight line to truth—one truth presumably. Although some Americans may agree with President Barak's interpretation of the judge's function, justices of the U.S. Supreme Court tend not to question the age-old symbols of impartiality, objectivity, neutrality, and legitimacy attached to their official positions. (Justice Scalia has been the most recent violator of this norm in his opinions that accuse the majority of following their own personal predilections, which, Scalia argues, happen to be those of the legal elite to which they belong.[30]) Therefore, as elaborated throughout this book, symbols of the U.S. Supreme Court displayed in its building, worn by its justices, written into its opinions, and communicated to all who visit it or follow its actions, have surely helped to maintain the generally positive image that the Court continues to enjoy and compliance with its rulings.

Indeed, the latter is the very essence of legitimacy, which has been defined in political science as "a political system's ability to win broad, voluntary public approval and acceptance for its decisions."[31] One explanation for the Court's legitimacy (which partially accounts for its success), namely, its expertise, impartiality, and wisdom (at least in comparison to the partisan political branches), has been labeled its "mythical role" in American life.[32] To the extent that the use of the word "myth" to describe the Supreme Court denotes a national narrative embodying the ideals of a society, the description is apt. Yet when modern academic observers refer to the mythology of the Supreme Court, they are more often thinking in terms of an unfounded or false belief about the institution.

Nevertheless, Americans still have more faith in the institution than other branches of government because the Court has preserved its positive image in the national narrative and avoided public displays that could undermine its standing. Charles Evans Hughes, who served the Court both as an associate justice and as its chief, wrote the following passage in 1927, but the words still resonate with accuracy:

When . . . we consider . . . the Court's activities, the thousands of determinations, the difficult questions with which it has dealt, and the fact that it has come out of its conflicts with its wounds healed, with its integrity universally recognized, with its ability giving it a rank second to none among the judicial tribunals of the world, and that today no institution of government stands higher in public confidence, we must realize that this is due . . . to the impartial manner in which the Court addresses itself to its never-ending task, to the unsullied honor, the freedom from political entanglements and the expertness of the judges who are bearing the heaviest burden of service and continuous intellectual work that our country knows.[33]

Hughes added, "Much of the criticism of the Court deals with what is occasional rather than typical."[34]

THE MEDIA AND THE COURT: WHERE TO DRAW
THE LINE

Much of what the media want to report is the "occasional rather than the typical." "Man Bites Dog!" is simply more interesting than the converse because it is atypical. Likewise, an airplane crash will garner headlines for days, whereas the thousands of successful flights that typically occur will go unreported. This fact of journalistic life is one that the Court will face in perpetuity. The Bork and Thomas nominations became media events, even circuses, because of their controversy; the numerous successful judicial appointments receive coverage but with demonstrably less fanfare than the nettlesome ones.

Yet so far the Supreme Court has survived the journalistic tendency to focus on the negative and the sensational. A recent trend may spare the Court even more in the near future; it has cut its opinion production almost in half over the last decade, which means it now issues decisions in approximately 90 cases annually.[35] (Reasons for the Court's diminished output include removal of mandatory jurisdiction cases from its docket by Congress in the late 1980s, uniformity of decisions in a federal judiciary guided by twelve years' worth of Reagan/Bush appointees, and a more conservative Court less willing to use the law to pursue a social agenda.) Although the Supreme Court will never be marginalized in the highly litigious American system, it is simply going to be in the news less often if it continues its current decision load.

If part of the problem with media reports on the Court is one of selection, that is, which stories to publish and how to edit them, or which part of oral arguments to broadcast, then should not complete coverage of oral arguments provide one area where those concerns do not apply? The good news is that televising oral argument sessions gavel to gavel would avoid the selectivity problem, in terms of the absence of sound bites. Some selection might occur, however, simply in choosing which oral arguments to cover. The really bad news is the problem that results from full coverage of government institutions. Former Senator William Cohen (R.-Maine) referred to this phenomenon when he observed that "the sense of majesty and mystique has been stripped away from Congress as a result of C-SPAN. Most people feel, 'Hey, wait a minute, he doesn't know any more about the issues than I do. So why should we defer to *his* judgment.' "[36] The Supreme Court would come across the airwaves looking much more dignified than Congress, but the overexposure factor is not to be underestimated. Even the most learned, intellectual debate at oral argument might quickly lose its appeal for the average television viewer, or familiarity could simply breed contempt.

Moreover, the typical C-SPAN viewer tends "to be vehemently anti-Washington, having spent so much time watching what politicians do there."[37] *The C-SPAN Revolution*, a 1996 book on the public affairs network, argues that "C-SPAN is to American politics what the Protestant Reformation was to Christianity. It lays everything out there so everyone can see. It gets rid of the middleman. People are able to judge for themselves who are the blowhards and who are the real speakers."[38]

These conclusions about the impact of C-SPAN viewing on the American public are even more significant because the number of adult viewers of the public affairs network has more than quadrupled since 1987. According to a 1994 survey, 8.6 percent of the population reported watching C-SPAN in the week before the poll was taken. If the C-SPAN audience brings a preconceived negative perception of government and Washington to its television viewing, even the Supreme Court, despite its traditional priestly image, may not be able to outweigh such ingrained public cynicism. Moreover, as Justice Stevens observed, we cannot anticipate an unforeseen negative impact that television could have on the oral argument process. The negative public image of Congress arguably derives from its very public nature in which it displays the elements of democracy the people find most disturbing (endless debates, mudslinging, posturing, pandering to interest groups).[39] Perhaps TV would reveal the best elements of the judicial process at the Supreme Court level (civility, reasoned deliberation, impartiality, professionalism), but television could also denigrate those virtues by overexposure and trivialization.

My suggested line on media access to the Supreme Court thus stops at the televising of oral arguments. Journalists already have access to the building, the oral arguments, the justices (on an individual basis), and officers of the Court. Although broadcasting oral argument sessions would fulfill a unique educative function, that benefit would come with an unacceptably high cost, that is, the risk of undermining the Court's image through sound-biting, simple overexposure, or unknown problems introduced by the presence of television cameras. The justices who argue against televising oral argument for fear of losing their relative anonymity are unpersuasive, but the institution's stature as a collegial body *is* enhanced when individual justices are not singled out for media hype. On several occasions, I have seen current and retired justices stroll through the crowded public areas of the Court unrecognized, and I once saw the chief justice walk through Washington's National Airport utterly unnoticed by the public. My observations confirm how successful the Court has been in maintaining its isolation from the public fray.

Nevertheless, people should have entrée to the high court to the extent that such access would facilitate public education about the institution without promoting incomplete, sensational, or tabloid-style coverage of the tribunal and its members. The Court should continue its efforts to welcome visitors; offer them informative films, displays, literature, lectures, and briefings; and accommodate them as space permits in oral arguments. (Sadly, the openness of the Court's edifice may fall prey to security concerns in the future. The Supreme Court has asked Congress for funds to build a 30-inch-high wall or other type of security barrier around the building's perimeter.[40]) Beyond the Court building, official tapes and transcripts of oral arguments and opinions of the Court should be made available on an unrestricted basis and through as wide a network as possible. For reasons of confidentiality and security, the Court does not offer public access through the Internet, but it should find ways in the future to connect safely to that universal conduit.[41] Northwestern University maintains an excellent Website on the Supreme Court, complete with audio versions of oral arguments and a "virtual tour" of the Court building. The release of justices' papers is obviously a personal decision for each member of the Court to make. Yet while protecting the confidentiality of their decision-making process, the justices should still allow timely access to papers and archival material.

By maintaining its public dignity and limiting breaches of its private work and its justices' personal lives, the Supreme Court can strike a blow for a bygone age when the line between the public and private realm had some meaning. Now it seems that individuals, government institutions, and the media maintain little, if any, distinction between those two realms. The overexposure of Congress and the president has resulted in loss of support for not only the public policy generated by these branches, but also for the institutions themselves and the government they constitute. This outcome diminishes one of the crucial contributions of the Founding Fathers, who knew that the success of the U.S. Constitution rested on their support for government institutions despite their political or personal differences. They learned quickly to separate men from institutions. The presidency could be valued even if the incumbent was not; Congress could maintain its respect even if its members were controversial.

The Supreme Court has managed to sustain its institutional strength for a host of reasons offered in this book. Its majesty and mystique have survived and remain strong as we enter the twenty-first century. Walter Bagehot, the distinguished nineteenth-century English constitutional scholar, warned that to maintain public reverence for the monarchy, "We must not let in daylight upon magic."[42] Although the Supreme Court of the United States is by no means a royal institution, its success in maintaining respect is nonetheless almost magical. To spoil the magic by exposing it to excess "daylight" might rob the nation and indeed the world of a stable and enduring emblem of the rule of law. The very fact that the Supreme Court operates beyond the white heat of television lights is in itself symbolic. As Justice Anthony Kennedy has explained, the absence of cameras in the high court

underscores for the public that we are different from the political branches. We operate on a different time line, a different chronology; we speak a different grammar; we decide by a different method; we announce our opinions; we give reasons for our opinions in a different way. And this is what sustains the separation of powers and makes for the individuality and strength of each of the branches of the government.[43]

By the dawn of the millennium, Chief Justice Charles Evans Hughes's 1932 declaration that the Supreme Court symbolizes the nation's faith in its enduring Republic had become a commendable truism.

NOTES

1. Tony Mauro, "The Court and the Cult of Secrecy," in *A Year in the Life of the Supreme Court*, ed. Rodney A. Smolla (Durham, N.C.: Duke University Press, 1995), 278.

2. Ibid., 279.

3. Ibid., 272, and Ruth Bader Ginsburg, response to author's question, talk to Public Leadership Education Network, U.S. Supreme Court, 11 January 1994.

4. Ruth Bader Ginsburg, "Communicating and Commenting on the Court's Work," *Georgetown Law Journal* 83 (1995): 2118–29.

5. William H. Rehnquist, C-SPAN, 2 July 1994.

6. Clarence Thomas, C-SPAN, 17 April 1994.

7. John Paul Stevens, "Remarks on the U.S. Supreme Court—Its Work, Its Workload, and the Appropriate Scope of Its Work," *Federal Bar Journal* 33 (March 1986): 109–11.

8. Linda Greenhouse, "Telling the Court's Story: Justice and Journalism at the Supreme Court," *Yale Law Journal* 105 (1996): 1537–61.

9. Frank Murray, comments to Supreme Court Summer Institute for Teachers, 23 June 1996.

10. Greenhouse, "Telling the Court's Story."

11. John Paul Stevens, *America and the Courts*, C-SPAN, 4 February 1995.

12. As quoted in Alan Green, *Justice for All: A Guide to the Supreme Court of the United States*, 3d ed. (Washington, D.C.: C-SPAN, the Benton Foundation, and the American Bar Association, 1993), 45.

13. Ibid., 48.

14. Ibid.

15. Ibid.

16. David Souter, response to author's question, talk to students from Sweet Briar College, U.S. Supreme Court, November 1993.

17. Anthony Kennedy and David Souter, *America and the Courts*, C-SPAN, 30 March 1996.

18. Antonin Scalia, remarks to foreign correspondents, U.S. Supreme Court, 16 November 1994.

19. Ibid.

20. Green, *Justice for All*, 48.

21. Ibid.

22. William J. Brennan, meeting with judicial fellows, U.S. Supreme Court, 8 December 1994.

23. Green, *Justice for All*, 48.

24. Benjamin N. Cardozo, *The Nature of the Judicial Process* (New Haven, Conn.: Yale University Press, 1921).

25. 297 U.S. 288 (1936).

26. Henry J. Abraham, *The Judicial Process: An Introductory Analysis of the Courts of the United States, England, and France*, 7th ed. (New York: Oxford University Press, 1998).

27. Greenhouse, "Telling the Court's Story," 1553.

28. Josef Sharon, *The Supreme Court Building, Jerusalem* (Jerusalem: Yad Hana-div, 1993).

29. Ahron Barak, remarks to Research Committee on Comparative Judicial Stud-ies, Hebrew University, 1 July 1996.

30. See his dissents in *Romer v. Evans*, 517 U.S. 620 (1996), and *United States v. Virginia*, 518 U.S. 515 (1996).

31. Thomas R. Marshall, *Public Opinion and the Supreme Court* (Boston: Unwin Hyman, 1989), 131.

32. See Gregory Casey's "The Supreme Court and Myth: An Empirical Investi-gation," *Law and Society Review* (Spring 1974): 385–419, and, for the role of myth in the American presidency, see also Thomas E. Cronin and Michael A. Genovese, *The Paradoxes of the American Presidency* (New York: Oxford University Press, 1998), 152–53.

33. Charles Evans Hughes, "Self-Inflicted Wounds and Popular Prescriptions," in *An Autobiography of the Supreme Court: Off the Bench Commentary by the Justices*, ed. Allan Westin (New York: Macmillan, 1963), 143.

34. Ibid.

35. See David M. O'Brien, "The Rehnquist Court's Shrinking Plenary Docket," *Judicature* 81 (September–October 1997): 58–65.

36. "The So-Long Senators: Bill Cohen, A Mid-Life Correction," *Washington Post*, 26 January 1996, F1–2 (emphasis in original).

37. Blaine Hardin, "Feasting on C-SPAN's Unedited Feed," *Washington Post*, 9 May 1996, A1, A18.

38. Ibid. See also Stephen Frantzich and John Sullivan, *The C-SPAN Revolution* (Norman: University of Oklahoma Press, 1996).

39. John R. Hibbing and Elizabeth Theiss-Morse, *Congress as Public Enemy: Pub-lic Attitudes Toward American Political Institutions* (New York: Cambridge Univer-sity Press, 1995).

40. Joan Biskupic, "Security and the Supreme Court: Funds Requested for Pro-tective Structure Around Building," *Washington Post*, 25 March 1998, A19.

41. Stuart N. Brotman, "Online Justice: It's Time for the Supreme Court to Get on the Internet," *Washington Post*, 19 November 1997, A21.

42. Walter Bagehot, *The English Constitution* (New York: D. Appleton & Co., 1877).

43. Anthony Kennedy, *America and the Courts*, C-SPAN, 30 March 1996.

Selected Bibliography

Abraham, Henry J. *The Judicial Process: An Introductory Analysis of the Courts of the United States, England, and France*. 7th ed. New York: Oxford University Press, 1998.

Ball, Milner S. "The Play's the Thing: An Unscientific Reflection on Courts under the Rubric of Theater." *Stanford Law Review* 28 (1975): 81–115.

Barnum, David G. "The Supreme Court and Public Opinion: Judicial Decision Making in the Post–New Deal Period." *Journal of Politics* 47 (1985): 652–65.

Baum, Lawrence. *The Supreme Court*. 5th ed. Washington, D.C.: Congressional Quarterly Press, 1989.

Bohte, John R., Roy B. Flemming, and B. Dan Wood. "The Supreme Court, the Media, and Legal Change: A Reassessment of Rosenberg's *Hollow Hope*." Paper presented at the Annual Meeting of the American Political Science Association, Chicago, Ill., September 1995.

Brennan, William J., Jr. "How Goes the Supreme Court?" *Mercer Law Review* 36 (Spring 1985): 781–94.

Brennan, William J., Jr. "Some Thoughts on the Supreme Court's Workload." *Judicature* 66 (December 1982/January 1983): 230–35.

Brigham, John. *The Cult of the Court*. Philadelphia: Temple University Press, 1987.

Brigham, John. "Exploring the Attic: Courts and Communities in Material Life." In *Courts, Tribunals and New Approaches to Justice*, ed. Oliver Mendelsohn and Laurence Maher. Australia: La Trobe University Press, 1995.

Brisbin, Richard A., Jr. "Toward a Conservative Constitutional Law?" *Judicature* 78 (March–April 1995): 256–60.

Burton, Harold H. "The United States Supreme Court." *Women's Law Journal* 34 (Summer 1948): 4–6, 33, 43–45.

Caldeira, Gregory A. "Neither the Purse Nor the Sword: Dynamics of Public Confidence in the Supreme Court." *American Political Science Review* 80 (1986): 1209–26.

Caldeira, Gregory A. "Public Opinion and the U.S. Supreme Court: FDR's Court-Packing Plan." *American Political Science Review* 81 (December 1987): 1139–53.

Cardozo, Benjamin N. *The Nature of the Judicial Process.* New Haven, Conn.: Yale University Press, 1921.

Casey, Gregory. "Popular Perceptions of Supreme Court Rulings." *American Politics Quarterly* 4 (January 1976): 3–45.

Casey, Gregory. "The Supreme Court and Myth: An Empirical Investigation." *Law and Society Review* (Spring 1974): 385–419.

Clark, Tom C. "The Court and Its Critics." *Villanova Law Review* 15 (September 1970): 521–26.

Clark, Tom C. "Internal Operation of the United States Supreme Court." *Journal of the American Judicature Society* 43 (August 1959): 45–51.

Cooper, Phillip J. *Battles on the Bench: Conflict inside the Supreme Court.* Lawrence: University Press of Kansas, 1995.

Cooper, Phillip J., and Howard Ball. *The United States Supreme Court: From the Inside Out.* Englewood Cliffs, N.J.: Prentice-Hall, 1995.

Cope, Alfred H., and Fred Krinsky, eds. *Franklin D. Roosevelt and the Supreme Court.* Lexington, Mass.: D.C. Heath and Co., 1969.

Davis, Richard. *Decisions and Images: The Supreme Court and the Press.* Englewood Cliffs, N.J.: Prentice-Hall, 1994.

Epstein, Lee, and Jack Knight. *The Choices Justices Make.* Washington, D.C.: Congressional Quarterly Press, 1998.

Epstein, Lee et al. *The Supreme Court Compendium: Data, Decisions, and Developments.* Washington, D.C.: Congressional Quarterly Press, 1994.

Faille, Christopher C. *The Decline and Fall of the Supreme Court.* Westport, Conn.: Praeger, 1995.

Fallows, James. *Breaking the News: How the Media Undermine American Democracy.* New York: Pantheon Books, 1996.

Frank, Jerome. *Courts on Trial: Myth and Reality in American Justice.* Princeton, N.J.: Princeton University Press, 1949.

Frankfurter, Felix. "Justice Roberts and the 'Switch in Time.' " In *An Autobiography of the Supreme Court: Off the Bench Commentary by the Justices,* ed. Alan Westin. New York: Macmillan, 1963.

Frantzich, Stephen, and John Sullivan. *The C-SPAN Revolution.* Norman: University of Oklahoma Press, 1996.

Gibson, James L., Gregory A. Caldeira, and Vanessa A. Baird. "On the Legitimacy of National High Courts." *American Political Science Review* 92 (June 1998): 343–58.

Ginsburg, Ruth Bader. "Communicating and Commenting on the Court's Work." *Georgetown Law Journal* 83 (1995): 2119–29.

Ginsburg, Ruth Bader. "Remarks for American Law Institute Annual Dinner." *Saint Louis University Law Journal* 38 (Summer 1994): 881–88.

Graber, Doris A. "The 'New' Media and Politics: What Does the Future Hold?" *PS: Political Science and Politics* 29 (1996): 33–36.

Green, Alan. *Justice for All: A Guide to the Supreme Court of the United States.* 3d ed. Washington, D.C.: C-SPAN, the Benton Foundation, and the American Bar Association, 1993.

Greenhouse, Linda. "Telling the Court's Story: Justice and Journalism at the Supreme Court." *The Yale Law Journal* 105 (1996): 1537–61.

Haltom, William. *Reporting on the Courts: How the Mass Media Cover Judicial Actions.* Chicago: Nelson-Hall, 1998.

Harrell, Mary Ann, and Burnett Anderson. *Equal Justice Under Law: The Supreme Court in American Life.* 6th ed. Washington, D.C.: The Supreme Court Historical Society, 1994.

Harriger, Katy J. "Cues and Miscues in the Constitutional Dialogue." *The Review of Politics* 60 (Summer 1998): 497–524.

Hibbing, John R., and Elizabeth Theiss-Morse. *Congress as Public Enemy: Public Attitudes Toward American Political Institutions.* New York: Cambridge University Press, 1995.

Hinckley, Barbara. *The Symbolic Presidency: How Presidents Portray Themselves.* New York: Routledge, 1990.

Irons, Peter, and Stephanie Guitton, eds. *May It Please the Court.* New York: The New Press, 1993.

Jackson, Robert H. *The Struggle for Judicial Supremacy: A Study of a Crisis in American Power Politics.* New York: Octagon Books, 1979.

Kammen, Michael. *A Machine That Would Go of Itself: The Constitution in American Culture.* New York: St. Martin's Press, 1994.

Kammen, Michael. "Temples of Justice: The Iconography of Judgment and American Culture." In *Origins of the Federal Judiciary: Essays on the Judiciary Act of 1789*, ed. Maeva Marcus. New York: Oxford University Press, 1992.

Katsh, Ethan. "The Supreme Court Beat: How Television Covers the U.S. Supreme Court." *Judicature* 67 (June–July 1983): 6–12.

Kessel, John H. 1966. "Public Perceptions of the Supreme Court." *Midwest Journal of Political Science* 10 (1966): 167–91.

Langston, Thomas S. *With Reverence and Contempt: How Americans Think about Their President.* Baltimore: Johns Hopkins University Press, 1995.

Lazarus, Edward. *Closed Chambers: The First Eyewitness Account of the Epic Struggles inside the Supreme Court.* New York: Times Books, 1998.

Lerner, Max. *Nine Scorpions in a Bottle: Great Judges and Cases of the Supreme Court*, ed. Richard Cummings. New York: Arcade Publishing, 1994.

Leuchtenburg, William E. *The Supreme Court Reborn: The Constitutional Revolution in the Age of Roosevelt.* New York: Oxford University Press, 1995.

Levinson, Sanford. *Constitutional Faith.* Princeton, N.J.: Princeton University Press, 1988.

MacColl, E. Kimbark. "The Supreme Court and Public Opinion: A Study of the Court Fight of 1937." Ph.D. diss., UCLA, 1953.

McGuire, Kevin T. *The Supreme Court Bar: Legal Elites in the Washington Community.* Charlottesville: University Press of Virginia, 1993.

McGurn, Barrett. *America's Court: The Supreme Court and the People.* Golden, Colo.: Fulcrum Publishing, 1997.

McGurn, Barrett. "Public Information at the United States Supreme Court." *American Bar Association Journal* 69 (1983): 40–45.

Marshall, Thomas R. *Public Opinion and the Supreme Court.* Boston: Unwin Hyman, 1989.

Mauro, Tony. "The Supreme Court and the Cult of Secrecy." In *A Year in the Life of the Supreme Court*, ed. Rodney A. Smolla. Durham, N.C.: Duke University Press, 1995.

Mishler, William, and Reginald S. Sheehan. "The Supreme Court as a Countermajoritarian Institution? The Impact of Public Opinion on Supreme Court Decisions." *American Political Science Review* 87 (1993): 87–101.

O'Brien, David M. *Storm Center: The Supreme Court in American Politics.* 4th ed. New York: W.W. Norton and Co., 1996.

Patterson, Thomas E. "Bad News, Period." *PS: Political Science and Politics* 29 (March 1996): 17–19.

Pearson, Drew, and Robert Allen. *The Nine Old Men.* New York: Doubleday, 1936.

Perry, Barbara A. *A "Representative" Supreme Court? The Impact of Race, Religion, and Gender on Appointments.* Westport, Conn.: Greenwood Press, 1991.

Powell, Lewis F., Jr. "The Burger Court." *Washington and Lee Law Review* 44 (Winter 1987): 1–10.

Powell, Lewis F., Jr. "Myths and Misconceptions about the Supreme Court." *New York State Bar Journal* 48 (January 1976): 6–10.

Powell, Lewis F., Jr. "What Really Goes on at the Court." *New York State Bar Journal* 52 (October 1980): 454–57.

Powell, Lewis F., Jr. "What the Justices Are Saying . . .". *American Bar Association Journal* 62 (1976): 1454–56.

Pritchett, C. Herman. *The Roosevelt Court: A Study in Judicial Politics and Values, 1937–1947.* Chicago: Quadrangle Books, 1969.

Pusey, Merlo. *The Supreme Court in Crisis.* New York: Macmillan, 1937.

Reeder, Robert P. "The First Homes of the Supreme Court of the United States." *Proceedings of the American Philosophical Society* 76 (1936): 543–96.

Rehnquist, William H. " 'All Discord, Harmony Not Understood': The Performance of the Supreme Court of the United States." *Arizona Law Review* 22 (1980): 973–86.

Rehnquist, William H. "The American Constitutional Experience: Remarks of the Chief Justice." *Louisiana Law Review* 54 (May 1994): 1161–72.

Rehnquist, William H. "The Changing Role of the Supreme Court." *Florida State University Law Review* 14 (Spring 1986): 1–14.

Rehnquist, William H. "Constitutional Law and Public Opinion." *Suffolk University Law Review* 20 (Winter 1986): 751–69.

Rehnquist, William H. "Convocation Address, Wake Forest University." *Wake Forest Law Review* 29 (1994): 999–1006.

Rehnquist, William H. "Remarks on the Process of Judging." *Washington and Lee Law Review* 49 (Spring 1992): 263–70.

Rehnquist, William H. "Sunshine in the Third Branch." *Washburn Law Journal* 16 (Spring 1977): 559–70.

Rehnquist, William H. *The Supreme Court: How It Was, How It Is.* New York: Quill, William Morrow, 1987.

Rehnquist, William H. "Who Writes Decisions of the Supreme Court?" *U.S. News and World Report,* 13 December 1957, 74–75.

Roberts, Owen. "Now Is the Time: Fortifying the Supreme Court's Independence." *American Bar Association Journal* 35 (January 1949): 1–4.

Roosevelt, Franklin D. "Reorganizing the Federal Judiciary," 9 March 1937. In *Free*

Government in the Making: Readings in American Political Thought, 3d ed., ed. Alpheus Thomas Mason. New York: Oxford University Press, 1965.

Rosenberg, Gerald N. *The Hollow Hope: Can Courts Bring about Social Change?* Chicago: University of Chicago Press, 1991.

Rosenberg, Gerald N., and Christopher M. Rohrbacher. "The Changing Meanings of Supreme Court Decisions: *Carolene Products* Footnote 4 as a Political Symbol." Paper presented at the Annual Meeting of the American Political Science Association, Boston, Mass., 3–6 September 1998.

Scheb, John M., II, and William Lyons. "Public Holds U.S. Supreme Court in High Regard." *Judicature* 77 (March–April 1994): 273–74.

Scheb, John M., II, and William Lyons. "Public Perception of the Supreme Court in the 1990s." *Judicature* 82 (September–October 1998): 66–69.

Schwartz, Bernard. *A History of the Supreme Court.* New York: Oxford University Press, 1993.

Segal, Jeffrey A., and Harold J. Spaeth. *The Supreme Court and the Attitudinal Model.* New York: Cambridge University Press, 1993.

Semonche, John E. *Keeping the Faith: A Cultural History of the U.S. Supreme Court.* Lanham, Md.: Rowman & Littlefield, 1998.

Slotnick, Elliot E. "Media Coverage of Supreme Court Decision Making: Problems and Politics." *Judicature* 75 (1991): 133.

Slotnick, Elliot E. "Television News and the Supreme Court: A Case Study." *Judicature* 77 (July–August 1993): 21–33.

Slotnick, Elliot E., and Jennifer A. Segal. "Television News and the Supreme Court." Paper presented at the Annual Meeting of the American Political Science Association, Chicago, Ill., September 1992.

Slotnick, Elliot E., and Jennifer A. Segal. *Television News and the Supreme Court: All the News That's Fit to Air?* New York: Cambridge University Press, 1998.

Stevens, John Paul. "The Supreme Court of the United States: Reflections after a Summer Recess." *South Texas Law Review* 27 (1986): 447–53.

Stewart, Potter. "Operations and Practice, a Comparison, the United States Supreme Court." *Canada-United States Law Journal* 3 (1980): 82–85.

Tanenhaus, Joseph, and Walter F. Murphy. "Patterns of Public Support for the Supreme Court: A Panel Study." *Journal of Politics* 43 (1981): 24–39.

Thomas, Clarence. "Commencement Address: Syracuse University College of Law." *Syracuse Law Review* 42 (1991): 815–22.

Totenberg, Nina. "Covering the Courts: Cases, Convention and Confirmation." Presentation at the 1992 Annual Convention of the Kentucky Bar Association, Lexington, Ky.

Van Wie, Nancy Ann. *Travels with Max! The Supreme Court.* N.p.: Max's Publications, 1994.

Wallen, Theodore C. "The Supreme Court—Nine Mortal Men." *Literary Digest*, 7 April 1934, 9, 45–47.

Warren, Earl. "Let's Not Weaken the Supreme Court." *American Bar Association Journal* 60 (June 1974): 677–80.

Wasby, Stephen L. *The Supreme Court in the Federal Judicial System.* 4th ed. Chicago: Nelson-Hall, 1993.

Westin, Alan F. "When the Public Judges the Court." *New York Times Magazine*, 31 May 1959, 16, 41–42.

White, Byron R. "The Work of the Supreme Court: A Nuts and Bolts Description." *New York State Bar Journal* 54 (1982): 346–49.

Whittaker, Charles E. "The Role of the Supreme Court." *Arkansas Law Review* 17 (February 1963): 292–301.

"Why Don't Americans Trust the Government?" *Washington Post*, Kaiser Family Foundation, Harvard University Survey Project, 1996.

Wohl, Alexander. "Read All about Them: Supreme Court Justices Have Become Popular Subjects for Biographers." *American Bar Association Journal* (May 1995): 46, 48.

Woodward, Bob, and Scott Armstrong. *The Brethren*. New York: Simon and Schuster, 1979.

Index

About the Author

BARBARA A. PERRY is Professor and Chair, Department of Government, Sweet Briar College. Professor Perry served as a judicial fellow at the United States Supreme Court (1994–95), where she received the Tom C. Clark Award. Her books include *A "Representative" Supreme Court? The Impact of Race, Religion, and Gender on Appointments* (Greenwood Press, 1991), and, with Henry J. Abraham, the seventh edition of *Freedom and the Court: Civil Rights and Liberties in the United States* (1998).

ISBN 0-275-96598-8

90000>

EAN

9 780275 965983

HARDCOVER BAR CODE